WILDLIFE & CONSERVATION VOLUNTEERING

THE COMPLETE GUIDE

the Bradt Travel Guide

Peter Lynch

edition
I

www.bradtguides.com

Bradt Travel Guides Ltd, UK
The Globe Pequot Press Inc, USA

Sperm, blue fin & minke whales
– Azores & Canada
see table page 28

Common & grey seals
– Ireland
see table page 27

Bottlenose dolphins & porpoises
– Scotland
see table page 24

Leopard & smooth-hound sharks
– USA
see table page 27

Howler & capuchin squirrel monkeys
– Costa Rica
see table page 22

Elephants, cheetahs & leopards
– Namibia
see table pages 24, 23 & 25

Macaws & pink river dolphins
– Peru
see table pages 26 & 24

Meerkats & great white sharks
– South Africa
see table pages 25 & 27

Condors
– Argentina
see table page 23

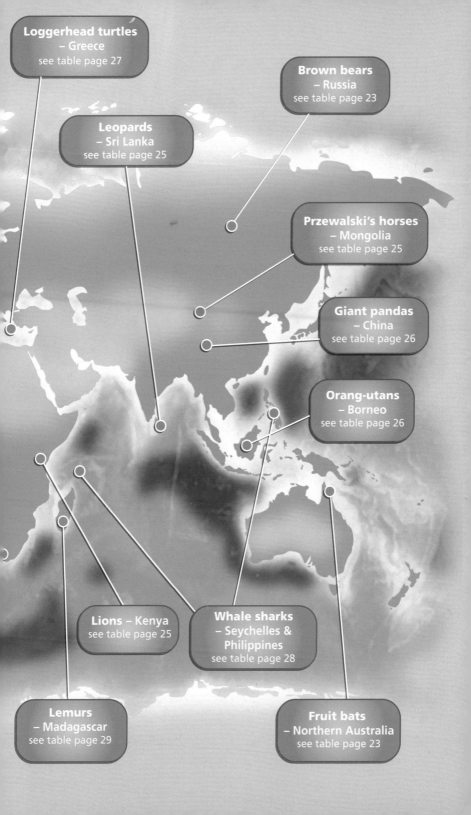

Loggerhead turtles
– Greece
see table page 27

Brown bears
– Russia
see table page 23

Leopards
– Sri Lanka
see table page 25

Przewalski's horses
– Mongolia
see table page 25

Giant pandas
– China
see table page 26

Orang-utans
– Borneo
see table page 26

Lions – Kenya
see table page 25

Whale sharks
– Seychelles &
Philippines
see table page 28

Lemurs
– Madagascar
see table page 29

Fruit bats
– Northern Australia
see table page 23

Volunteering Activities

Monitoring wildlife
Cheetah fitted with a radio tracking collar being released, Namibia (BE)

Wildlife surveys
Capuchin monkeys, Costa Rica (KW/E)

Marine conservation
Random sampling for diversity of fish species, Bahamas
(DC/E)

Sustainable management of habitats
Belarus wetlands
(CR/E)

Measuring climate change
Arctic Circle
(PK/E)

above   Aerial view of the Brazilian rainforest. The Amazon has the highest diversity of plant species on earth; one hectare can contain more than 750 types of tree (I)

below   Rainforests once covered 14% of the earth's surface, but logging and land clearance have reduced it to just 6% (PL)

above   **Monitoring fish stocks in an Amazonian lake** (PL)

below   **Earthwatch volunteer accommodation: a restored 19th-century riverboat** (PL) page 167

Sparring Przewalski's stallions –
otherwise known as the Mongolian wild
horse – have been listed as 'critically
endangered' on the IUCN Red List.
Reintroduction programmes are taking
place in Hustai National Park (HNP) page 25

AUTHOR

Born and educated in the UK, Peter Lynch is a travel
writer contributing to newspapers, magazines and books
in America, Australia, the Far East and the UK. Prior to
this he spent several years teaching biology, leading field
trips and working on health and education community
development projects. He has a PhD in educational
psychology, is a member of the British Guild of Travel
Writers, and has participated in community and
conservation volunteer projects since the 1990s.

AUTHOR STORY

Ecology has been a passion of mine for most of my life and the opportunity
to spend so much time researching and writing this book has been a joy.
I am really grateful for the enthusiasm with which Bradt took up my
initial idea; their commitment to highlighting quality issues and wanting to
know which companies really are making a difference never faltered from
day one.

I've travelled widely to research the book and one of the key lessons hit
home to me was the interconnectedness of global problems: wildlife and
environmental conservation cannot be disentangled from political, social
and economic issues; the policies designed to resolve the latter, often have
a knock-on effect on the former. In fact, it is estimated that three species of
plant or animal life become extinct every hour. If this statement is true, the
need for conservation volunteering has never been greater.

At the time of writing, the credit crunch continues to bite deeper, but
surprisingly the volunteer sector seems to be bucking the trend and
experiencing a mini boom. Conservation volunteer organisations are finding
that people being made redundant or opting for early retirement, are
reassessing their options and deciding to use the opportunity to do
something they've always wanted to do. So if you've toyed with the idea of
volunteering in the past, but put plans on the shelf for fear of leaving an
unstable job market, then maybe its time to get them down and dust them
off. There's never been a better time to make the leap. You can use the time
away from work to contribute in a meaningful way and enhance your CV
at the same time. Conservation volunteering offers all this and more,
so go for it!

First published February 2009

Bradt Travel Guides Ltd,
23 High Street, Chalfont St Peter, Bucks SL9 9QE, England; www.bradtguides.com
Published in the USA by The Globe Pequot Press Inc, 246 Goose Lane,
PO Box 480, Guilford, Connecticut 06437-0480

Text copyright © 2009 Peter Lynch
Maps copyright © 2009 Bradt Travel Guides Ltd
Illustrations © 2009 Individual photographers
Editorial Project Manager: Emma Thomson

British Library Cataloguing in Publication Data
A catalogue record for this book is available from the British Library
ISBN-13: 978 1 84162 275 0
All details and prices were correct at the time of going to press. Bradt cannot be held
responsible for injury, etc, sustained while on a project reviewed in the book.

Photographers Andrew Bannister/Images of Africa (AB/IOA), ArcoImages/TIPS (AI/TIPS),
Azafady (A), Biosphere Expeditions (BE), Caroline Rodgers/Earthwatch (CR/E), Crispin
Zeeman/Buddha34 (CZ/B), Dale Curtis/Earthwatch (DC/E), Eve Carpenter/Earthwatch
(EC/E), Frans Lanting/FLPA (FL/FLPA), Grant Pedan/Earthwatch (GP/E), Hamid Rad (HR),
Heather Angel/Natural Visions (HA/NV), Helen Johnson/ Earthwatch (HJ/E), Hustai
National Park (HNP), Imagestate/TIPS (I/TIPS), Katie Wilson/Earthwatch (KW/E), Niall
Riddell/Earthwatch (NR/E), Peter Kershaw/Earthwatch (PK/E), Peter Lynch (PL),
Photononstop/TIPS (P/TIPS), Prof James Crabbe/Earthwatch (JC/E), Reinhard Dirscherl
(RD/TIPS), Russ Schleipman/Earthwatch (RS/E), WorldPictures/Photoshot (WP)
Cover Black rhino, Kenya (AB/IOA), Inspecting an Atlantic puffin chick, Rost, Norway
(FL/FLPA), Volunteer and meerkats, South Africa (HJ/E)
Back cover Whale shark (RD/TIPS); Studying meerkats (GP/E); Gorilla (AI/TIPS)
Title page Ringtail lemur, Madagascar (A); Preparing to fit a radio tracking collar on a
captured cheetah, Namibia (BE); Hawksbill turtle, Indian Ocean (HR)
Black & white photographs All pictures taken by the author

Mixed Sources
Product group from well-managed
forests, and other controlled sources
www.fsc.org Cert no. TT-CoC-002424
© 1996 Forest Stewardship Council
FSC

Map by ArtInfusion
Designed and formatted by ArtInfusion
Printed and bound in Malta by Gutenberg Press Ltd

FOREWORD

As a small boy I had only one ambition: to become a game warden in Africa. So, after leaving school in 1949, I packed my bags and went to Kenya to follow my dream only to be politely told that I was not wanted! My dreams shattered and stranded without a penny to my name I sold bird paintings on the coast to raise my fare home.

Back in England I was faced with two choices: to drive buses or starve as an artist. The Slade School of Fine Art rejected me for having 'no talent whatsoever' but it was my great good fortune to meet professional artist, Robin Goodwin, who took me under his wing and spent three years teaching me.

I started my career as an aviation artist and, in 1960 the RAF flew me as their guest from Aden to Kenya, where they commissioned my first wildlife painting – I never looked back.

It was at this time that I became a conservationist overnight when I came across 255 dead zebra at a poisoned waterhole in Tanzania. It was the first of many horrors that convinced me that I had to do something to protect this planet's magnificent wildlife from the barbarity and cruelty of man. Throughout my career I have tried to do all I can to repay the enormous debt I owe to the elephants, tigers and other wildlife that have given me so much success and in 1984 I founded my conservation charity the David Shepherd Wildlife Foundation (DSWF).

Over the last 25 years, DSWF has given away over £4 million in grants to save critically endangered mammals in the wild and I am hugely proud of the small and dedicated team that has helped achieve so much. But, whether in the UK office or abroad on the frontline of conservation, it is the volunteers from all walks of life including fellow artists, who make the real difference to our fight to save wildlife. Without them, we could not hope to achieve half of what we do. Their time, enthusiasm and passion are invaluable and after the animals themselves it is they who inspire me most.

Follow your dreams – as a volunteer you too can truly help make a world of difference to saving wildlife.

David Shepherd

David Shepherd CBE, Wildlife artist and conservationist
(*www.davidshepherd.org*)

CONTENTS

ACKNOWLEDGEMENTS

There are so many people who need to be thanked for helping me get this book to its conclusion. Great thanks must go to all the companies who contributed the core information about themselves, but especially to the people at Archelon, Biosphere Expeditions, British Trust for Conservation Volunteers, Global Vision International and the Earthwatch Institute who enabled me to experience a wide range of conservation volunteer activities.

Many scientists and professionals helped shape my thinking, including Dr Stephen Morse at Reading University with whom I discussed the criteria for comparing different organisations; Dr Jamie Lorimer (Oxford University); Rachel Hine (Centre for Environment and Society at University of Essex); and Tom Griffin (originally at the University of the West of England) for having produced such useful research papers. Thanks also to Kate Simpson, who I never managed to contact, for her pioneering thinking on ethics and responsible travel and Dr Richard Bodmer (Canterbury University) for some fascinating discussions whilst in the middle of the Amazon.

I would especially like to thank the volunteers who shared their insights and enthusiasm about their conservation experiences: Andrew Hayes, Ceri Gibson,Christopher Margetts, Daniel Quilter, Eve Carpenter, Izzy Jones, Mandy Hengeveld, Rebecca Joshua and Yolanda Barnas.

To everyone at Bradt who appreciated the value of the book, beyond its publishing potential, and seemed to have a vision that reached beyond my own. But special thanks must go to my editor, Emma Thomson, who pulled together my sometimes disparate themes into its more coherent final form.

My good friend Dr Ian Clark who helped gather information, commented on my grammar and was always so encouraging. Finally, thanks to my best friend and partner Sheena. Without a doubt the book would never have been completed without her understanding, support and patience.

Feedback request

We are keen to include more volunteer feedback in future editions of *Wildlife and Conservation Volunteering*, so please send us any comments and suggestions you might have about the book. Any stories relating to your experiences on any of the projects mentioned within these pages – good or bad – would also be very gratefully received. Email the author at ✉ conservationvolunteer@peter-lynch.co.uk or check out his blog ⌂ www.peter-lynch.co.uk. Alternatively, send your comments to Bradt Travel Guides Ltd, 23 High Street, Chalfont St Peter, Bucks SL9 9QE, England; ✉ info@bradtguides.com. Your personal information won't be published without your express permission.

INTRODUCTION

It's easy to sit in our lounge watching a David Attenborough documentary and 'tut' about environmental destruction. To criticise the loggers and hunters and ask: 'Don't they realise what they're doing to the planet?' without realising we – by default – are implicated in the process. Just by sitting at home it's possible to contribute to unfair business practices, habitat destruction and wildlife decline – Amazonian rainforest is destroyed to raise cattle for burgers and provide biofuel for our cars; hardwood trees are logged in Indonesia to supply food and quality kitchen cabinets; and vast tracts of land in Africa are given over to growing coffee to produce beans for our morning lattes, instead of producing food for local people.

However, therein lies our power. A business can only sell what individuals will buy. The most socially conscious action we could take would be to stop buying exotic foods flown in from the third world, to stop buying products made from tropical hardwoods, and to look in horror at people buying gas-guzzling cars. This would reduce carbon emissions, reduce corporate land-grabbing, and enable local people to control their lands again.

Of course, not all problems arise as a result of the West's excessive resource consumption. Third-world countries inflict damage on themselves too. For example, 90% of Madagascar's rainforests have been cut by locals for saleable charcoal or cleared to make way for rice production. Understandable given the fact that 70% of the island's 19 million inhabitants live on less than a dollar a day, but nevertheless it's critical they find the delicate balance between social development and environmental protection so that the remaining 10% of forest is preserved.

So, what about volunteer organisations? A quick web search throws a plethora of conservation volunteer outfits, each of which claim to be eco-friendly and ethically motivated, but often they are weaving a green smokescreen around their actual tour-operator status. This is not to say that they are bad companies, but the questions to ask are: 'How good are they?' and 'How much of the cash you pay actually contributes towards conservation as opposed to UK overheads, publicity or shareholders?'

Companies rarely explain these things, and their standards and criteria are usually unspecified. Some are excellent, some are average and some fall below the ideal. In order to help you differentiate between them, all the companies listed in this book have been audited on the basis of nine categories (see *The Audit Criteria* page IX), including an analysis of each company's website, official documentation, their terms and conditions, volunteer comments, and discussions with company staff and volunteers.

As the title suggests, this book focuses specifically on environmental conservation volunteering ie: issues to do with habitats, endangered wildlife, rainforest destruction and human-wildlife conflict resolution. It doesn't cover community projects, education or emergency relief.

Maybe we can't change the world on our own, but a small contribution from millions of individuals can have a significant impact. So get out there and do something – make a difference!

HOW TO USE THIS BOOK

STEP 1: GETTING STARTED

Think through exactly what you want to do and why. The table on page 18 will help you clarify your preliminary thoughts about why you want to become a conservation volunteer and what you hope to gain from it. It will help you review your personal motivations, assist in selecting project options and highlight the practical issues. Alternatively, *Chapter 5* should whet your appetite for the variety of projects on offer.

STEP 2: DECIDING ON YOUR PURPOSE

After refining your search criteria, you should have narrowed your selection process down to the point where you can choose a project according to species or country. For the former move to Step 2A; for the latter jump to Step 2B. Alternatively, if money is the deciding factor, jump to Step 2C.

STEP 2A: CHOOSING VIA SPECIES

Use the table in *Chapter 3* on page 22 to browse for specific animals with which you might be interested in working. If you wanted to work with whales, for example, you are not restricted to one or two destinations but could join projects in the UK, Azores, Canada, Brazil, Bahamas, America, Mexico or South Africa.

STEP 2B: CHOOSING VIA COUNTRY

Having identified the country that most interests you, use the table on page 22, to find out which organisations are running programmes there, or look up your country of choice in *Appendix 1 The Country Guide*.

STEP 2C: CHOOSING VIA COST

The table on page 30 shows the cheapest and most expensive project fees offered by all of the companies audited in the book, so you can find one that meets your price range. If you have time, consider fundraising a portion of the money.

STEP 3: CHOOSING A PROJECT

Once you have identified the organisations that run projects working with the species, or in the country, you have selected, you need to identify which one best suits your needs. Read *Chapter 2 Types of Volunteer Organisations* to establish which type of company is most appropriate for you and then go directly to the companies listed in *Chapter 4*.

STEP 4: FUNDRAISING

Once you've chosen a company and have an idea of how much the project is going to cost, turn to *Chapter 6* for advice on fundraising.

STEP 5: PRACTICALITIES

Finally, consult *Chapter 7 Before You Go* for general information on booking tickets, visa services, what to take, etc.

THE AUDIT CRITERIA

THE SCORING SYSTEM

The scoring scheme developed and used in this book is unique. No other publication has ever delved so deeply into the 'how', 'why' and 'what' of conservation volunteer organisations, or tried to quantify their variable and often hyperbolic claims.

The raw data comes from an analysis of websites, company documentation, terms and conditions, as well as first-hand experience, previous volunteer comments, and email and telephone discussions with senior staff in each organisation.

Every organisation in the book has been asked for exactly the same data and asked to answer the same specific list of questions (see *Audit Categories* overleaf), so they can be fairly and legitimately compared. Because different organisations have different strengths and weaknesses, we abandoned a star-rating system in favour of using bargraphs because they highlight, where necessary, the subtle differences in scoring achieved for different categories by different companies.

There are nine categories in total, which should allow you to compare organisations according to the criteria that are most important to you. The list of questions found under each category was devised specifically to prevent bias affecting the results. So, for example, the credibility ratings have nothing to do with what a company say about themselves, how big they are, or if they have a great website or a massive advertising budget. Instead, the author only gathered evidence-based information that was verifiable, ie: safety procedures had to be confirmed with documentary proof.

Categories such as entertainment or the potential enjoyment value haven't been assessed because these were considered too subjective to measure and are a bonus – rather than the purpose – of conservation volunteering.

One final note: readers should be aware that some of the categories do not allow for the fact that organisations may have different priorities. For example, Frontier don't enter for any eco-tourism awards because they consider themselves to be a science-driven organisation and as a result score lower on credibility, whilst Coral Cay Conservation and i-to-i doubt the veracity of the current carbon-offsetting schemes, so have decided not to support them and therefore achieve lower scores in the environment and culture category. To prevent biased scorings, each category contained several questions where companies could score differently.

AUDIT CATEGORIES

1. CREDIBILITY

This category covers endorsements made by third-party organisations.
* What is the source of scientific conservation advice?
* Do they have any independently adjudicated awards?
* What do the media say about them?
* Is there a responsible tourism policy?
* Is it audited externally?
* Are they member of any key conservation/sustainable tourism organisations?
* Do any third-party organisations (ie: businesses, universities, governments) sponsor or make financial contributions?
* How long have they been in business?

2. ORGANISATION

This category provides an overview of how the company operates, their range of options and how projects are organised.
* What destinations do they go to?
* How many conservation projects/expeditions are available each year?
* How many conservation volunteers are recruited and sent each year?
* What sort of tasks and activities do volunteers undertake?
* What percentage of projects/expeditions are environmental/ conservation/animal care-oriented as opposed to teaching or community work?
* Do they retain contractual responsibility for volunteers on-site or is it passed to in-country NGOs or someone else?
* Is a booked placement assured, or do they retain the right to move volunteers to different projects or countries?
* Do they have regular open days or 'meet the staff' events?
* Are there named in-country project leaders?
* Are projects science-led with named scientists or other specialists?
* Do volunteers know who else will be on the project prior to departure?
* Are qualifications possible, eg: NVQ, BTEC, thesis study, PADI qualification?
* Are there written details about previous projects on the website or on request?
* Is there a facility to contact previous volunteers before booking?

3. WHERE THE MONEY GOES

This category looks at the cash implications, commitment and how much goes to the project (see table on page 30 for a comparison of fees).
* How much does it cost?
* Is a transparent public record of cash flow publicly available?
* What is included in the fee, what extras are there beyond board and lodgings, ie: welcome pack, expedition briefing, health assessment

form for your GP, equipment, pre-departure training, insurance, emergency evacuation, carbon off-setting (flights and local transport), follow-up reports, etc?
- What is not included, ie: visa, vaccinations, food, local transport?
- What are the payment arrangements, initial financial commitment, refunds and drop-out penalties; what degree of flexibility is there after booking?
- What percentage of a volunteer's contribution is spent in-country, ie: how big are the overheads?

4. PRE-DEPARTURE PREPARATION

Some volunteers will require a higher level of detail and information before departure and this category indicates what is available.
- Is there a pre-departure training event or detailed written advice?
- Is the in-country training explicit before departure?
- Are written project aims and objectives available before departure?
- Are details of environmental field conditions and anticipated activity (fitness requirements) levels provided or a health assessment required from a GP?
- Is there a clear job brief, do volunteers have a good idea of what they will be doing on a daily basis before departure?
- What details about equipment, packing, visa guidance are provided?
- Are there clear travel directions, and what assistance is provided?

5. IN THE FIELD

This category outlines how the company organises its projects and gives a feel for what life will be like.
- What are the stated or intended conservation benefits of specific projects?
- Who is legally responsible for volunteers at each project worksite – the sending company or local agent?
- Are projects long-term and ongoing over several years, or a one-off?
- What is the level of accommodation and comfort? Are there a choice of accommodation options?
- What is the work/leisure ratio? Is it a full working week, or is there plenty of time off?
- What local people – scientists, organisers, leaders, guides, drivers, cooks, etc – are employed?

6. ENVIRONMENT AND CULTURE

This category indicates the level of ethical forethought the company has made towards the local people and their environment.
- Are volunteers encouraged to carbon offset their travel?
- Is the carbon offset cost for the volunteer's international flight paid for within the basic fee, eg: with www.climatecare.org

- Is all the in-country project travel and activity carbon offset?
- Are there written guidelines about how volunteers should minimise their impact on the local environment?
- Is detailed cultural advice about local communities and traditions provided before departure?

7. SAFETY MEASURES

This category itemises the plans and procedures that companies may have in place to minimise risks.

- Is the new British Standards Institute BS8848:2007 (see page 221) in place and to what standard is it upheld? .
- Are on-site risk assessments carried out by company staff for each project? Is proof available for inspection?
- Are company staff at the project site 24/7, as opposed to a local contactor available by phone?
- Is a written emergency protocol in place and are field staff trained in emergency procedures – to what standard?
- What safety kit is on-site with volunteers – medic, satellite phone, medical kit?
- Is 24/7 emergency assistance/evacuation in place?

8. DEMONSTRABLE ACHIEVEMENTS

This is potentially the most important criterion for assessing organisations because it highlights exactly what conservation outcomes have resulted from past volunteer activity. If there is no tangible evidence of achievement, how are you to know if the conservation activity is worthwhile?

- Are there professionally written-up field records of past volunteer conservation activity including project progress? Are they made publicly available?
- Are there verifiable public records of past conservation outcomes for up to five cited achievements? Are they publicised on the website or in company literature? Are they published in the media or in scientific journals?

9. POST-TRIP FOLLOW-UP

This section considers the degree of follow-up after your project time is over and how interested organisations are after you return home.

- Are evaluation forms completed by all volunteers?
- Are the results published or available on request?
- What post-project follow-up is provided – reunions, lectures, updates, newsletters, etc?
- Is any organised support or advice available to ex-volunteers to help them develop local community action or establish an environmental project at home?

OVERVIEW OF HIGH-SCORING ORGANISATIONS

These conservation volunteer organisations exhibited exceptional strengths in the following categories:

Credibility CVA scores maximum and BTCV scores exceptionally highly.

Organisation Blue Ventures and VSO score maximum and Coral Cay and Operation Wallacea score exceptionally highly.

Where the money goes CVA and VSO score maximum and Azafady and BTCV score highly.

Pre-departure preparation Earthwatch, BTCV, Trekforce, GVI, Raleigh, VSO score maximum and Travellers Worldwide and ACE score exceptionally highly.

In the field Blue Ventures, GVI and Operation Wallacea score maximum and Biosphere, Travellers Worldwide, Earthwatch, Azafady, Coral Cay and GOP score very highly.

Environment and culture Earthwatch scores highly.

Safety BTCV, CVA, Raleigh and Operation Wallacea score maximum and Blue Ventures, Earthwatch, Trekforce and Biosphere score exceptionally highly.

Demonstrable achievements Earthwatch score maximum and Archelon, Frontier and Operation Wallacea score highly.

Post-trip follow-up None scores well in this category but Earthwatch and CVA score better than most.

NB An organisation's absence from a specific category here does not indicate they are bad (they may in fact be very good)– it's just that other organisations have scored more highly.

1 CONSERVATION: WHAT ARE THE ISSUES?

THE LOOMING CRISIS

In order to appreciate the value of volunteering, we need to see it in the context of the earth's environmental status. In 2008 the Living Planet Report – a dossier measuring the health of worldwide ecological diversity compiled by the likes of WWF, the Zoological Society of London and the Global Footprint Network – concluded that the planet is headed for an ecological 'credit crunch'. It found that three quarters of the world's population live in countries where consumption levels are outstripping the environment's ability to renew itself. Over the last few months, brokerages and insurance firms may have lost £1.3 trillion, but nature has permanently lost £2.9 trillion worth of resources. If these demands continue, director-general of WWF International, James Leape, believes we will need two planets by 2030 to provide the resources necessary to accommodate the growing population and maintain our current standard of living.

It's sobering stuff. But is it a shock? Conservation wasn't brought to the forefront of political discussion until 1992, when world leaders met at the United Nations Rio Earth Summit to adopt the Convention on Biological Diversity, which outlined international measures that could help preserve vital ecosystems and biological resources. The shocking statistics put to them *then* by leading scientists encouraged 150 nations to sign a declaration and generated a plethora of promises, projects and initiatives about developing alternative energy sources, stopping rainforest destruction, reducing car use and reducing pollution. However, 15 years on little has changed. At the 2007 convention, a report revealed that 90% of the world's tropical rainforests – which contain 80% of all identified living species – had been wiped out and that around ten million hectares continue to be destroyed every year. That's an area three times the size of Belgium. Elsewhere, 41% of mammals are in decline and 28% under direct threat. Unless urgent action is taken, by 2050 up to 20% of the earth's remaining plant species will be extinct.

Is it really all our fault? It's easy enough to link deforestation to a decrease in biodiversity, but what about issues like global warming? A minority argue that climatic factors such as these are a symptom of natural shifts in the earth's evolution and can't be attributed to CFCs or the burning of fossil fuels. Increasingly isolated scholars like Richard Lindzen, professor of atmospheric sciences at MIT, believe the warming phase is just a result of natural variability in the long lifespan of the earth and that human contribution is minimal, or that it could be due to a subtle change in the Earth's orbit or the intensity of the sun's radiation which has triggered the warming effect.

What about issues like overpopulation? In fact, boom-and-bust population cycles are a well established biological pattern – infinite growth and consumption is impossible within a finite environment – but if we don't balance our exponential population growth in relation to resource consumption then nature will find a way to regain the balance. Indeed, since the Cambrian explosion of diverse life forms, 500 million years ago, tens of thousands of creatures have appeared, proliferated and become extinct. (Interestingly, the average life span of a species is 4 million years and *Homo sapiens* [us] are nearing the end of that grace period.) It becomes clear then that, in fact, conservation is about saving ourselves, as well as wildlife. The planet is not as fragile as we think. It's an ever-changing biosphere that will carry on with or without us for millions of years to come. But our ability to survive as a species relies on fragile variables and if our mismanagement of resources continues at a rate the earth can't adapt to, then we may experience the long-lasting detrimental effects sooner rather than later.

According to the Living Planet report, the following need to happen in order for the earth's population to live within the bio-capacity of the planet:

1. Halt and then reverse human population growth.
2. Reduce consumption in affluent countries and allow a more equitable consumption by people in poorer countries.
3. Reduce the amount of resource/energy used to produce goods and services by increasing efficiency, minimising waste, recycling more and to start producing and consuming as locally as possible (ie: reduce unnecessary transportation).
4. Improve land management by reclamation, terracing, irrigation and reduce urbanisation, salinisation and desertification.

When faced with these facts, most of us ask: what can we do to help? Perhaps the best environmental contribution we could make would be to grow our own food, recycle everything, get rid of the car and reduce our power consumption. But let's be realistic! We all enjoy holidays and need to get away from time to time. Conservation volunteer projects allow you to travel AND contribute to a worthwhile cause. But what exactly does it involve?

CONSERVATION VOLUNTEERING: WHAT'S IT ALL ABOUT?

Conservation volunteering can range from preserving wildlife, and protecting the environment from destructive change, to developing more sustainable ways of living and reducing pollution. But the key factor common to all is that you get involved in the conservation process: you measure the leaves and plant the trees, instead of just passively marvelling at the rainforest as a tourist might do. Instead of just passing through, you have the opportunity to really get to grips with an unfamiliar culture; you work with local people, as opposed to staring at them. You're able to get a hands-on feel for the problems and issues associated with a particular environment, and play an active role with the chance to participate in solutions.

To put it into context: on a recent conservation project in Africa someone told me the story of a small boy who, while watching the umpteenth safari vehicle drive pass, asked his father, 'Why don't white people have legs?' This sums up the difference: as a conservation volunteer you'll have your feet firmly on the ground. You'll be expected to work without pay – in fact, you can expect to pay handsomely for the privilege – but you'll learn things that no escorted tour group ever will.

ISSUES OF CONCERN

It's commendable taking part in any conservation project, but volunteers want to be safe in the knowledge they're investing their time and money in a company that puts these resources to the best possible use. How do prospective volunteers choose between them and what do they need to watch out for?

It's not easy to tease out the differences among the raft of companies offering gap year projects, ecotourism, 'voluntourism' and working holidays; all have an element – to varying degrees – of personal enlightenment, social and cultural exchange, environmental improvement or preservation, education, economic benefit, and sustainability. However, the cold truth is that most organisations are not philanthropic; most are run as businesses – albeit doing altruistic things – which are set on making a profit. Volunteers need to keep an eye open for dubious ethics, complacency, superiority and even (some researchers claim) neo-colonialism.

NEO-COLONIALISM

The issue of neo-colonialism is one of the great concerns for some researchers. Indeed, most space on conservation volunteer organisation's websites is dedicated to the benefits volunteers will receive, but there's a notable absence of how the local environment or local people will benefit. One particular research study (see page 217*) identified how company websites and open days are full of uncritical volunteer comment and buzzwords like 'rewarding', 'meaningful', 'making a difference', 'valuable', 'humanitarian', 'life changing'. The absence of any host community voice is conspicuous. While studying at the University of the West of England, Tom Griffin also found that the only difference between tourism and volunteering was the marketing jargon they used. Volunteering, he said, was commonly differentiated from general tourism by claiming 'uniqueness, being more real, being part of the community, [and] being distant from familiar western culture'. But when companies are focused solely on the volunteer rather than the destination communities, what sort of impact can they really make?

Questions about the true helpfulness of a project arise: what happens to indigenous people deprived of access to their lands because it has been designated as an officially protected area? Are volunteers angering communities by taking on jobs locals could do? How will your money be spent? Volunteers should quiz organisations about these issues and ask them to demonstrate the tangible benefits local people are receiving from the project. Any reputable company should ensure the wishes of local people are paramount at all times and guard against a few powerful businessmen, landowners or the government reaping the financial benefits.

On another note, there's a tendency in the West to glamorise the exotic culture of indigenous peoples; our own loss of connection with the land often encourages our distaste for signs of development in under-developed countries. Volunteers shouldn't expect indigenous peoples to sit in a time warp. We all have televisions, use mobile phones and wear designer trainers, so don't be surprised if the people you meet also have these things or aspire to have them. The effects of globalisation may undermine many traditional cultures and therefore seem regrettable, but if they make life easier it is certainly not our place to halter development where it is wanted.

If you're concerned about appropriate ethical behaviour, it's worth bearing the following in mind:

- Respecting local people and their traditions doesn't just mean being polite, pleasant, or not offending sensibilities. It means recognising you are not superior because you happen to have been born into a wealthy nation, and that indigenous knowledge is of equal value, even though it may be different from yours.
- Make sure that, as relatively wealthy visitors, you do not skew the local economy by lavish spending, but also guard against bartering down to the cheapest possible price.
- Don't push your cultural values (religious, political or otherwise).
- Don't flaunt your wealth, ie: iPods, cameras, clothes, etc. Try to adopt a lifestyle that is not too dissimilar from that of the local people.

HOW USEFUL ARE VOLUNTEERS?

Another area of concern is the value of data gathered by volunteers. Some researchers argue that any results or surveys gathered by volunteers cannot be relied upon because they aren't properly trained and aren't au fait with the issues at hand. This kind of professional appropriation does go some way to preserving the integrity of conservation, but a swathe of recent studies has shown that with appropriate training, diligence and commitment volunteers *are* capable of monitoring biodiversity and endangered species almost as well as professional conservationists.

Indeed, the Wildlife Conservation Research Unit at Oxford University found that conservation techniques, eg: identification, trapping, recording data, etc, taught to volunteers, without lengthy training, were sufficiently accurate to yield reliable data, verified by professionals. Elsewhere, a New Zealand study at an endangered kakapo nesting site replaced 11 full-time nest monitors with a revolving series of 200 volunteers and found no diminution of standards over four breeding seasons.

Other examples of volunteers helping scientific research include: the Shark Trust inviting divers, beachcombers and walkers to register details of skate and ray egg cases that had washed up on Britain's beaches online, so they could identify potential nursery grounds; and Ecocean liaising with dive operators who run whale shark encounter trips to ask divers to take photographs of the skin patterning behind the gills of each shark and submit them to an online database, which immediately compares them with existing records so marine biologists can build up a global overview of the endangered species.

MEASURING THE DIFFERENCE

Exactly what a conservation project achieves is the most important measure of it's worth. With some organisations there is an absence of details concerning the quantifiable outcomes of their projects. There are numerous cowboy outfits in the marketplace that are quite happy to milk money from volunteers and the field is full of stories about counting the same turtles that were counted by a previous group, painting a school that was painted a month earlier or collecting worthless data that sits unused.

In such cases, volunteers often ask if there are any accreditation schemes listing responsible organisations. There are a couple: the Year Out Group (🖰 *www.yearoutgroup.org*) is an umbrella association whose code of practice (see the website for details) provides the basis for the standard of service expected of the group's member organisations; and the Foreign & Commonwealth Office runs a 'Know Before You Go' campaign (🖰 *www.fco.gov.uk/en/travelling-and-living-overseas/about-kbyg-campaign/*), which lists over 250 partners. However, there are problems with both. Whilst, the Year Out Group ensures companies are financially sound, have crisis management plans and agree to a code of practice, it doesn't guarantee the quality or effectiveness of specific projects. Meanwhile, several companies suggest that taking part in the KBYG campaign gives them official UK government approval, but this isn't the case. The Foreign Office has had to issue the following statement: 'the FCO does not endorse any of the companies who are part of the KBYG campaign... [and we do not] monitor their quality'. In fact, the only UK government-approved scheme is the BS8848:2007+A1:2009 (see page 221), which sets out a national standard for safe operational management of fieldwork and expeditions and is drawn up by the British Standards Institute. Companies which display this certification can be counted on as being more reliable. However, companies aren't required to follow the scheme and this is where this book comes into its own; it assesses companies on a host of other criteria to evaluate their worth.

THE CONSERVATION VOLUNTEER EFFECT

"Africa needs 'community benefit tourism' at a time when international aid flows are declining. Tourism is the largest voluntary transfer of resources from the rich to the not-so-rich in history and it offers Africa a unique opportunity to harness the power of the world's largest and fastest growing industry to improve the lives of its people. Tourists from Britain bring and leave more cash on the continent than the British government gives in aid to Africa. And it's the same for other rich countries, but if tourism does not benefit communities then it will not be truly sustainable".

Lelei LeLaulu, president of Counterpart International and co-founder of the World Tourism Forum for Peace and Sustainable Development

This quote rings true for all nations. Taking part in conservation volunteer projects has several positive knock-on effects. Research studies have identified three benefits of the volunteering process: the first was the benefits accrued by the destination, but the second two were an increase of awareness and self-development in volunteers. Similarly, the University of Essex's Centre for Environment and Society found that 'an increased connectedness to nature' – an invariable outcome of conservation volunteering – results in 'higher environmental awareness [and] an increase in environmentally friendly practice by volunteers on returning home.'

Essentially, conservation volunteering establishes a two-way beneficial process: while volunteers bring about change by contributing money and hands-on help to a specific conservation issue, the engagement in the project can also bring about personal development in the volunteer's life, not to mention enhance their CV. There are numerous stories of conservation volunteers who, on returning home, have started growing their own food, become local wildlife diversity officers, created habitats for endangered wildlife, sought alternatives to pesticide use, become conservation leaders, or created wildlife gardens in schools so they can teach city children about the environment. The personal benefits and knowledge to be gained from conservation volunteers projects are unlimited.

2 TYPES OF VOLUNTEER ORGANISATIONS

What started in the 19th century as the 'grand tours' of aristocrats and missionaries, has morphed over the years into mass tourism and charity, and now evolved to incorporate elements of conservation. Today, conservation volunteering is a major commercial business sector, marketed just like any other part of the tourism industry. This chapter looks at the different types of companies and how they operate.

CONSERVATION OPPORTUNITIES

The choice of conservation volunteer activities available is extensive. Generally projects attempt to clarify the unknown and slow down or ameliorate the negative impact of human activity. A selection of typical projects routinely on offer within the wildlife and conservation sector include:

- Game parks, animal rescue and rehabilitation centres, animal sanctuaries, work in nature reserves, eco-parks or national parks.
- Rainforest conservation, eg: reforestation, sustainable development (ie: growing coffee within the rainforest), guided trips.
- Marine and coastal conservation, eg: beach cleaning, turtle protection, fish and coral surveys, boat-based whale and dolphin surveys, and sustainable development in tropical coastal communities.
- Resolving human-wildlife conflicts, eg: desert elephants and village water supplies, hippo attacks, crocodiles nesting in village fishing areas.
- Sustainable tourist development, eg: solar and fuel-efficient projects to reduce rainforest cutting.
- Building and repairing nature trails, managing habitats, environmental education, assisting in visitors centres or construction work to support sustainable tourism infrastructure.
- Wildlife and botanical surveys, eg: monitoring endangered species, relocating animals, reintroduction of species.
- Sustainable management of river health, wetland health, urban conservation and land management.

Note: Volunteers should steer clear of projects that commercially exploit animals under an eco banner. Any suggestions of swimming with captured dolphins, or feeding and cuddling cute animals should be regarded with great suspicion.

CHARACTERISTICS OF DIFFERENT ORGANISATIONS

On the surface volunteer organisations appear to offer similar opportunities. However, their involvement with the projects they're offering can vary considerably. Most organisations imply that they organise and run specific conservation projects. Some actually do, but many do not. Most of the time it is an NGO or charity based overseas that actually organises and runs the projects; they are the people engaged in conservation. Placement agencies may merely agree to find and send them volunteers.

For some travellers it may not matter by what route they come to a project, but for others it may. It's certainly worth bearing in mind that, in some cases, being aware of the operations of various organisations can help you save money (see page 12). For example, you could find that on any one overseas project, volunteers booked their placement through a variety of UK-, USA- and European-based organisations with their fees varying accordingly; a similar set up as buying a package tour from a holiday company.

When deciding which organisation to book with, volunteers should consider factors such as how confident they are when far from home. Nervous travellers, for instance, would be better suited to a privately run expedition than, say, a field-based organisation that requires a high level of self reliance. Organisations can be divided to the following general categories:

Internet directories

Internet directory services list conservation volunteer opportunities. They don't have any specific company allegiance. However, the information is not unbiased as the service provider usually writes the entry content. Furthermore, it is not always possible to identify which organisation is offering a project until you enquire through the website. Choose one of these if you haven't made up your mind where to go or what to do. They're an ideal tool for getting a feel for what's on offer.

Placement organisers

These organisations match up volunteers, as individuals or groups, with conservation volunteer opportunities abroad. They're also often described as clearing houses. The best organisations know what projects they will be running, when and where, several months in advance. Other organisations have lists of overseas projects that have requested volunteers and when individuals contact them they try to match them up. This can result in being 'bumped off' your chosen project or, for example, being placed on a turtle project during a period when there are no turtles. Furthermore, quite often a project booked with one placement agent is also likely to be offered by several other placement agents. They quite often give them different names, and the price can vary considerably (see box on page 12).

Placement organisers are all a bit different, but usually you can expect them to:
- Arrange an airport pick-up or have a nearby meeting point
- Arrange additional overnight accommodation if required
- Have a local co-ordinator who will provide some local orientation, deal with serious problem, but who is also likely to be supervising many other projects

- Issue you with a 24-hour emergency home-country telephone contact
- They may also arrange flights, side trips, or onward travel

Essentially, a placement service will make most of the arrangements between you and the organisers of the conservation project, but will not be on site with you 24/7 (if at all). In fact, they have very little direct involvement with your chosen project and this is why they are invariably vague about a volunteer's specific daily activities – they don't control the schedule; the local project supervisor identifies what needs to be done. Their operational responsibility often ends as soon as you are left at the project site. From there on the in-country project leaders are in charge. These outfits are ideal for volunteers who don't want to be looked after or organised quite so much, but still want to keep clear lines of communication open with home.

Privately run expeditions/NGOs
These hands-on organisations plan and run their own in-country projects, leading organised groups on expeditions with a prepared agenda. They are mostly, but not always, charities or NGOs. These privately mounted expeditions tend to target specific scientific projects. Groups have a designated leader who meets you at the pick-up point and remains on-site with the team 24/7. They take responsibility for general problems, project organisation and liaising with the local community and officials. These projects are ideal for volunteers who haven't travelled much, or are cautious and want to be with someone who will take overall responsibility.

Hybrids
Some organisations are a hybrid of placement organiser and privately run expedition, ie: they lead their own expeditions AND recruit and place volunteers with partner organisations as a means of augmenting their income and supplementing core charity conservation projects. Be sure to check whether you are booking one of their own expeditions or a placement run by another organisation.

Field-based organisations
Field-based conservation organisations tend to be grassroots outfits that focus on a specific species or habitat and are run locally in the destination country. They range from local NGOs and government-supported projects to private enterprises. In most cases, you can contact and arrange a placement with them directly, cutting out the middlemen and any additional finder's fee charged by a placement organisation.

The upside of this is that the cost is likely to be low or even nil, apart from board and lodgings. The downside is that your accommodation is likely to be very basic, or you may even need to bring your own tent. You will also have to find your own way from the airport to the project site, which may involve a few local buses and a bit of hiking. But perhaps the most problematic issue will be unpredictable language problems; there may be limited English speakers on the project and you will have no emergency back-up support, except that provided by your personal travel insurance.

These organisations have the least amount of media coverage, so you need to find placements via word of mouth from previous volunteers, or via websites like Green Volunteers (🕮 *www.greenvolunteers.com*) that lists the details of around 500 conservation volunteer opportunities around the globe. These organisations are best suited to confident experienced travellers, capable of handling problems on their own. The conservation work is likely to be just as meaningful – if not more so – than any organised trip. For more advice on planning your own placement see page 33.

Eco-friendly package-holiday companies

There are also eco-friendly package holiday companies, which mainly offer travel itineraries with a token volunteering element incorporated. These organisations may offer hundreds of projects in dozens of countries, may look the most impressive but they are less likely to have direct involvement or a genuine long-term commitment to any given project or purpose. You need to be wary of telesales staff that may be reading from a crib sheet or working on sales commission.

SUBTLE DIFFERENCES BETWEEN COMPANIES

In addition to operating differently, some organisations place different emphases on core topics. The lists below outlines some of the different stances companies take.

MONEY ISSUES

- Some organisations spend more on advertising and self-promotion than they do on the conservation projects they promote.
- Some organisations spend over 70% of your fee on and around the project in the country you go to, whereas others may spend as little as 30%.
- Some organisations require a totally non-refundable deposit.
- Some organisations will refund most of the placement fee up until a certain point in time and others demand it very early and never let it go.
- Higher fees do not necessarily mean that more of your cash goes to help the project – some placements are just overpriced.
- Take out travel insurance before handing over any cash because it provides some cover for cancellations. Check the details carefully because insurance policies may not pay out if the reason is deemed inadequate or you have just changed your mind (see page 182).

ETHICS AND RESPONSIBILITIES

- Some companies have good ethical and responsible travel principles while others are notably vague or make no actual commitment.
- Some organisations include carbon offsetting of your international airfares within your fee; others may encourage you to do so at an additional cost,or not mention it at all.
- Some organisations fund the carbon offsetting of all of the project's additional energy consumption while in the field, whereas others do not.
- Some organisations are very clear about ensuring that their projects do not add an environmental burden on the country visited – consumption of water and other resources and waste left by volunteers – while others don't mention it.
- Some organisations emphasise respect and consideration for local cultures and ensure that local communities benefit from volunteer visits; others don't.
- Some organisations have a vision of what they want to achieve and work on projects year-on-year, while others will send volunteers on any overseas project that match volunteers' requirements.

EFFECTIVE ORGANISATION

- Some organisations have qualified leaders who accompany volunteers in the field, organise project activity, solve problems and liaise with local communities, whereas others just send you.
- In-country co-ordinators can be full-time employed staff (European or local), or contracted staff supervising several projects and may only be available during office hours if there is a problem.
- Some organisations have pre-departure training days where you meet other participants and learn about the project and the country, whereas others tell you little until you get there.
- Some organisations carry out their own risk assessment in the field according to UK Health and Safety standards; others are less rigorous.
- Some organisations provide details of what you will actually be doing – aims and objectives, daily or weekly job brief – whereas others are vague and merely indicate activities you may be 'helping with'.
- Some organisations have good follow-up and keep volunteers in touch with project development after you return home, while others forget you.

CREDIBILITY

- Some organisations have been around for 20–50 years, whereas others are new kids on the block.
- Some organisations explicitly publicise their past achievements,

whereas others are vaguer and only list general worthy achievements.

- Some organisations have third-party sponsors such as Land Rover, Vodaphone, financial institutions, universities or government departments; this can increase their funding and credibility. Others eschew all commercial associations.
- Some organisations have won awards, or have been reviewed in the national press or other credible media outlets.
- Some organisations interview volunteers. You shouldn't take this as a slight, but instead see it as proof that they care who goes on their projects. They want to make sure it's right for you and you're right for the project. You should think carefully about a travelling with a company that sends anyone, anywhere.
- Some organisations reserve the right to change your project and even your destination without recompense.

EFFECTS ON THE FEES

As stated above, many organisations are incredibly vague about who exactly is running the placement you will be on. This is so you don't bypass them and lose them their finder's fee. Two revealing comments made to me by prominent individuals in the industry were: 'this is a wholesale business: you buy project places cheaply abroad and retail them on to volunteers' and 'some companies use the supermarket strategy of "stack them high and sell them cheap".' Essentially, two organisations might, in effect, 'buy' a volunteer placement from an NGO in Namibia for £400. One might sell it to a prospective volunteer for £800, while another sells it for £1,000.

The difference could be to cover larger overheads, a corporate profit margin, or expensive marketing. Some real-life examples (based on Autumn 2008 prices) include:

Example A: Two weeks on the Namibia-based desert elephant project run by Elephant–Human Relations Aid (EHRA) costs £799 if booked with Real Gap, £600 booked with GVI and £480 if booked directly with EHRA.

Example B: Two weeks working on a range of conservation projects in Australia with Conservation Volunteers Australia (CVA) costs £550 (based on £1,100 for four weeks) if booked with Frontier, £431 with Projects Abroad, £399 with Real Gap and £270 if booked directly with CVA.

It's clear to see that by bypassing a placement agency and contacting the NGO directly, volunteers quite often end up paying a fraction of the cost. However, placement agencies may provide significant additional services for their fee, including pre-departure advice, airport meet-and-greet, internal transfers, onward travel planning, etc. In addition to this, their higher prices might also include extras such as local travel costs, full-board meals and better class of accommodation, which can easily push up the cost of a self-organised placement. Like any other expensive purchase, volunteers should question what the seller has to say and maintain a healthy degree of caution and scepticism and never take anything for granted.

TERMS AND CONDITIONS DISCLAIMERS

Before purchasing any placement be sure to read the terms and conditions attached to the contract. The terms and conditions of most companies are intended to limit their responsibilities and liabilities and disclaim liability in the event you do anything foolish. The list below provides a guide to the more unusual terms and conditions, but volunteers must study a company's terms and conditions carefully before signing up for a trip, so you know what you are agreeing to and what you are legally signing away.

T&C A force majeure is 'an abnormal and unforeseeable event that no human foresight could anticipate, ie: circumstances beyond the organisation's control such as fire, lightning, explosion, earthquake, storm, hurricane, flood, landslide, outbreak of infectious disease, imposition of quarantine, government or other official intervention, the threat or outbreak of war, riot, civil commotion, the threat or an act of terrorism, loss, theft or damage to strategic equipment, hijacking, nuclear disaster and even any other event or circumstance considered to be beyond the organisation's control. If one is invoked you could lose your full project fee.

A In the first instance it's worth doing some research into the destination you propose to travel to. How likely is it any of the above will happen? Secondly, it's important to find out what your chosen organisation will do in such circumstances. What is the company contingency or evacuation plan? Will you get a refund? Will your travel insurance cover the bill?

T&C Most organisations have a clause allowing them to cancel a trip if there are insufficient numbers; they will normally offer an alternative or a refund.

A Check whether a full refund will be provided

T&C All organisations include a clause stating volunteers will be sent home if found to be using drugs, even if it's locally acceptable.

A Apply suitable judgement

T&C All organisations disclaim liability for accidents, disasters and personal injury except when the result of their own negligence. They will of course assist injured volunteers, but will not accept liability.

A Seek redress from travel insurance policy and recognise potential risks

T&C No liability is usually accepted for the acts or omissions of third-party contractors (eg: jungle guides, drivers, etc, not associated with the company), including negligence.

A Be aware of altered liability during different project activities insurance cover

T&C If you have a serious complaint this must be raised in writing with field staff during the project; if not, a complaint may not be accepted as legitimate on your return home.

A Be clear on what the company's obligations are and what disclaimers you have signed and agreed to

T&C No liability is accepted if you experience visa or immigration problems, or are refused entry at the project destination.

A Check passport and visa entry requirements and plan well in advance

T&C Any problems with your flights or travel arrangements that prevent you reaching an agreed assembly point are down to you and the airline.

A Seek redress from carriers or travel insurance

T&C No liability is accepted if you don't, or can't, keep to an agreed arrival timetable.

A Check the cancellation clauses. In what circumstances will you forfeit your booking payments? Travel insurance may or may not cover this; it depends on how good the reason is

Also...

- If your behaviour endangers the project or anyone on the project they will send you home without any recompense.
- No liability is accepted if you commit a criminal act. You will be asked to leave the project and make your own way home without recompense. Travel insurance policies also disclaim liability if a criminal act is committed by the policy holder.
- Most organisations expect you to have independent travel insurance cover, although some provide emergency evacuation or basic insurance cover. Make sure your policy covers volunteering activities and manual work if necessary.
- If you damage project equipment due to negligence, you will be charged for it.
- All organisations disclaim liability for any infectious diseases you might contract.
- No organisation will guarantee seeing or experiencing specific wildlife.
- Special diets are difficult to cater for and are unlikely to be generally available, although some companies do cater for vegetarians.

CANCELLATIONS

If you are concerned that you might need to cancel a proposed trip, do not book it – as in some cases you will be legally liable for the full cost even if you haven't paid the final balance. The downside is you run the risk of not getting the placement you want, but on the other hand you will have safeguarded your money and there's always the chance you'll able to negotiate a last-minute placement. A travel insurance policy may cover you if you need to cancel a trip for health reasons, etc, but never if you just change your mind.

MARINE SURVEYS

Mandy Hengeveld

'Masks on, regulators in mouth, BCDs inflated, bums over the edge, fins crossed, dangly bits between your legs, clear behind... 3, 2, 1 ... GO!'

With a swift backwards roll, the team of surveyors enter the welcoming turquoise waters of the South China Sea. You'd think we were at an army drill camp, but the reassuring words of the boat marshal ensure that all divers enter the water safely.

The waters of the Perhentian Islands are an inviting 29°C and extremely clear. From boat or shore you can see the outlines of the fringing reefs and watch groups of damselfish dart around in the shallows. These damselfish are part of the seemingly endless assortment of fish, corals, algae and invertebrates that together form a close-knit community consisting of tens of thousands of individual organisms.

It's the variety and types of these organisms that we've come to study, but the super thing is none of us can predict what our survey team will see during our data-collection dives. A passing school of barracuda? A towering colony of dazzling blue coral? Each dive holds an element of surprise.

It's easy to get distracted watching the complex symbiotic relationships found between different types of organisms on coral reefs, such as the interaction between sand-dwelling gobies and their blind shrimp partners; the shrimp diligently digs out a burrow for both animals, while the goby stands guard, ready to alert the blind shrimp of any approaching danger.

The highlight was finding a group of ghost shrimps hidden amidst the branches of a colonial tree coral. It was the first sighting to be recorded in the area and it had taken us two months of diving these waters to find them; we were ecstatic.

Mandy Hengeveld was a marine project scientist at the Perhentian Islands, Malaysia, with Coral Cay Conservation

ENDANGERED PRIMATES
Ceri Gibson

When we booked our trip, our group leader put volunteers in touch with each other as well as past volunteers who provided useful information about the project, so by the time we arrived at Mombasa Airport it felt like a much-anticipated reunion of good friends. Our Colobus Trust hosts met us at the airport and we were off.

The accommodation was described in the catalogue as clean and basic, but this didn't do Colobus Cottage justice. We had direct beach access with a sea breeze in the bathroom, were 'serenaded' by bushbabies on the veranda most nights and awoken at 05.00 every morning by Sykes monkeys dancing on the corrugated iron roof.

Surveying included visiting sacred forest areas, known as *kayas*, in search of non-habituated colobus, Sykes and vervet monkeys. These dense forests are held in great esteem by the local people, for historical and spiritual reasons. Permission had to be sought from village elders, and guides accompanied us during these visits. Although exhausting and at times scary, these trips were a real bonus to the holiday. We were not only permitted somewhere very few tourists are allowed, but the guides and Colobus Trust staff passed on their incredible knowledge about trees and wildlife.

We also cared for sick monkeys in the clinic and looked after rescued monkeys being rehabituated. These tasks were particularly heart wrenching, especially having to scare the monkeys into the corner of the cage before feeding, so they didn't become familiar with humans prior to release. I found it particularly difficult to be really scary rather than making a game of it, but knowing the monkeys would be safer in the wild following the treatment was a huge incentive. During my clinic day I cared for an old female Angolan colobus. She was injured and exhausted and by the expression on her wizened face I knew she was terrified of being away from her troop. A couple of days later I woke to the knowledge that she had not survived; it was heart-breaking!

I really felt a part of the team when asked to give a tour of the Trust to some English tourists and was pleasantly surprised at how much I'd picked up during my short stay. A highlight was the two-night break to Tsavo East and West. It was booked through a local tour guide at a fraction of the cost I would have paid has I booked through an operator at home. Our drivers were great and we saw the 'big five' and much more.

Unfortunately, the Trust managers vigorously discouraged contact with the local community, but all other aspects of my experience were incredible. I feel very privileged to have gained insight into monkey shenanigans and the background work that goes into protecting both them and their habitat. The conservation volunteer holiday really did combine an unforgettable experience with achieving something valuable.

Ceri Gibson travelled with the British Trust for Conservation Volunteers on their endangered primates 'holiday' to Diani Beach, Kenya.

3 CHOOSING AN ORGANISATION

'Which is the best project?' has to be one of the most frequently posed questions on travel site chat room forums. However, it's a rather pointless one because 'best' is subjective: nobody else can answer it for you; it depends on why you want to go. Now you're aware of the range of organisations in the industry and how they operate, you can set about choosing a project that meets your requirements. With so many options to choose from it can be difficult to pinpoint where to go, what to do and which organisation is the best to go with. This chapter takes you step-by-step through the process.

DECIDING ON YOUR PURPOSE

First of all, it's important to be clear about the purpose of your conservation volunteer trip. Are you going to learn new skills or reassess your career options? Do you want to develop your language skills? Is it for adventure and out-of-the-ordinary experiences? Are you just after a relaxing holiday with a conservation element attached? Do you want to be able to travel during/after the project? You might just want to get out there and back safely. Whatever your reasoning, choosing the right company and the right project is crucial if you are to get exactly what you want out of the trip.

Secondly, different organisations offer trips with different emphases, so you need to ensure that the one you choose meets your expectations. Some outfits specialise in long-term gap year-style trips, whereas others cater for those on a fortnight vacation; there are trips led by scientists and others that emphasise working with local communities; some attract a young crowd who favour a party atmosphere, others can be more studious and quiet. The goals and outcomes of these different types of projects will vary enormously, and so will the work. Find a company that is going to work in the way that meets your purpose.

To help you focus on which companies might fit your purpose, fill in the table on page 18, ticking which statements are a priority for you. Alternatively, if you've already seen a couple of companies who run projects you are interested in, you can compare the two outfits by filling in the companies names and ticking which statements apply to them, so you can compare their advantages and disadvantages at a glance.

TABLE 1: WHAT ARE YOUR PRIORITIES?

	A priority?	Company name:	Company name:
IN A NUTSHELL			
→ They are a charity			
→ They are a commercial organisation			
→ They run their own expeditions			
→ Company staff are actively involved in running the project			
CREDIBILITY			
→ They have won awards			
→ There is positive media coverage about the company or projects they arrange			
→ Projects are scientifically based			
→ They have been in business for a long time			
→ They have responsible travel policies for eco and ethical tourism			
→ Evidence of long-term commitment			
→ They continue to support the project after you depart			
→ Third-party organisations endorse or support the work of the organisation			
ORGANISATIONAL ARRANGEMENTS			
→ The primary emphasis is on meeting the project's conservation priorities			
→ The primary emphasis is on meeting the interests of the volunteer			
→ Most participants are younger than 25			
→ Participants age is immaterial			
→ A balanced gender mix is important			
→ I want to know exactly who will be in charge at the project site			
→ I want to attend an open day and meet staff, fellow volunteers and past volunteers			
MONEY			
→ The total cost of the project is crucial			
→ It's important that the fee directly benefits the project and local people			

→ I want all the fee to go directly to the project → I don't what to pay the final balance until close to the departure date → I want to be able to cancel after booking and get most of my money back → I want to know what all the extra costs are → I don't want any hidden extras; I want everything to be arranged			
PRE-DEPARTURE PREPARATION			
→ I want a pre-departure training programme → I want to know what the in-country training programme involves → I want to read project reports about previous volunteer activities → I want to know what the specific project aims and objectives are → I want a clear job brief– exactly what I will be doing on most days → I want to know what the fitness requirements are, ie: long walks or heavy lifting → I want to be able to talk to past volunteers about my project			
IN THE FIELD			
→ I don't care what type of accommodation I have → I don't want to rough it too much → I don't want to take a sleeping bag, sheets or any other living equipment → I'm happy to help with cooking, washing up and general cleaning → I don't want to get involved with cooking or general domestic chores → I would prefer to work in a group with other volunteers like myself → It's important that I meet and work with local people on the project → I would be happy working alone → I would prefer working in a team → I am confident in an overseas environment			

→ I like to have things well planned and don't like badly organised activities			
→ I'm easy going and enjoy winging it			
→ I need to keep in touch with home so want easy internet and/or telephone access			
→ I couldn't bear to be without my mobile phone			
ENVIRONMENT & CULTURE			
→ I want to be sure that the project is environmentally friendly			
→ I want to ensure that my trip is as carbon neutral as possible			
→ I want to engage with local people and get to know the local culture			
SAFETY			
→ The organisation works to the British Standard Institute BS8848:2007 (see page 221)			
→ I want to know that an in-country risk assessment has been carried out for the project			
→ I want to know what the emergency planning procedures are if something goes seriously wrong			
→ I would like there to be trained first-aiders or medics on site			
ACHIEVEMENTS			
→ I want to read or view video evidence of past activities at my project site or similar sites			
→ I would like to know what published evidence there is of practical achievements and environmental successes by the company			
POST-TRIP FOLLOW-UP			
→ I want to be able to make my post project views known			
→ I want to continue supporting my project after retuning home			
→ I want to continue my conservation involvement once back home			
→ I want to see the company supporting conservation initiatives once I've returned home			

Now that you have built a personal profile of your ideal conservation volunteer organisation, go through the list again and extract your top ten priorities and mark them in the table below. You can refer back to this condensed list when choosing a conservation volunteer organisation to travel with.

TABLE 2: TOP TEN PROJECT PRIORITIES

1.
2.
3.
4.
5.
6.
7.
8.
9.
10.

CHOOSING VIA COUNTRY

Some volunteers want to work with a certain species of animal, but others are more interested in a particular country, and as long as you're not tying yourself to an endemic species, ie: koalas or kangaroos found only in Australia, the project possibilities are endless. For example, if you want to work with big cats there are opportunities in India, Thailand, Arabia, Eastern Europe, Central and South America and many African countries. Whilst whale and dolphin projects are found in the UK, Spain, Greece, Canada, New Zealand, the Amazon, Brazil, USA and the Azores, and there are reforestation projects in Scotland, Nepal, Central and South America, the Far East and Australia.

In the first instance, the table on page 22 is primarily intended for volunteers who know which species they'd like to work with, but it has also been designed so that volunteers can select a country – albeit from different sections of the table – and find out which organisations run projects there.

Alternatively, you can look up the country of your choice in the *Country Guide* appendix on page 199 where a list of organisations operating in that particular country is provided, alongside general background information on the destination such as special security and political issues, visas, flight distance, cost of getting there and any health advice.

CHOOSING VIA SPECIES

More often than not volunteers have a firm idea about the species of animal they'd like to help protect or monitor. Bearing this in mind, the following table summarises the variety of species covered by volunteer organisations audited in this guide. They are cross-referenced so you can look up a particular species, identify countries where projects are happening and find organisations that lead expeditions or send volunteers there.

Please note that different companies going to the same country and working with the same or similar species may be offering the exact same project, or they may be working with different local partners in a different part of the country.

It's also worth remembering that specific project opportunities may change from year to year. Sometimes scientists have completed their research and no longer require volunteers, or changes in the local situation have made a project unviable or unsafe. Occasionally a project is cancelled at the last minute if the organisation cannot fill all the available places.

Species	Country	Organisations
Animal rescue centre/sanctuary	Argentina	i-to-i 104
	Australia	Cape Tribulation Tropical Research Station 64, CVA 68, Frontier 84, GlobalXperience 92, Real Gap 123, Travellers Worldwide 130
	Bolivia	Inti Wara Yassi 102, Quest 116
	Belize	Personal Overseas Development 110
	Brazil	Ecovolunteer 76
	Cambodia	Personal Overseas Development 110
	Costa Rica	Frontier 84, GlobalXperience 92, i-to-i 104, Real Gap 123
	Estonia	BTCV 58
	Ecuador	Frontier 84, i-to-i 104, Real Gap 123
	Ghana	Frontier 84
	Guatemala	GlobalXperience 92, Frontier 84, Real Gap 123
	India	GlobalXperience 92, i-to-i 104, Real Gap 123
	Ireland	Irish Sea Sanctuary 148
	Kenya	Frontier 84
	Malaysia	Frontier 84, Travellers Worldwide 130, Way Out Experience (WOX) 140
	Namibia	Frontier 84, GlobalXperience 92, Real Gap 123
	South Africa	Africa Conservation Experience 42, Frontier 84, GlobalXperience 92, GVI 89, i-to-i 104, Operation Wallacea 107, Real Gap 123, Travellers Worldwide 130
	Sri Lanka	Greenforce 94, i-to-i 104, Travellers Worldwide 130
	Swaziland	Frontier 84
	Thailand	Ecovolunteer 76, Frontier 84,

	USA	GlobalXperience 92, i-to-i 104, Personal Overseas Development 110, Real Gap 123, Starfish Ventures 128 Ecovolunteer 76, GlobalXperience 92, GVI 89, Real Gap 123
	Venezuela	Real Gap 123
	Zambia	Frontier 84
Bats	Australia	Cape Tribulation Tropical Research Station 64, CVA 68
	Brazil	Earthwatch 71
	UK	Wildlife Trusts 156
Bears	Borneo	Way Out Experience (WOX) 140
	Russia	Ecovolunteer 76
	Slovakia	Biosphere Expeditions 52
Cheetahs	Botswana	Africa Guide 41
	Namibia	Biosphere Expeditions 52, Earthwatch 71, Frontier 84, Real Gap 123
	South Africa	Africa Conservation Experience 42
Chimpanzees	South Africa	GlobalXperience 92
	Southwest Cameroon	GVI 89
	Uganda	GVI 89
Condors	Argentina	Earthwatch 71
Coral reefs and fish	Bahamas	Earthwatch 71, Greenforce 94
	Costa Rica	Asociacion ANAI WIDECAST Marine Programme 47
	Cuba	Operation Wallacea 107
	Belize	Personal Overseas Development 110
	Ecuador	Real Gap 123
	Egypt	Coral Cay Conservation 65, Operation Wallacea 107
	Fiji	Frontier 84, Greenforce 94, Real Gap 123
	Greece	Frontier 84, GlobalXperience 92
	Honduras	Biosphere Expeditions 52
	Indonesia	Operation Wallacea 107
	Madagascar	Blue Ventures 55
	Mexico	GVI 89
	Philippines	Coral Cay Conservation 65

	Mozambique	Operation Wallacea 107
	Seychelles	Africa Guide 41,
		Earthwatch 71, GVI 89
	Tanzania	Frontier 84
	Thailand	Frontier 84, Personal Overseas Development 110, Projects Abroad 113
	Tobago	Coral Cay Conservation 65
Crocodiles and other reptiles	Australia	CVA 68
	Brazil	Earthwatch 71
	Egypt	Operation Wallacea 107
	Guatemala	Frontier 84, Real Gap 123
	Honduras	GlobalXperience 92, i-to-i 104
	Mexico	Projects Abroad 113
	Peru.	Earthwatch 71, Operation Wallacea 107
	South Africa	Real Gap 123
	Zambia	Earthwatch 71
Dolphins	Azores	Biosphere Expeditions 52
	Bahamas	Earthwatch 71
	Brazil	GVI 89
	Greece	Earthwatch 71, GlobalXperience 92, GVI 89
	Italy	Ecovolunteer 76, Frontier 84, GVI 89
	Kenya	Africa Guide 41, GVI 89
	Peru	Earthwatch 71, Operation Wallacea 107, Real Gap 123
	South Africa	Africa Conservation Experience 142, GlobalXperience 92, i-to-i 104, Travellers Worldwide 130
	UK	Earthwatch 71
Elephants	Botswana	Africa Conservation Experience 42, Frontier 84
	Kenya	Earthwatch 71
	Namibia	EHRA 81, GVI 89, Africa Guide 41
	South Africa	Edge of Africa 79, Travellers Worldwide 130,
	Sri Lanka	BTCV 58, Frontier 84, GVI 89, i-to-i 104, Travellers Worldwide 130
	Thailand	Ecovolunteer 76, Frontier 84, GlobalXperience 92, i-to-i 104, Personal Overseas Development 110, Starfish Ventures 128

	Zambia	GlobalXperience 92
	Zimbabwe	Real Gap 123
Gorillas	Southwest Cameroon	GVI 89
Hippos	Malawi	Africa Guide 41, Frontier 84, GlobalXperience 92, Real Gap 123
Horses	Mongolia	Ecovolunteer 76, GlobalXperience 92
	South Africa	Africa Conservation Experience 42, Africa Guide 41, GlobalXperience 92, i-to-i 104, Real Gap 123
	USA	Earthwatch 71
Kiwis	New Zealand	CVNZ 68, Real Gap 123
Leopards	Botswana	Africa Conservation Experience 42, Frontier 84
	Namibia	Biosphere Expeditions 52, Frontier 84
	South Africa	Africa Conservation Experience 42, Edge of Africa 79
	Sri Lanka	Frontier 84
Lions	Botswana	Frontier 84
	Kenya	Earthwatch 71
	Namibia	Biosphere Expeditions 52
	South Africa	Africa Conservation Experience 42, i-to-i 104
	Zimbabwe	Real Gap 123, Travellers Worldwide 130
Meerkats	South Africa	Africa Guide 41, Earthwatch 71, Edge of Africa 79,
National Parks	Australia	CVA 68
	Costa Rica	Projects Abroad 113, Frontier 84
	Honduras	Operation Wallacea 107
	Mongolia	Ecovolunteer 76
	New Zealand	CVNZ 68
	Portugal	BTCV 58
	South Africa	Africa Conservation Experience 42, Africa Guide 41, Edge of Africa 79, GVI 89
	USA	Real Gap 123, Responsible travel.com 126

	Venezuela	Real Gap 123
	Zambia	GlobalXperience 92
	Zimbabwe	Real Gap 123
Orang-utans	Indonesia	Ecovolunteer 76, Frontier 84, GlobalXperience 92, GVI 89, Way Out Experience-Orang-utan Project 140
	Malaysia	Frontier 84, Real Gap 123, Travellers Worldwide 130
Otters	Brazil	Earthwatch 71, Ecovolunteer 76, GlobalXperience 92
	Peru	Earthwatch 71, Operation Wallacea 107,
	USA	Earthwatch 71
Pandas	China	Frontier 84, Greenforce 94, i-to-i 104, Quest 116, Real Gap 123
Parrots and macaws	Australia	CVA 68
	Peru	Biosphere Expeditions 52, Earthwatch 71, Operation Wallacea 107, Personal Overseas Development 110
Penguins	Australia	CVA 68
	South Africa	Earthwatch 71, Greenforce 94, Travellers Worldwide 130
Rainforest and reforestation	Australia	Cape Tribulation Tropical Research Station 64
	Brazil	GlobalXperience 92
	Colombia	Ecovolunteer 76
	Costa Rica	Earthwatch 71, i-to-i 104, Projects Abroad 113
	Ecuador	Earthwatch 71, GlobalXperience 92, GVI 89, i-to-i 104
	Honduras	i-to-i 104, Operation Wallacea 107
	Madagascar	Azafady 49
	Nepal	BTCV 58
	Papua New Guinea	Coral Cay Conservation 65, Trekforce 133
	Peru	GlobalXperience 92, Greenforce 94, Personal Overseas Development 110, Projects Abroad 113, Travellers Worldwide 130

	Puerto Rico	Earthwatch 71
	Sri Lanka	Frontier 84
	UK	Trees for Life 152
	USA, Hawaii	Real Gap 123
	Venezuela	Real Gap 123
Rhinos	Kenya	Earthwatch 71
	South Africa	i-to-i 104, Africa Conservation Experience 42
	Swaziland	Ecovolunteer 76, GlobalXperience 92
	Uganda	Africa Guide 41, GVI 89, Real Gap 123
	Zimbabwe	GVI 89, Real Gap 123
Seals	Australia	CVA 68
	Ireland	Irish Seal Sanctuary 148
	South Africa	Africa Conservation Experience 42, GlobalXperience 92, GVI 89
	Turkey	Ecovolunteer 76, GVI 89
	USA, Alaska	Earthwatch 71
Sharks	South Africa	Greenforce 94, Real Gap 123, Travellers Worldwide 130
	USA	Earthwatch 71
Toucans	Brazil	Ecovolunteer 76, GlobalXperience 92
Turtles	Australia	CVA 68
	Azores	Biosphere Expeditions 52
	Cape Verde Islands	Frontier 84
	Costa Rica	Asociacion ANAI WIDECAST Sea Turtle Programme 47, Earthwatch 71, Frontier 84, GlobalXperience 92, i-to-i 104, Real Gap 123
	Cuba	Operation Wallacea 107
	Greece	Archelon 45, GVI 89
	Guatemala	Frontier 84, GlobalXperience 92, Real Gap 123
	India	GlobalXperience 92, Real Gap 123
	Mexico	Earthwatch 71, Projects Abroad 113
	Nicaragua	Frontier 84
	Panama	GVI 89
	Seychelles	GVI 89
	Sri Lanka	Frontier 84, i-to-i 104

	Thailand	Ecovolunteer 76, Frontier 84, i-to-i 104, Starfish Ventures 128
	Trinidad	Earthwatch 71
	Vanuatu	GVI 89
	Uruguay	Frontier 84
	USA	Earthwatch 71
Vultures	Croatia	Ecovolunteer 76
	Mongolia	Earthwatch 71
	Spain	GVI 89
Whales	Azores	Biosphere Expeditions 52
	Bahamas	Earthwatch 71
	Brazil	Ecovolunteer 76 GlobalXperience 92, GVI 89
	Canada	Earthwatch 71, Ecovolunteer 76, GlobalXperience 92
	Kenya	GVI 89
	South Africa	Africa Conservation Experience 42, GlobalXperience 92, Travellers Worldwide 130
	UK	Earthwatch 71
Whale sharks	Kenya	Frontier 84
	Mozambique	Frontier 84, GlobalXperience 92, Real Gap 123
	Philippines	Coral Cay Conservation 65
	Seychelles	GVI 89
Wolves	Canada	Earthwatch 71
	Portugal	Ecovolunteer 76
	Russia	Ecovolunteer 76
	Slovakia	Biosphere Expeditions 52
	USA	Real Gap 123
Wombats, Bandicoots, Koalas, Echidnas, Fruit bats, Goannas, Wallabies	Australia	Cape Tribulation Tropical Research Station 64, CVA 68, Frontier 84, GVI 89, Real Gap 123
Other Birds	Australia	CVA 68
	Brazil	Earthwatch 71
	Bulgaria	BTCV 58
	Germany	BTCV 58
	Japan	BTCV 58
	New Zealand	CVNZ 68

	South Africa	Operation Wallacea 107
	Spain	Biosphere Expeditions 52
	UK	RSPB 51
	USA	Earthwatch 71
Other cats	Altai	Biosphere Expeditions 52
	Bolivia	Inti Wara Yassi 102
	Brazil	Biosphere Expeditions 52, Ecovolunteer 76, GlobalXperience 92
	Oman	Biosphere Expeditions 52
	Peru	Biosphere Expeditions 52
	South Africa	Africa Conservation Experience 42
Other primates	Bolivia	Inti Wara Yassi 102
	Ghana	Frontier 84
	Honduras	Operation Wallacea 107
	Kenya	BTCV 58
	Madagascar	Africa Guide 41, Azafady 49, BTCV 58, Frontier 84, GVI 89
	Peru	Earthwatch 71, Operation Wallacea 107
	South Africa	Edge of Africa 79
	Tanzania	Frontier 84
	Thailand	Ecovolunteer 76, GVI 89, GlobalXperience 92, Starfish Ventures 128

CHOOSING VIA COST

Comparing organisations on the basis of cost is less effective than other methods because it is rare to find projects that can be matched on an exact like-for-like basis. The level of provisions offered by different organisations can vary dramatically. One project may be cheaper than another because volunteers are expected to bring their own tent and cook for themselves, whilst another offers air-conditioned cabins with three full-time cooks; one might employ local group leaders, whilst another employs professional scientists or vets; and one project might stop when the volunteer work is complete, whilst another will use a percentage of project fees in follow-up campaigning and in-country government lobbying for environmental protection. Essentially, the cheapest project doesn't necessarily offer the best value for money and the most expensive isn't always the most environmentally effective. Indeed, cheaper projects may have hidden extras such as airport collect and drop off, training and preparation, essential pre- and post-project accommodation costs, even food and daily transport might be extras.

If money isn't an issue, volunteers can pick and choose among organisations according to other criteria. However, for many the cost of a project is a key factor in the decision making process and often the main limiting factor. If you don't have time to fundraise, the number of projects open to you will be restricted according to your budget. Volunteers choosing this method should be prepared for the fact that the project may not match their expectations. Bearing this in mind, I would strongly suggest volunteers to organise at least some type of fundraising (see *Chapter 6* for details) so they can get the most out of their time away. Nevertheless, the following table has been compiled to point you in the right direction. It summarises the cheapest and most expensive projects offered by the companies audited in this book.

Volunteers should bear in mind that prices may vary with the season (ie: increase during the high season when the weather is at its best) and fluctuations in the exchange rate. As a rule, airfares, insurance, visas, etc, aren't included in quoted fees and whilst longer projects are usually more expensive, their unit day costs tend to be lower.

Organisation	Lowest Price	Highest Price
Africa Guide	Desert elephants, Namibia: £600 (14 days) = £42/day	Lemurs, Madagascar: £2,200 (56 days) = £40/day
African Conservation Experience	Rhinos, South Africa: £3,220 (28 days) = £115/day (inc flights)	Rhinos, South Africa: £5,270 (84 days) = £63/day (inc flights)
Archelon	Turtles, Greece: £130 (accom & food not inc) = £2/day if you stay 10 weeks	Turtles, Greece: £216 (accom & food not inc) = £2/day flat rate which allows you to stay as long as you want
Asociacion ANAI aka WIDECAST	Turtles, Costa Rica: £12 reg + £5/day (camping & food not inc)	Turtles, Costa Rica: £12 reg + £12/day (inc accom in ranger station or local cabin)
Azafady	Lemurs, Madagascar: £1,600 (28 days) = £57/day	Lemurs, Madagascar £2,200 (70 days) = £31/day
Biosphere Expeditions	Arabian leopard, Oman: £1,260 (14 days) = £90/day	Lammergeyers, Spain: £880 (7 days) = £126/day
Blue Ventures	Non-diving, Madagascar: £700 (21 days) = £33/day	Reef diving, Madagascar: £3,250 (84 days) = £38/day (inc full dive training)
British Trust for Conservation Volunteers	Wetland conservation, Germany: £395 (14 days) = £28/day	Rural conservation, Nepal: £695 (14 days) = £49/day

Cape Tribulation Tropical Research Station	Rainforest conservation, Australia: £22/day (for volunteers)	Rainforest conservation, Australia: £31/day (for students/researchers)
Coral Cay Conservation	Two week project: £650 qualified diver (14 days) = £46/day or £2,950 (112 days) = £26/day	£750 trainee diver (14 days) = £54/day or £3,050 (112 days) = £27/day
Conservation Volunteers Australia & CV New Zealand	General conservation work, Australia or New Zealand: £93 (5 days) = £19/day	General conservation work, Australia or New Zealand: £670 (42 days) = £16/day
Earthwatch Institute	Whales & dolphins, UK: £895 (11 days) = £81/day	Climate change, Arctic: £3,195 (11 days) = £290/day
Ecoteer	Ecotourism intern, Asia: no fee	Turtles, Seychelles: £1,010 (56 days) = £18/day
Ecovolunteers	Vultures, Croatia: £279 (14 days) = £20/day	Whales, Canada: £958 (14 days) = £68/day
Edge of Africa	Coastal ecology, South Africa: £650 (14 days) = £46/day	Meerkat research: £1,300 (28 days) = £46/day
Elephant Human Relations Aid	Desert elephants, Namibia: £480 (14 days) = £34/day	Desert elephants, Namibia: £2,880 (84 days) = £34/day
Flat Holm project	Habitat management, island off Welsh coast: no fee (few weeks to 6 months) food & accom provided	—
Frontier	Turtle & rainforest, Nicaragua: £1,095 (21 days) = £52/day	Reef diving, Fiji: £1,695 (28 days) = £60/day or £3,995 (140 days) = £28/day
Gap Year	Cheetahs, South Africa: £1,250 (28 days) = £45/day	Whales, South Africa: £2,290 (14 days) = £164/day
Global Vision International	Reef diving, Mexico: £795 (14 days) = £57/day = £41/day	Marine & rainforest, Costa Rica: £1,445 (35 days)
GlobalXperience	Turtles, Guatemala: £295 (7 days) = £42/day	Rainforest, Peru: £2,295 (42 days) = £55/day

Greenforce	Wildlife & culture, Tanzania: £1,300 (21 days) = £62/day	Wildlife& culture, Tanzania: £2,300 (70 days) = £33/day
Green Volunteers	Black bears, USA: no fee	Rhino, Swaziland: £665 (14 days) = £48/day
International Voluntary Service	Environmental projects: £15 reg + £130 flat-rate (unwaged) placement fee regardless of length of stay	Environmental projects: £35 reg + £150 flat rate (unwaged) placement fee regardless of length of stay
Inti Wara Yassi	Animal sanctuary, Bolivia: £73 (14 days) = £5/day	Animal sanctuary, Bolivia: £90 (14 days) = £6.50/day (paying for better accom)
Irish Seal Sanctuary	Seals, Ireland: no fee except food & accom	Seals, Ireland: no fee except food & accom
i-to-i	Turtles, Costa Rica: £395 (7 days) = £56/day	Dolphins, South Africa: £1,295 (28 days) = £46/day
Operation Wallacea	Reef & rainforest, Indonesia: £950 (14 days) = £68/day	Reef & rainforest, Indonesia: £2,800 (56 days) = £50/day
Personal Overseas Development	Reef conservation, Belize: £595 (7 days) = £85/day	Rainforest, Peru: £1,095 (14 days) = £78/day
Projects Abroad	Rainforest, Costa Rica: £1,345 (14 days) = £96/day or £2,395 (90 days) = £27/day	Reefs & mangrove swamp, Thailand: £1,545 (14 days) = £110/day
Quest Overseas	Rainforest & cities, Brazil: £3,980 (70 days) = £57/day	Conservation & community work, southern Africa: £4,750 (42 days) = £113/day
Raleigh International	Environmental, Borneo: £1,500 (28 days) = £54/day	Environmental, India: £2,995 (70 days) = £43/day
Real Gap Experience	Koala sanctuary, Australia: £329 (14 days) = £23.50/day	Lion conservation, Zimbabwe: £1,999 (28 days) = £71/day
Responsible Travel	Elephant care, Thailand: £285 (7 days) = £41/day	Cheetah conservation, Botswana: £1,390 (14 days) = £99/day

Royal Society of the Protection of Birds	Wild bird protection, UK: no fee; accom provided, but not food	—
Starfish Ventures	Dog rescue, Thailand: £700 (14 days) = £50/day	Gibbon sanctuary, Thailand: £900 (28 days) = £32/day
Trees for Life	Planting trees, Scotland: £50 (7 days) unemployed volunteers	Planting trees, Scotland: £100 (7 days) employed volunteers
Trekforce Worldwide	Sustainable tourist development: £1,200 (14 days) = £86/day	Sustainable tourist development: £4,100 (5 months) = £27/day
Travellers Worldwide	Rainforest, Peru: £995 (14 days) = £71/day	Orang-utan conservation, Malaysia: £2,995 (56 days) = £53/day
Voluntary Service Overseas	Paid volunteer placements	—
Wildlife Trusts	Wildlife surveys, UK: annual membership fee £30	—
Worldwide Opportunities on Organic Farms	No fee; accom & food provided in return for 5 days labour	—

ARRANGING YOUR OWN PLACEMENT

Arranging your own conservation volunteer placement with an overseas grassroots conservation project is not as difficult as you might think. However, the DIY option is not suited to everyone. If you wouldn't normally arrange an annual overseas holiday by booking your own flights, finding your own accommodation and travelling there independently, it might not be for you.

The best approach is obviously by word-of-mouth recommendation from someone you know and trust; random trolling of the internet is probably the worst approach. The second-best approach would be to use a book or internet directory such as Green Volunteers or Ecoteer that lists hundreds of grassroots organisations. They cannot guarantee a problem-free trip, but if there are serious concerns about an organisation these would probably come to light and you might be able to contact previous volunteers.

There are absolutely no generalised standards for projects sourced from these directories; each project is totally independent, so volunteers have to take them as they find them. Each project registers with a specific website-listing directory and is responsible for posting the details of the project. The degree of vetting will be minimal or non-existent and an important consideration is that there will be no in-country back-up or support from the UK.

Some projects may not make a specific charge, but you may be left to arrange your own board and lodging. Others will charge you to work on the project, but provide board and lodging or camping facilities free of charge. Compared with a pre-booked placement package, arranged in your home country, it does mean you are very much on your own. Generally the following will be true:

- There will be no airport meet-and-greet service.
- You have to find your own way to the project which may involve using a mixture of unfamiliar local transport.
- There will be no organised in-country cultural or programme orientation.
- You will have to cope with language difficulties on your own.
- Nobody is charged with 'looking out for your interests'.
- There will be no local contacts (co-ordinators) to help resolve any problems that arise.
- Any legal or liability issues will fall under local jurisdiction so may be incomprehensible, expensive and not to your usual expectations.
- The project is unlikely to have been vetted or approved to any specific standard.
- You may have to pay for/find your own accommodation or take a tent and sleeping bag.
- You will probably have to pay for/arrange your own meals.
- The nature of the work may be relatively unspecified and you will have to agree this with whoever is running the project.

A good point is that all the cash you pay will contribute directly to the running of the project. There will be no top slicing for home-country advertising, office overheads, company executives or corporate profits. You might not sign a contract of commitment, so potentially you can walk away if it doesn't live up to expectations without losing a shed load of cash.

By their nature many conservation projects are in out-of-the-way places and may require journeys on two or three local buses and then a hike, which can be very daunting or near impossible without some language capability. Many projects do not accept large groups of males but it pays to be careful when travelling alone to an unknown project in an unfamiliar country. Women, in particular, should take especial care.

The DIY option will always be cheaper but it also requires a great deal more confidence and independence from a volunteer. It may be the ideal option for people who have previously visited the country and who have a reasonable level of local language skill. It may be an absolute disaster for the inexperienced traveller, or those of a timid or cautious disposition.

If you are planning to arrange your own project placement, detailed background research is an absolute necessity ideally find someone who has already been there; search and ask for information on conservation and gap-year chat rooms; email and/or telephone the people running the project.

Your sole back-up will be your travel insurance so make sure you have the best possible policy (see page 182), check that your mobile phone will work at the location and ensure you have your insurance company emergency contact details readily to hand.

A FINAL WORD OF ADVICE...

When you eventually speak to someone don't just accept their word, as it's too easy for them just to say 'yes' to everything you ask and you might just be speaking to a telesales person. Request evidence – copies of policies, evidence of past achievements, previous training programme schedules, samples of the daily work routines from previous projects, and if you can, speak to someone who has previously volunteered on your chosen project with that company.

ECOTOURISM DEVELOPMENT

Daniel Quilter

I had butterflies in my stomach as I flew out of Heathrow. But I said to myself: 'Come on, this is it: sink or swim. It's time to fly the nest!'

I was taking a year out to travel after finishing an environmental science degree at Plymouth University. The course had promoted my enthusiasm in ecotourism, but I was saddled with student loans and debts and couldn't afford the usual conservation placement. Instead, I decided to work while travelling and an agency found me a placement at an eco-lodge in Asia.

On the first morning I woke up and thought, 'God, what the hell am I doing? I am in Borneo on my own. How the hell am I going to survive?' I sweated a great deal that first day – whether it was nerves or heat, I don't know – but I ended it enjoying a huge plate of 30p noodles with a German lad (who was sharing my dorm) and watching a perfect sunset overlooking the nearby islands of the Tunku Abdul Rahman Marine Park.

I was thrown into the deep end regarding work: my main task was to produce a guide for the city of Kota Kinabalu, as well as helping to improve Borneo Backpackers hostel and shadowing tour groups to identify possible improvements. I experienced a mixed bag of nerves and excitement, but the young staff in the office helped me to find my feet and taught me some useful swear words in the process.

Days off were amazing. I was invited to my new friends' homes, a unique experience denied to tourists. Some of them lived in rich family townhouses and others in poorer rural homes in the jungle, but it made no difference. Everyone was welcoming and proud to have you visit their home, nothing was too much effort and they always smiled.

Daniel Quilter's experience as an intern at a Borneo rainforest lodge led him to found the conservation volunteer company Ecoteer.

WHAT WILL IT COST?

The price of conservation volunteering trips can vary enormously from
£200–3,000 excluding airfares, which are rarely included in published costs.
The fee that each volunteer pays is the core funding that enables most
conservation projects to function. It usually includes board and lodgings, and
payment of local staff and equipment costs, so it's never going to be cheap.

Budgeting for a conservation volunteer trip, like a holiday, depends on
where you're going, how long you will be away, and what you will be doing.
On average, a short two-week trip abroad is likely to cost £1,000, plus
£700–£1,000 for flights and up to £500 for visas, insurance, vaccinations,
equipment and a whole range of other incidental costs. That's potentially
£3,000–4,000; even on a shoestring it'll rarely be less than £2,500. If you don't
already have sufficient funds in the bank you may need to put fundraising on
your agenda. See *Chapter 6* for details.

However, conservation volunteering needn't cost much at all; you don't
have to fly around the world to engage in important environmental activities.
You could join a UK-based project run by the likes of British Trust for
Conservation Volunteer or Wildlife Trusts for as little as £100. See pages 58,
154–6 and 216 for details.

STANDARD EXTRAS

With a few exceptions (which are referred to in the specific organisation
audits) there are a number of additional costs that a volunteer needs to
budget for in addition to the basic project fee. Additional costs are likely to
include any international or onward internal flights and any associated taxes,
entry visa, vaccinations, travel insurance, pre- and post-project
accommodation and perhaps transport to and from the airport to a team
assembly point. It will also be necessary to budget for a daily spending
allowance that covers drinks, snacks, taxis, side visits and other daily
incidental expenses.

It is also likely that you will need to buy some special kit, eg: for diving
projects and/or clothes suitable for hot and humid or cold environments.
However, don't rush out and buy everything in the UK. Instead, research what
you could buy in the country you plan to visit; in most instances you'll find
things can be bought on arrival at a fraction of the cost. On recent trips I have
bought a £10 multi-purpose waterproof cape for £2 in Peru, £45 lightweight zip-
off trousers for £5 in Thailand and bush-trekking gear for half price in Australia.
Organising yourself this way saves money and boosts the local economy.

SUSTAINABLE ECOTOURISM
Izzy Jones

Getting to Gallon Jug in Belize had been long and bumpy road: I had spent a year fundraising over £4,000, by walking across England, holding a concert with Barclays Bank and running an early-morning car boot sale on a grey March Sunday.

Now that I was finally, and literally, on the road to Gallon Jug I found it more rollercoaster-like than bumpy. I was also sweating more than I had ever done on a hockey pitch. I had come to Belize, with a group of other volunteers, to embark on a ten-day jungle training programme; a prelude to our sustainable conservation and community-based work.

I didn't know anybody that had set foot in a rainforest, and I didn't have the first idea about how to use a machete, and yet I was about to spend the next two months in the jungle. I did question why, all those months ago in the sixth form centre, I had thought this to be a good idea.

Ten days later I knew everyone, had spent a few nights in a jungle hammock and was semi-skilled at machete use. I had learnt to light fires, cross rivers, stretcher a casualty, and how to clean one's basher (hammock cover) after a troop of howler monkeys had thrown fruit onto it in the middle of the night.

Our main mission was to build a one-and-a-half-mile boardwalk linking a Ketchi Mayan community to a visitors centre built by Trekforce the previous year. We were completing a long-term project to introduce sustainable ecotourism to the area, helping to protect the unique ecosystem of Aguacaliente Wildlife Sanctuary.

Most days were long and hard. We got up in the dark at 05.30, fetched our own water and made porridge for breakfast. Then from 07.00–12.30 we were out on the trail digging holes, packing posts in, and carrying wood. There was a quick break for lunch and then it was back to work from 14.30 until 17.00. Evenings were dinner, diary writing, music, parties for special occasions and chilling out after a hard day's work. Not every day was like this; we did have some playtime thrown in.

Diary entry: Day 29 *Tried to work, but rain made it impossible, so had whole day off! Spent morning chilling out – wrote letter to family. We decided to go to Phil's (resident volunteer) for the day. Got swimming things, clean cut-offs and T-shirt ready. Set off in the back a pick-up truck owned by one of the villagers.*

On the way back in the pick-up it was dark and raining – good to feel the wind in my hair again! Feel so contented and happy; wish the feeling would never end. Walked back along the very muddy trail in the rain – trying to dodge the holes filled with water! Wrote diary in the candlelight, then went to bed. One of the best times of my life today.

We managed to complete the project and we left Laguna and Aguacaliente feeling proud that our blood, sweat and tears had helped the villagers by aiding ecotourism and protecting the sanctuary from illegal hunting and fishing.
Izzy Jones travelled with Trekforce Worldwide and spent three months in Belize

4 THE AUDIT

This chapter is the heart of the book. It covers 50 conservation volunteer organisations that have been audited according to strict scoring criteria. The evaluated categories are summarised in the box below. For a full explanation see *The Audit Criteria* page IX. It's important to note that whilst all the overseas conservation volunteer providers have been assessed for the nine categories, much of the criteria is irrelevant for referral agents, UK domestic organisations or unavailable for small locally based NGOs. As a result, these organisations have entries that focus on key information rather than the full assessment criteria.

Organisations have been listed alphabetically because outfits offering conservation volunteering projects run the full gamut – from hands-on companies who plan and lead their own expeditions to clearing houses who put together packages for overseas organisations seeking volunteers – and therefore can't be categorised according to type. There's just too much crossover between categories.

SUMMARY OF AUDIT CRITERIA

Each organisation has been evaluated on the following nine categories and been graded using a bargraph, so that readers can compare those factors that are most important to them.

1 Credibility Includes scientific validity, awards won, media coverage, membership of key organisations and third-party sponsorship or endorsement.

2 Organisation Includes general organisation, clarity of purpose, leaders, educational options, open days, volunteer contact and field planning.

3 Where the money goes Includes cost, deposit, extras, cancellation penalties, in-country spend.

4 Pre-departure preparation Includes training, aims and objectives, job specification and volunteer liaison, field contacts, health and environment.

5 In the field Includes intended benefits, project longevity, accommodation, work/leisure ratio and local benefits.

6 Environment and culture Includes carbon offsetting, environmental impact and cultural preparation.

7 Safety Includes British Standards Institute BS8848:2007 status (see page 221), explicit details and comprehensiveness of safety procedures, risk assessment and emergency planning.

8 Achievements Includes verifiable reports of past project activities and tangible (ie: recorded) conservation outcomes and achievements.

9 Post-trip follow-up Includes evaluation, level and extent of follow-up and post-project support.

See page IX for a more detailed explanation of the methodology used to collect and analyse the company data.

AFRICA GUIDE
✉ administrator@africaguide.com; 🖰 www.africaguide.com

A South Africa-based company providing comprehensive coverage across 52 African countries and island groups. It is an internet directory so does not organise or arrange trips directly, but lists 270 operators who offer 600 tours, treks and safaris of which 27 have focused conservation volunteer options.

Background
Phil and Vera arrived in Africa in the 1990s and have travelled widely throughout the continent. Vera started the website as a pet project in 1996 to pass on her accumulated knowledge of travel in Africa to other travellers. Now they use the internet as part of a mobile lifestyle travelling extensively and running the Africa Guide website from wherever they happen to be in the world.

Directory and method
As well as conservation volunteering the website includes overland trips, tours, safaris and a useful range of travelogues of experiences in a range of African countries. Useful project information is provided on the website, as well as previous volunteer comments.

After filling in contact details they are forwarded to the project placement provider who then contacts the enquirer with further information.

The website has an exceptionally useful background database on health, geography and culture throughout Africa. Many of the projects will simply redirect you back to one of the organisations that are already in this book, but there are also links to a number of smaller, more specialised African organisations.

Examples of projects
Madagascar Lemur Venture
It costs £2,200 for 56 days and includes a week's accommodation whilst training in Fort Dauphin. For the rest of the programme it's basic camping and volunteers need to bring their own tent. The work focuses on lemur behaviour, feeding ecology, conservation biology, population estimates, home range studies, community natural resource management and habitat management. Unspecified placement provider. It runs all year round.

Lake Malawi Hippo Expedition
It costs £950 for 28 days and most days are spent aboard a boat on Lake Malawi. Accommodation is camping and volunteers must bring their own tents, sleeping mats and sleeping bags. Scuba-diving courses can be included for an additional fee. The work is primarily a hippo census, but with some additional tree planting and lakeside school visits. Unspecified placement provider.

AFRICAN CONSERVATION EXPERIENCE
0870 241 5816; www.conservationafrica.net; available in English, French & Dutch

African Conservation Experience is a UK-registered company focusing on conservation projects in southern Africa. They are a placement service, but differ from many others because their own staff are present and actively involved with each project. Their speciality is in game parks, animal sanctuaries and whale and dolphin studies. Only a few of the projects are research-based; most are more practically orientated.

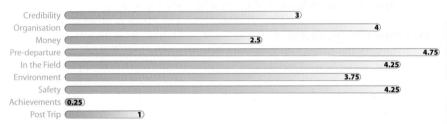

Credibility	3
Organisation	4
Money	2.5
Pre-departure	4.75
In the Field	4.25
Environment	3.75
Safety	4.25
Achievements	0.25
Post Trip	1

Background
Rob and Marian Harris founded ACE in 1998. Rob is South African and ACE has developed into a family business shared with their son, who is still based out there. They work closely with their South African partners and build on their local knowledge and experience.

Credibility
Projects are designed in partnership with game rangers and local conservationists, but are more practically oriented than scientific. They have media coverage in *BBC Wildlife* and other publications and a good responsible travel policy. All the field staff have the status of honorary rangers with the South African National Parks.

Organisation
They are South Africa specialists and focus on game parks. They use tracking and ranger skills, and are involved in behaviour monitoring, sanctuaries, rehabilitations centres and some veterinary work. Bookings are with well-established partner organisations, so are generally assured, and volunteers can work from two to 12 weeks.

Most projects are conservation oriented with some community or teaching elements added in; there are named leaders with specialist knowledge that are detailed on the website. Volunteers have a wide age range and include gap year students, career breakers and people taking sabbaticals. Volunteers are put in touch with each other before departure and invited to contact previous volunteers. Field ranger courses are available and are recognised by the Field Guide Association of South Africa and the UK. Open days are held twice a year, usually on UK university campuses.

Where the money goes

A two-week project costs around £2,000, but this includes airfares as well as carbon offsetting, airport transfers and internal transport.

A £250 non-refundable deposit is required at booking and the balance due eight weeks before departure. Cancellation penalties operate on a sliding scale from eight weeks down to two weeks before departure, after which all fees are forfeit.

Around 60% of the volunteer's fee is spent in and around projects in southern Africa. An unusual and unattractive condition of the Africa Conservation Experience contract is that any return visits to a project within five years following your visit must be booked via ACE.

Pre-departure preparation

There is no pre-departure training, but downloadable project files and online videos give a good idea of what project life is like. Qualified project co-ordinators introduce volunteers to the bush environment, guide on-site activities and look after safety issues. A fitness requirement for different projects is indicated and there is a good kit list, but there is little about environmental conditions.

Objectives and goals for each project are set and there is an overview of volunteer tasks.

In the field

The intended conservation benefits are clearly outlined on the website. Each project has its own named co-ordinator with photograph and biography on the website and they are employed directly by ACE. All projects are long-term, locally based enterprises and the majority of staff are local people. Volunteers are expected to work a normal five-day week with weekends off.

Accommodation is usually shared in twin rooms, which can be viewed on the website's photo gallery, and unlike many conservation projects they can cater for special dietary requirements.

Environment & culture

Carbon offsetting is a priority and ACE covers all volunteer international flights through ClimateCare. Volunteers are provided with information in their departure pack on how to reduce water usage and to minimise their impact on the wildlife and environment of southern Africa. Cultural orientation is provided on arrival.

Safety

ACE have declared themselves as meeting the standards of BS8848:2007 and include this in each volunteer's information pack.

Project leaders are first-aid trained and on site 24/7; they also have additional field guide qualifications including emergency training, dealing with firearms and dangerous game.

First-aid kits are on site and more remote projects have additional equipment such as stretchers, oxygen and IV drips. Risk assessment procedures are in place and carried out at each project location and a major incident protocol outlines what to do in an emergency.

Demonstrable achievements
Demonstrable conservation achievements are a weak area and only the whale and dolphin project has been written up and published. Volunteers must assess the relative worth of each project as it's presented.

Post-trip follow up
There is little post-project follow-up, although volunteers receive a feedback form on arrival back in the UK and the website is kept up to date with 'news' about various projects.

ARCHELON: THE SEA TURTLE PROTECTION SOCIETY OF GREECE

☎/F 0870 241 5816; ✉ stps@archelon.gr; 🖰 www.archelon.gr/index_eng.php

This is a tightly focused NGO operating since 1983, whose primary objective is to protect loggerhead sea turtles and their habitats in Greece through developing and implementing management plans, monitoring, research, habitat restoration, raising public awareness and rehabilitating sick and injured turtles.

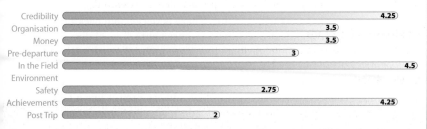

Credibility	4.25
Organisation	3.5
Money	3.5
Pre-departure	3
In the Field	4.5
Environment	
Safety	2.75
Achievements	4.25
Post Trip	2

Background

During their summer holidays in 1977 Dimitris and Anna Margaritoulis discovered many loggerhead turtles (*Caretta caretta*) nesting on the island of Zakynthos. Although turtles have probably nested there for millions of years and local people were well aware of them, the scientific community knew nothing about this site. Dimitris and Anna got more involved, collecting data that demonstrated the importance of Zakynthos as a nesting site and urging the Greek government to protect the beaches.

Credibility

An award-winning, single-focus project, locally conceived and led with its own scientists and working links with WWF and IUCN. There are informative stories in *The Teacher, Altitude Magazine,* the *Reading Eagle* and a number of foreign-language media outlets. They receive strong support from corporations such as Alpha Bank, Blue Star Ferries and Ford. They are weak on written procedures and protocols, but strong on action planning and effectiveness.

Organisation

There are Greek loggerhead turtle specialists working at every stage in the animals' lifecycle from nesting to hatching, involving adult tracking and rehabilitation of injured turtles as well as educating locals and tourists. Bookings are made directly with Archelon and individual sites are organised by volunteer leaders. Volunteers tend to be young, often with a background in biological sciences and they usually stay for most of the summer. Recruitment is via universities and word of mouth.

Where the money goes

Flat rate fees are between £100–187 for a minimum of four weeks, but usually between six and eight weeks at no additional cost. A daily food kitty of £1.50–2.00 covers all essentials and volunteers are responsible for all housekeeping and site management chores. Project transport is provided but you have to find your own way to and from the project site.The volunteer's entire fee is spent in and around the project.

Pre-departure preparation
Signing up is via the web and straightforward. There is little in the way of pre-departure planning, but the aims and objectives are very clear and volunteers know what they will be doing. There is reasonable packing advice, but not much regarding health or fitness requirements. Travel directions are reasonable, but a little inadequate if you are unfamiliar with Greece.

In the field
The intended conservation benefits are clear and the project has a long-term development plan. Project sites are rough and ready, accommodation may be dormitories or more usually tented camps and volunteers may need to bring their own camping equipment. Expect basic amenities, dawn beach patrols and two or three different shift duties a day. Most site locations have bars and tavernas within walking distance.

Environment & culture
No information is provided about carbon offsetting, general environmental conditions or cultural issues.

Safety
Safety issues are not elaborate and volunteers are expected to be sensible and responsible for their own actions. Volunteer leaders are on site 24/7 and deal with all organisation and safety issues. First-aid kit, fire extinguishers and mobile phones are on site.

Demonstrable achievements
Regular updates and news reports are on the website and scientific papers are produced for EU and other funding bodies along with presentations to international marine turtle conservation groups. Practical conservation achievements include:
- Purchased land behind Sekania Beach on Zakynthos in 1992 to prevent building and development on this important loggerhead nesting site.
- Work monitoring the impact of fishing activity on the sea turtle populations resulted in a Presidential Decree in 1999 establishing the National Marine Park of Zakynthos.
- A project (2002) aims to reduce deaths of turtles caught in fishing gear.

Post-trip follow up
Evaluation forms are completed by volunteers, and newsletters and the website keep ex-volunteers informed about ongoing activity.

ASOCIACION WIDECAST, SEA TURTLE PROGRAMME

☏ +506 261 3814; ✉ info@osaseaturtles.org or volunteers@latinamerican seaturtles.org;🖰 www.osaseaturtles.org or www.latinamericanseaturtles.org

WIDECAST (the Wider Caribbean Sea Turtle Conservation Network) organise a number of projects in Costa Rica to protect hawksbill, leatherback and other sea turtle nests from human poachers and more recently from beach erosion. Generally there is project activity at one of the locations from early March through to the end of October each year. The peak nesting period for the turtles is April and May with the first hatchling turtles emerging from mid-May through to the end of the season. The Talamanca region has been declared a UNESCO World Heritage Site and 'biodiversity hotspot'.

Background

Since 1986 ANAI, the Costa Rican NGO has been working with community groups and volunteers in Costa Rica's Talamanca region. They have been supporting and building expertise in local communities to help them preserve their environment and develop eco-friendly forms of sustainable tourism. ANAI ran most of the turtle projects but in 2008 they formally handed over the management and operation to WIDECAST, run by local people and local scientists, many of whom previously worked with ANAI.

Volunteer opportunities

Each season, as part of their conservation effort, the project recruits national and international volunteers to help with ongoing research and conservation work. Volunteers can work on any of several project sites on the Caribbean or Pacific coasts and can volunteer from one week to seven months between March and October. Long-term research assistant placements are available to undergraduate and postgraduate biologists (free board and lodgings, but no pay). Conservation programmes are linked with ecotourism efforts in the area and aim to provide an alternative income for participating communities. Schools are also welcome to work on the project as part of the environmental education programme.

Where the money goes

There is a registration fee of £18 and the project fee is £12 per day (about £168 for two weeks), but this does not include meals or accommodation. Accommodation (board and lodgings) can be arranged with local host families for around £9 per night or there is a camping option for around £4 per night. They can also arrange an airport pick-up for £15. Applications to work at any of the beach locations are made via their online application form.

Demonstrable achievements

Before the project began, the poaching rate was over 95% but with the presence of night patrols and the hatcheries on the beach, the survival rate had increased to over 90% last season.

These well-established projects have been recognised with two major conservation awards, although they were given to ANAI, the previous organiser:

- ANAI and the Talamanca Initiative were recipients of the United Nations Equator Prize in 2002, which recognises.
  'extraordinary accomplishments in reducing poverty in the tropics through conservation and sustainable use of biodiversity'.
- WIDECAST marine biologist, Didiher Chacón-Chaverri, was the winner of the 2005 Whitley Award sponsored by WWF-UK.
  Didiher and WIDECAST are committed to the establishment of marine protected areas and the effective protection of turtles and coral reef ecosystems.

AZAFADY

☏ +44 (0)20 8960 6629; ✉ claire@azafady.org; 🌐 www.madagascar.co.uk

This UK-registered charity works in partnership with its other half, the Azafady NGO in Madagascar, and recruits volunteers from around the world. They work with the 65 local Malagasy staff on integrated conservation and development projects intended to improve health, reduce environmental degradation and improve the livelihood prospects of the poorest rural people.

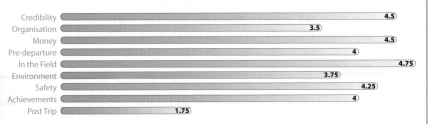

Credibility	4.5
Organisation	3.5
Money	4.5
Pre-departure	4
In the Field	4.75
Environment	3.75
Safety	4.25
Achievements	4
Post Trip	1.75

Background

Brett Massoud visited Madagascar in the early 1990s on a botanical palm survey from Australia and fell in love with the country and its people. He had seen his home town move from being run-down to a thriving community and wanted to see something similar in Madagascar, so when he moved to the UK he set up Azafady.

Credibility

The science and planning of projects are in collaboration with the Malagasy Ministry of Environment, Water, Forests and Tourism, the Parc Botanique et Zoologique de Tsimbazaza (PBZT), the Malagasy Ministry of Higher Education and, from time to time, external specialists. They have won a string of awards including Best Volunteering Organisation in the 2007 Responsible Tourism Awards; Sting and Trudie Styler Award for Conservation and Human Rights; four Walt Disney Foundation awards for conservation research; and Flora and Fauna International Fund cash awards for conservation research.

Media coverage includes *Metro*, *Big Issue*, *The Times* and *Geographical Magazine* and a 20-minute documentary film produced in February 2007. They are members of BOND and Care International and lead a regional committee for the environment in Madagascar. They have received funding from the World Bank, the EU and commercial sponsorship from Natural Deco.

Organisation

They are Madagascar specialists and go nowhere else. Lemur projects focus on a captive breeding programme at the national zoo involving the practical maintenance of lemur populations and assisting with feeding and caring for the animals. Fieldwork involves conservation biology by studying lemur behaviour, feeding ecology, population monitoring, home range studies, natural resource management and habitat management. In addition, volunteers may get involved with training in sustainable agricultural techniques, reforestation, environmental education, water and food hygiene as well as a range of other community activities.

Around 140 volunteers travel with Azafady each year. There is a wide age range, but students make up the majority of the long-term placements. There are plenty of past project reports on the website, although they are not always easy to find. All projects have long-term plans and undergraduate dissertation options are possible. They have no capacity to run open days in the UK, but volunteers are put in touch with a previous volunteer once placement is confirmed.

Where the money goes

Fees are considered charity donations and are £1,600 for four weeks and £2,200 for eight weeks on the Pioneer Lemur project; the Lemur Plus community development project is £2,000 for ten weeks. All are inclusive of project transport and language classes. A £500 non-refundable deposit is required on booking and the balance is due three weeks before departure. Cancellation penalties are virtually non-existent so fees are rarely, if ever, forfeited and volunteers can usually arrange a deferment if necessary.

Around 90% of all volunteer donations to Azafady are spent in and around projects in Madagascar; UK overheads are minimal and they spend nothing on commercial promotions and so have an unjustified low profile.

Pre-departure preparation

There is no pre-departure training in the UK because most of the organisation is based in Madagascar but there is good general advice on risks and issues in their survival guide and specialist medical advice booklets. Volunteers need to be prepared for physical work in a hot climate with adventurous road journeys and long walks to reach remote project sites. The general purpose is clear but there is only an indication of general tasks a volunteer is likely to perform. Similarly the aims, although sound, are fairly generalised and there is an absence of specific conservation objectives, primarily because they are first and foremost a sustainable development NGO.

The planning guidance is excellent in terms of health, potential risks, fitness requirements and essential kit. Travel planning and arrival information is well covered, which is important, as an overnight stay in the capital Antananarivo is necessary before flying on to the main base at Fort Dauphin.

In the field

The intended conservation benefits are clear and projects all operate on a long-term basis. Accommodation in Antananaviro is quite good, but in the field it's basic camping all the way and at times there is no piped water or electricity. Volunteers normally work a five-day week with weekends off to explore the country. Azafady employ more than 90 local people in a wide range of roles including administration, construction, project staffing, health education and government liaison.

Environment & culture
Volunteers do not pay to offset their carbon emissions because they get involved in tree planting, which far exceeds the carbon footprint from their flights. Azafady expect to obtain full Defra offset accreditation by 2009. Because of the high level of interaction with local people, language classes and a booklet are provided in addition to a team of Malagasy staff who travel and work with the group to offer translation and advice on Malagasy culture. Surprisingly, there is little reference to how volunteers can minimise their impact on the local environment during their stay.

Safety
They aim to be BS8848:2007 self-certified by the end of 2008. Medical facilities are generally poor in Madagascar, even in city centres, therefore serious emergencies may need to be evacuated to South Africa so ensure you have good insurance, covering manual work in remote areas. First-aid equipment and satellite phones are carried and field co-ordinators have first-aid qualifications and local field staff have regular training in first aid. Nevertheless volunteers are advised to take a comprehensive personal medical kit. Risk assessments are carried out at all sites and externally audited and there are clear emergency protocols including air evacuation.

Demonstrable achievements
Field records, reports and publications are collated through the Parc Botanique et Zoologique de Tsimbazaza (PBZT), part of the Malagasy Ministry of Higher Education, but are not currently made available. The website has a number of professionally written research papers; newsletters provide updates about what is happening on various projects.
- In 2007 Azafady volunteers planted over 3,500 trees at the Sainte Luce area in collaboration with the English NGO SAFAD. Three researchers from Cranfield University are supporting the environment team on reforestation design and monitoring methods using GIS mapping. The government have now agreed to plant a further 8,000 trees.
- The mangroves of Sainte Luce were also studied to find a suitable site for a ecotourism venture. Tours using *pirogues* (local canoes) are being planned.

Post-trip follow up
Evaluation questionnaires are completed and there are a few quotes on the website. A very informative newsletter is produced every six months but there is little other follow-up in the UK as most staff are based in Madagascar.

BIOSPHERE EXPEDITIONS

0870 446 0801; ⊠ uk@biosphere-expeditions.org or info@biosphere-expeditions.org; ⊕ www.biosphere-expeditions.org; available in English, German and French.

They are a hands-on, not-for-profit organisation arranging and running their own scientific research and conservation expeditions. They take around 400 volunteers per year to the Altai Republic, Azores, Brazil, Honduras, Namibia, Oman, Peruvian Amazon and Slovakia. Expeditions are adventurous conservation projects, in two-week blocks, providing an insight into the practicalities of conservation in the field. They have offices in Germany, France, America and Australia.

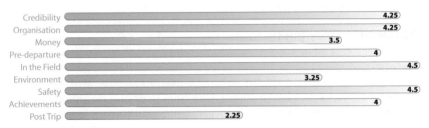

Credibility	4.25
Organisation	4.25
Money	3.5
Pre-departure	4
In the Field	4.5
Environment	3.25
Safety	4.5
Achievements	4
Post Trip	2.25

Background
Founded in 1999 by Dr Matthias Hammer, a biologist who became disillusioned with the ivory tower mentality of academia. An army background coupled with some student expeditions made the idea of founding a practical and scientific conservation organisation a predictable career move.

Credibility
Projects are designed and proposed by conservation scientists with a first-hand knowledge of the country and the issue. They are regular award winners including best in Sustainable Travel Award from Islands Magazine, 2008; highly commended in the 2007 First Choice Responsible Tourism Awards; Best for Conservation of Endangered Species category and winner of the Best Volunteering organisation 2006 by First Choice Responsible Tourism Awards. They have also been listed in *The Independent* as one of its Top 10 Outdoor Pursuits for 2004. They have extensive media coverage and have been featured in *The Independent*, *Lonely Planet*, *Wanderlust*, *Condé Nast Traveller*, *Radio 4* and *MTV* and widely on German television. A range of commercial sponsors support their work by providing Land Rovers, Motorola radios and satellite phones, Woodsmoke bushcraft training for staff, and expedition equipment from Cotswold Outdoor and Globetrotter Ausrüstung.

Organisation
They accept full responsibility for volunteers and booked places are assured in normal circumstances. Past volunteers can be spoken to at regular open

days and extensive previous project write-ups are available on their website. They run long-term projects using scientific objectives overseen by local scientists with clear conservation goals. They are actively involved in every project with an expedition leader making sure things happen as planned by linking volunteers with scientists and the local community. Volunteer teams are 12 or fewer to maximise research efficiency and minimise each project's environmental impact; student thesis study may be possible.

Activities include biodiversity monitoring, radio tracking predator species, game counts and data management. Expedition team members come from all over the world, all walks of life and include a wide age spectrum, but generally volunteers are more mature than those found on many student-dominated gap year-style projects.

Where the money goes

A two-week expedition costs around £1,225–1,450 but there are less expensive week and weekend taster expeditions in the UK and Germany; the taster fee is refunded if a full project booking is made. A post-trip report contains a detailed budget of how the expedition contribution was spent.

Once volunteers arrive at the in-country assembly point all costs are covered and the in-country carbon footprint of the expedition is offset with ClimateCare.

A £300 non-refundable deposit is required after which you become liable for the full cost, although the balance is not due until four weeks before departure. A full refund (minus deposit) is available for cancellations over 100 days before departure. After this, cancellation penalties are on a sliding scale until 20 days before departure when all monies are forfeited.

Around 66% of a volunteer's fee is spent in and around project activity, benefiting the project directly and the community locally; the rest goes towards administrative back-up, as well as researching and setting up new expeditions.

Pre-departure preparation

There is excellent pre-departure information, but no specific expedition training events. Open days to meet the staff, previous volunteers and expedition reviews are available as well as UK-based weekend taster events to discover if expedition life is really for you.

Volunteers know the names of their expedition leaders, scientists and other volunteers before departure. A written expedition briefing is provided before signing up, including the purpose, aims and objectives, exact location, field training, a general work schedule, fitness requirements, field conditions, accommodation, packing advice, health and safety risks, travel details, photographs and previous volunteer comments. A unique touch is live diary feeds sent to pending volunteers detailing current expedition activities. They provide a great sense of pre-departure involvement, and there are plenty of video clips.

In the field

The project purpose is explicit and Biosphere staff are on the project site 24/7 and contribute to field activities. Accommodation is always locally owned and varies from simple bed-and-breakfast style to Amazon lodge research centres and tent basecamps. Training in research methodology is provided and local people are always employed.

All projects are long term and are primarily work based, but time off is built in for relaxation or to visit local attractions.

Environment & culture

Carbon offset of flights with ClimateCare is strongly encouraged and there is a 50% uptake. They offset the carbon debt incurred from the assembly point onwards and provide guidelines on how volunteers can minimise their environmental impact, but there's not much on cultural issues.

Safety

They are working towards BS8848:2007 accreditation and currently implement it wherever possible, but do not have an implementation date. Company staff are based at the project site 24/7 and carry out a risk assessment before volunteers arrive and have written procedures for every eventuality. Field staff have first-aid and wilderness medical training, first-aid kits are carried at all times, as well as telecoms equipment.
They have an emergency medical and air evacuation contract with SOS (*www.internation alsos.com*) and access to a 24-hour medical phone line.

Demonstrable achievements

Biosphere write up scientific reports for all expeditions and detail their conservation outcomes via media coverage, scientific research papers and web reports:

- In 2003 they took the first ever photographs of Falzfein's thick-tailed three-toed jerboa in the Ukraine.
- In 2006 while working with WWF and a local NGO they helped create a snow leopard protection corridor in central Asia.
- In 2006 research data was used to help the bid to upgrade Kinburnska Kosa Regional Landscape Park to a national park.

Post-trip follow up

Evaluation forms are completed in the field. Sometime after the end of each expedition volunteers receive an expedition report with full details on all conservation work done, the data collected, how this information was used and the results of the expedition. This report is made available to the public, the scientific community and relevant decision makers. The report also contains a detailed budget on how the expedition contributions were spent. Where applicable, results are also published in scientific journals and several scientific papers are posted on the Biosphere website. Open days and reunions keep volunteers in touch with projects and each other.

BLUE VENTURES

☎ 020 8341 9819; ✉ via web link only; 🖱 www.blueventures.org

They are a hands-on, registered not-for-profit organisation arranging and running award-winning projects, dedicated to marine conservation, education and sustainable development in tropical coastal communities. Annually 100–120 volunteers work on their Madagascar projects along with field research teams and local communities on coastal and rainforest projects.

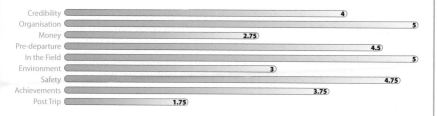

Credibility	4
Organisation	5
Money	2.75
Pre-departure	4.5
In the Field	5
Environment	3
Safety	4.75
Achievements	3.75
Post Trip	1.75

Background

In 2000 biology student, Alasdair Harris, discovered that Madagascar, with almost 6,000km of extraordinarily diverse coastline, had no institutional capacity for underwater research or exploration – a fundamental prerequisite for the development of conservation and environmental management. He raised funds for a series of underwater research and exploration expeditions, but realised there was a greater need for continuity. He established BV with a friend, Tom Savage, whose practical business approach provided a reality check to Alasdair's biological enthusiasm. It is a social enterprise based on an entirely non-profit business model that provides continuity and sustainability to future work.

Credibility

Projects are designed in partnership with governmental and academic institutes in Madagascar, as well as local NGOs. They won the Skål Eco-tourism Award in 2006, the Equator Prize, Best Volunteering Organisation in 2006 and were highly commended in the Responsible Travel Awards. They have good media coverage and have been featured in *National Geographic*, *The Independent Ethical Travel Guide* and *Sportsdiver*. Aqua Lung (diving) and ESRI (satellite surveying) support their work with equipment and discounts.

Organisation

They are marine conservation specialists working in Madagascar focusing on diving, coral and fish surveys, marine farming, carbon offsetting initiatives, education and sustainable development with coastal and rainforest communities.

Bookings are for pre-planned projects, which are always long term with named leaders; dissertation studies and medical electives are possible.

Volunteers tend to be dive enthusiasts of all ages with PADI training provided from beginners to dive masters. Past volunteers can be contacted on request and previous project reports are available on their website. Open days are mainly in the London area and at specialist exhibitions.

Where the money goes

A three-week project costs around £1,300, and all costs are covered from the assembly point onwards, but volunteers need to make their way there from the international airport. PADI training is included along with all scuba equipment except personal wetsuit, mask and flippers; there is also an expedition medic on site.

A 10% non-refundable deposit is required at booking and the balance is due six weeks before departure. No refunds are available, but postponing and rescheduling is possible. Around 70% of each volunteer's fee gets spent in and around the project.

Pre-departure preparation

A telephone interview is standard. There's no pre-departure training, but an excellent pre-departure guide is provided along with a good introduction to Madagascar. Intensive study of marine guides for species identification is required. The aims and objectives of the research are clearly outlined, as are the health and fitness requirements and the environmental conditions. There is good planning advice as well as useful packing and travel directions.

In the field

The intended conservation benefits are clear and projects have ten-year development plans. Accommodation is in shared beachside bungalows with showers and Western-style toilets. Working days are long and entertainment is self-generated. Lots of local people work with the projects, including Malagasy biologists and social scientists and there is a higher than average qualified staff to volunteer ratio. A scholarship programme is available for local Malagasy people who want to develop their marine conservation knowledge.

Environment & culture

Carbon offsetting is not included in the fee, but volunteers engage in some carbon-offset projects within local communities. There is good advice about how volunteers can minimise their environmental impact (everything coming in must go out) and learn about local customs and traditions.

Safety

They are BS8848:2007 self-certified for overseas fieldwork expeditions. Good risk assessment protocols are in place and vessels have VHF radios, satellite phones, first aid and oxygen. The on-site doctor has a medical station and with the dive manager can cope with most on-site emergencies and a well-formulated evacuation protocol is in place.

Demonstrable achievements

Regular field research reports are updated on their website, detailing recent activities and scientific articles are written up for professional journals. Practical conservation achievements include:

- In 2004 they created of the world's first community-run marine protected area for octopus.
- Developed an 800km² protected area at the Andavadoaka project benefiting more than 10,000 people by protecting coral reefs, mangroves, seagrass beds and other threatened habitats. The area will also implement sustainable development projects including ecotourism and sea cucumber farming.
- Developing an online marine species identification website for the western Indian Ocean.
- A unique forest of dwarf baobabs near Andavadoaka is being mapped as a potential ecotourist attraction and assessing threats to its health.
- Twice every month volunteers work with local fisherwomen to sample the species and weight of all catches landed in on Andavadoaka Beach. Results of this monitoring programme are providing an unprecedented long-term data set, which is enabling identification of temporal changes in landings.
- Blue Ventures organises Club Alo Alo, an environmental education programme designed to introduce local schoolchildren to ecological principles.

Post-trip follow up

Questionnaires and debriefings are conducted in the field and newsletters circulated to past volunteers. The website is updated on project activities and a Facebook page keeps volunteers in touch with each other.

BRITISH TRUST FOR CONSERVATION VOLUNTEERS (BTCV)

☎ 01302 388828; ✉ information@btcv.org.uk; 🖰 www.btcv.org.uk

BTCV is a registered charity and one of the UK's oldest conservation organisations. Volunteer leaders accompany all projects in the UK and overseas. Destinations include mainland Europe, Iceland, Africa, Nepal, USA, New Zealand and Australia. It is ideal for UK residents uncertain about the idea of conservation volunteering, because they can try out volunteering near home at moderate cost.

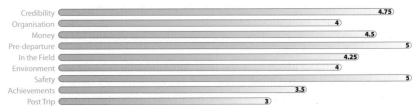

Credibility	4.75
Organisation	4
Money	4.5
Pre-departure	5
In the Field	4.25
Environment	4
Safety	5
Achievements	3.5
Post Trip	3

Background

In 1959 Brigadier Armstrong founded the Conservation Corps. David Bellamy was part of the first project to clear dogwood at Box Hill in Surrey. In 1970 the Corps morphed into the British Trust for Conservation Volunteers (BTCV) and HRH Duke of Edinburgh became the patron.

Credibility

In essence BTCV is a traditional grassroots organisation eschewing fancy marketing in favour of practical fieldwork. It has won awards for its environmental, sustainable communities and charity work and is a significant player in national conservation and environment strategies. It doesn't court the media, but local projects get good local media coverage. They attract funding to support their work from English Nature, Norwich Union, Royal Bank of Scotland, Prudential, Rio Tinto, National Lottery grants and the EU.

Organisation

It has a 100% focus on conservation and sustainable development. Although mainly based in the UK it currently runs 37 overseas conservation projects with 17 overseas partners. Projects include building and repairing nature trails, managing habitats, reforestation, working on nature reserves and biodiversity surveys.

Bookings are for pre-planned projects, which are usually long term and have a clear conservation purpose. Unlike most placement services BTCV provide details of the host organisation with webs links when available. It's not usually possible to contact past volunteers. Volunteers come from a wider age range than typical gap-year projects.

NVQs are only available on UK-based projects and open days are limited to an annual event, but there are offices all over the UK.

Where the money goes

Project costs range from £220–1,450. Full audited accounts are available and all internal transport and insurance is included.

A £100 non-refundable deposit is required at booking and final payment is due eight weeks before departure. Cancellation charges are on a sliding scale until 27 days before departure, when all payments are forfeited.

Changes or transfers between projects can be made up to eight weeks before departure for an administration fee of £25 and a full refund is made if BTCV have to cancel a project.

Approximately 65% of each volunteer's fee gets spent in and around projects, but the specific amount varies depending on the country and how new the project is.

Pre-departure preparation

Excellent background is provided about overseas partners and the project leader personally contacts each volunteer for an individual pre-departure briefing. Only a quarter of projects have a detailed daily schedule; others give a general idea of day-to-day activities.

Good information is provided about field conditions, and health hazards and fitness issues are discussed with the project leader along with a health and safety briefing.

An interesting web link to the Department for International Development is provided when there is relevant information.

In the field

Good general background to the projects is provided, but not in any scientific detail. Accommodation ranges from simple to basic, including dormitory style, homestay and tented camps. There are close working links with the local community and projects have a strong work focus with one day off per week. Volunteers can expect to contribute to daily domestic chores.

Environment & culture

Carbon offset for international flights and in-country volunteer activity is covered within the fee but environmental care and cultural advice is limited – though augmented during one-to-one discussions with the group leader before departure.

Safety

BTCV became BS8848:2007 self-certified in July 2008. There are good risk assessment protocols in place and staff (volunteer leaders) are on site 24/7. New contingency plans and emergency protocols have been revised in line with BS8848:2007 and are available for inspection on their website. Volunteers are covered by BTCV insurance whilst engaged in volunteer activities, which includes repatriation.

Demonstrable achievements

Overseas projects are not usually well written up as volunteer leaders only work for the two-week project slots. Practical conservation achievements include:

- Construction of artificial nesting islands for sandwich terns on Bulgaria's Pomorie Lake.
- During 2006 and 2007 volunteer projects constructed 1,000m of vital mountain footpath in the remote Semonkong region of Lesotho in southern Africa.
- Carried out major environmental restoration in the Nevada Desert during 2007.
- They have been engaged in environmental protection by creating hiking trails in Iceland for decades.

Post-trip follow up

Questionnaire feedback is sought from all volunteers with a return rate of 48%. Newsletters are distributed but more importantly volunteers are introduced to the wider BTCV organisation and made aware of the conservation opportunities within the UK.

CAMPAIGNING ORGANISATIONS

COUNCIL FOR THE PROTECTION OF RURAL ENGLAND (CPRE)
📞 020 7981 2800; ✉ info@cpre.org.uk or campaigns@cpre.org.uk;
🖰 www.cpre.org.uk

CPRE is a national charity that helps people to protect the English countryside where it is under threat, to enhance it where possible and to keep it beautiful, productive and enjoyable for everyone. It campaigns for a sustainable future for the countryside, by highlighting threats and promoting positive solutions using research and active campaigning to influence public opinion and decision makers at every level.

Volunteer opportunities
There are nine regional groups, 43 county branches and 200 district groups, covering the whole of England. Volunteering opportunities exist at CPRE's regional groups and county branches as well as at their national office. Volunteer activities include responding to planning applications, producing publicity, lobbying MPs, fundraising, helping at special events, distributing leaflets or helping in the office.

Demonstrable achievements
The continued existence and quality of so much of the English landscape is a testament to CPRE's 80 years of successful campaigning. CPRE led the campaign to create the town and country planning system, national parks, areas of outstanding natural beauty and green belts. Even so, the countryside continues to face a multitude of threats so CPRE still campaigns to protect and enhance our landscape heritage for the benefit of all.

FRIENDS OF THE EARTH
📞 020 7490 1555; ✉ contact via the website; 🖰 www.foe.co.uk. It also has offices in 70 other countries.

Friends of the Earth is made up of two distinct organisations – a charity and a limited company – which enables them to operate in a more flexible way: Friends of the Earth Trust focuses on campaigning, research, education and publishing; whereas Friends of the Earth Limited focuses on influencing political parties and business practices. Their key campaigning areas are monitoring biodiversity, climate change, corporate responsibility, safe and healthy food, fair trade, transport and waste.

Volunteer opportunities
There are over 70 international Friends of the Earth groups and 200 local groups within England, Wales and Northern Ireland, including the Channel Islands and Isle of Man (Friends of the Earth Scotland is a separate organisation).

Local groups work to improve the environment in their own area, as well as joining in with national and international campaigns. Look on the national website to find your local group or see what they have recently been up to.

Their most famous campaign was the dumping of 1,500 non-returnable bottles outside Schweppes headquarters to make a point about corporate responsibility in waste and recycling.

Demonstrable achievements

- The establishment of palm oil plantations to meet the growing demand for one of the world's most popular vegetable oils is driving devastating rainforest destruction in southeast Asia. Friends of the Earth want to see a law put in place that prevents UK companies from acting irresponsibly both here and overseas. Over 90 local groups have been taking action on palm oil.
- Over 100 local groups have been pushing the 'Big Ask' campaign to commit the government to reducing CO_2 emissions by around 3% every year. Groups have been lobbying their local MPs and asking them to sign up the Early Day Motion 178 in favour of the climate change bill. Thousands of postcards have been filled in by the public in support of this campaign. So far almost 400 MPs are supporting the campaign.
- A new super-port, proposed by Associated British Ports (ABP), would have destroyed wildlife areas of national and international importance in Dibden Bay near Southampton. However, objection from local Friends of the Earth campaigners, alongside other community groups, resulted in the government's decision to reject the project.

GREENPEACE

📞 020 7865 8100; ✉ info@uk.greenpeace.org; 🖰 www.greenpeace.org.uk.
It has offices in dozens of other countries.

Greenpeace was formed in 1970 when a group of activists in Vancouver chartered a boat and set sail to oppose American nuclear testing in the Aleutian Islands. It is now a large international organisation with its headquarters in the Netherlands and there are 41 country-specific branches around the globe.

They seek to defend the natural world and promote peace by investigating, exposing and confronting environmental abuse by governments and corporations around the world. They also champion environmentally responsible and socially just solutions, including scientific and technical innovation.

Volunteer opportunities

It is possible to join the crew of a Greenpeace ship, but volunteers need to be very experienced and fully qualified for any paid role and the competition for these high-profile positions is very intense. Check out the opportunities on the Greenpeace International website (🖰 *www.greenpeace.org/ international/about/faq/questions-about-working-or-vol*) or write to them

(*Greenpeace Marine Services, Ottho Heldringstraat 5, 1066 AZ Amsterdam, The Netherlands;* ☎ *+31 20 718 2000*). There is plenty of campaigning action on land, so contact the UK office for further information and sign up for newsletter updates to find out about current issues.

Demonstrable achievements
Their goal is to ensure the ability of the earth to nurture life in all its diversity. To this end Greenpeace have played a pivotal role in the adoption of:

- A ban on toxic waste exports to less developed countries.
- A moratorium on commercial whaling.
- A United Nations convention providing for better management of world fisheries.
- A Southern Ocean Whale Sanctuary.
- A 50-year moratorium on mineral exploitation in Antarctica.
- Bans on the dumping at sea of radioactive and industrial waste and disused oil installations.
- An end to large-scale driftnet fishing on the high seas.
- A ban on all nuclear weapons testing – their first ever campaign.

CAPE TRIBULATION TROPICAL RESEARCH STATION
☏ +61 07 4098 0063; ✉ hugh@austrop.org.au; 🖰 www.austrop.org.au

The Cape Tribulation Tropical Research Station is a not-for-profit organisation established in 1988 when the Cape Tribulation tropical region became a UNESCO World Heritage Site. It is part of the Daintree rainforest region and is beside the Coral Sea, 100 miles north of Cairns in far north Queensland. Its purpose is to provide a focus for researchers and students to carry out both pure and applied research in the region.

Volunteer opportunities
Volunteers should apply by email explaining what their interests are, what skills they might bring and which dates they want to work. Research projects are possible if they come with external funding. In general, volunteers will be expected to contribute wherever work is most needed.

A whole host of practical trade skills are needed to help run and maintain the research station as well as assistance with research and general station activities. This could include radio tracking bats, counting figs, rainforest regeneration, gardening, horticulture, constructing buildings, digging holes and running the 'bat house' (visitors' centre), or whatever else needs doing.

In the field
Most volunteer placements are for two or three weeks and they can accommodate up to 20 volunteers in four two-room bunkhouses. The station facilities are fairly basic, but there is a good range of field equipment, microscopes, radio-tracking gear, plant drying facilities, survey gear, etc, as well as excellent workshop facilities. They prefer volunteers to be over 20 years old and capable of working a full day, six days a week. In addition to individual or team projects, volunteers are also expected to contribute to the domestic duties of running the research station.

Fees are calculated on a daily basis for board and lodgings and for volunteers this is around £17, but research students pay £27 for the use of additional research facilities.

This is a real, working, tropical research station and not a tourist or gap-year venue so expect to work hard and participate in their environmentally friendly approach to sustainable living.

Demonstrable achievements
The successful reforestation and increased rainforest vegetation around the station, has now attracted a wide range of native species, including jungle fowl, scrub turkeys, goannas, bandicoots, melomys (climbing rodent), uromys (white tailed rat) and cassowaries. Their work on non-lethal flying fox deterrents, for use by local fruit farmers, is helping to reduce unnecessary deaths.

The 'bat house' is a rescue and rehabilitation centre for orphaned flying foxes, many of which continue to return and roost there.

CORAL CAY CONSERVATION

\ 020 7620 1411; ✉ info@coralcay.org; 🖰 www.coralcay.org

Coral Cay Conservation works specifically in the fields of coral reef and tropical rainforest conservation. They run their own expeditions, always in partnership with local NGOs, collecting scientific information to produce habitat maps and provide conservation management recommendations. Work is based on understanding the wishes and aspirations of local communities rather than imposing what outsiders feel the community should be doing. Key destinations include Tobago, Philippines, Papua New Guinea and Fiji.

The Coral Cay Conservation Trust is a UK-registered charity that funds community-based education and training programmes that Coral Cay is participating in. Coral Cay Expeditions is the not-for-profit business arm that recruits volunteers, and deals with the practicalities of getting them on site and looking after them.

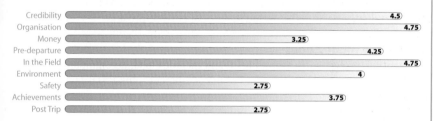

Credibility	4.5
Organisation	4.75
Money	3.25
Pre-departure	4.25
In the Field	4.75
Environment	4
Safety	2.75
Achievements	3.75
Post Trip	2.75

Background

Coral Cay Conservation was created in 1986 after a team of university students visited Belize to examine the effects of fishing and tourism on the world's second-largest barrier reef. Founder and marine biologist, Peter Raines, saw that coral reefs were being degraded at an alarming rate. With insufficient scientists to survey the reefs he conceived the idea of establishing a volunteer programme to train volunteers in baseline survey work. This information is used to help scientists establish protection policies for coral reefs under threat.

David Bellamy, CCC's president, has been actively involved since day one.

Credibility

Projects are designed in partnership with overseas government agencies or local NGOs. CCC takes responsibility for all aspects of projects, all of which are long standing, some in excess of ten years. They have won a string of awards including the BA Community Volunteer Award and the Philippines Best Managed Reef. Media coverage includes *Wanderlust*, *BBC Wildlife*, *Dive* magazine along with *BBC Newsreel* and newspaper features.

They work with key agencies like the Belize government's Coastal Zone Management Unit, the University College of Belize, Coral Reef Initiative, Project AWARE Foundation and the International Ecotourism Society.

They have received sponsorship funding from the Darwin Initiative, P&O and the Jack Petchey Foundation for scholarship places.

Organisation

CCC are coral reef conservation specialists, but also engage in rainforest and some community activities. Key tasks include reef diving, trekking, rainforest and marine biodiversity surveys, education of local young people and fishermen.

Bookings are for pre-planned projects that are all long term and led by top marine scientists and there is scope for students to carry out dissertation research.

Projects are not conceived and implemented in the UK. CCC are usually asked by local organisations, NGOs, or governments to come and join, or establish, reef research. There are four long-standing project areas that have 400 volunteers per year these tend to be a mix of young and career gappers.

They hold regular open days and pre-departure meetings providing opportunities to meet other members of the expedition team and gain final briefings and updates. The website contains a detailed bibliography of all projects, publications and monthly updates of current projects.

Where the money goes

A two-week project costs around £800 and includes food, accommodation, airport pick-up plus expedition and scuba equipment, plus PADI training as required.

A £100 administration fee is required at booking. This is refunded if a booking is refused, but contributes to the fee if accepted. A non-refundable deposit of £500 is then due 12 weeks prior to departure.

Project cancellation more than eight weeks before departure results in the administration fee and deposit being forfeited. Cancellations of less than eight weeks before departure result in all fees being forfeited. There is some flexibility with changing departure dates, but only on a case-by-case basis.

Around 75% of a volunteer's contribution is spent on and around conservation projects. They have an excellent scheme of providing scholarship places for disadvantaged kids from the UK, as well as local young people.

All volunteers have to become members of the Coral Cay Conservation Society, which costs £25 per annum; the reason is to promote a sense of common endeavour.

Pre-departure preparation

A pre-departure training meeting is held in the UK and an in-country 'skill development programme' is outlined on the web along with plenty of detail about expedition life, including diaries, accounts and volunteer stories.

The scientific aims and objectives are well laid out and volunteers know the type of work they will be doing. Medical forms need to be completed and scuba divers need an additional PADI medical statement. Good kit lists are detailed for both marine and terrestrial expeditions.

In the field

Projects are part of an integrated conservation approach. As well as scientific activities, they also work with local schoolchildren, village community leaders, resort guests, dive instructors and tourism guides.

Expect basic conditions, including shared dormitories and washing facilities. Sometimes there are local cooks, but volunteers may be required to assist with food preparation.

Projects involve a full and busy work programme, but a holiday element can be added on for an additional cost. Local people play a significant role in aspects of the project – not just cooks, guides and drivers, but also as major organisational players.

Environment & culture

Carbon offsetting is encouraged – but is the responsibility of volunteers – although they are planning to develop their own rainforest carbon-offset scheme. Well thought out environment protection guidelines require that everything that goes into the forest must also leave the forest. Local briefing on customs and culture is provided on arrival and a scholarship scheme is available to Filipino, Tobagan, Papuan citizens wishing to make an active contribution towards the protection and sustainable use of their coral reefs.

Safety

They have fully implemented the British Standards Institute's BS8848:2007 on a self-declared basis. All expeditions have a permanent team of qualified and experienced expedition staff who are trained in first aid and on site 24/7. Medical staff are usually present on marine expeditions and first-aid kits are in place.

Details of on-site risk assessments were not available for inspection, nor was it possible to inspect their emergency protocols for handling field emergencies.

Demonstrable achievements

- Helped establish seven marine and forest protected areas and were instrumental in having the Belize barrier reef declared as a UNESCO World Heritage Site.
- Established a 'reef ranger' training programme for local students to monitor and report on the state of their own reef – snorkel and monitoring equipment provided by CCC.

Post-trip follow up

Most volunteers complete evaluation questionnaires. Monthly project updates are posted on the website along with ongoing news and staff diaries. A subscription newsletter keeps ex-volunteers up to date with general developments and the CCC Society aims to maintain a long-term commitment.

CONSERVATION VOLUNTEERS AUSTRALIA (CVA) AND CONSERVATION VOLUNTEERS NEW ZEALAND (CVNZ)

☏ 0800 032 501 (freephone within Australia) or +61 3 5330 2600 from elsewhere; ✉ info@conservationvolunteers.com.au;
🖰 www.conservationvolunteers.com.au. There are 21 regional offices around Australia with contact details on the website.

They are a long-established, hands-on registered charity arranging and running conservation projects across the whole of Australia and New Zealand. They organise placements but actively supervise all projects, setting clear safety standards and outcomes. The majority of volunteers taking up Australian conservation placements offered by UK or USA companies will actually be working on CVA projects.

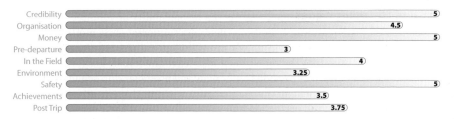

Credibility	5
Organisation	4.5
Money	5
Pre-departure	3
In the Field	4
Environment	3.25
Safety	5
Achievements	3.5
Post Trip	3.75

Background

CVA is an incorporated not-for-profit organisation founded in 1993 and originally called the Australian Trust for Conservation Volunteers. It changed to the trading name of Conservation Volunteers Australia (CVA) in 2000 and in 2006 CVA took over the management of Conservation New Zealand although CNZ still operates as an independent NGO. A third arm of CVA is 'Naturewise', a more upmarket organisation offering conservation holiday experiences ranging from two days to one week. The time spent undertaking conservation activities typically makes up 30–40% of the trip with the other time spent touring, such as bush walks, island tours, wildlife viewing and visiting national parks.

Credibility

All projects are designed to meet rigorous conservation parameters. They have won numerous awards, including United Nations Global 500 Honour Roll for Environmental Achievement, five Banksia Environmental Foundation Awards, Best Responsible Travel Programme and more. Projects get good national newspaper and radio coverage. They are members of the World Conservation Union of the Conservation Volunteer Alliance and Ecotourism Australia and receive financial support from Shell, Vodafone, Rio Tinto and Toyota.

Organisation

There are over 2,000 projects each year covering all of Australia and New Zealand and around 50% of volunteers come from overseas countries. Activities include biodiversity studies, coastal conservation, environmental education, carbon offset initiatives, river health, sustainable land management and urban conservation.

Bookings are for pre-planned projects that work with conservation scientists, rangers, land managers and qualified team leaders to manage the volunteers. A range of conservation and volunteer training courses is available. Monthly open days are provided in every state, prospective volunteers can speak to past volunteers, but no details are provided about who else is on a specific project.

About 50% of overseas volunteers book directly with CVA and 50% pay over the top through home-country placement agencies, located throughout Europe, Asia and the USA (see CVA website for details). But with CVA or CVNZ this offers few, if any, advantages for English-speaking volunteers.

Where the money goes

With CVA a two-week project in Australia or New Zealand costs around £270 all-inclusive from the appropriate state assembly point and includes a wildlife guide and annual membership of CVA or CVNZ.

There is an AU$100 non-refundable deposit and generous cancellation penalties on a sliding scale of 15% up to 30 days before commencement, 30% up to 14 days before commencement, and full forfeiture within 14 days of the project start date. Volunteers can reschedule prior bookings. Up to 87% of revenue gets spent on and around conservation projects.

Pre-departure preparation

Pre-departure training is unrealistic with so many overseas volunteers and in-country training varies from project to project, but CVA has a rigorous screening and selection process for projects. Job clarity is rather generalised, but their health and fitness information is excellent as are packing and domestic travel directions.

In the field

The intended conservation benefits are fairly clear, but all projects are ongoing and actively managed for effectiveness. Typical accommodation can include caravans, hostels, shearers' quarters, bunkhouses or tented camps. All staff are local, but there is a disappointing level of Aboriginal involvement. However, CVA promises not to displace the work of any existing paid staff. Work schedules are usually weekdays with the weekends as free time.

Environment & culture

Carbon offsetting is encouraged and CVA has policies to minimise project emissions and aims to be one of the first NGO carbon credit providers in Australia. There is excellent advice to volunteers on minimising their environmental impact and good information about respecting Aboriginal culture.

Safety

BS8848:2007 is not relevant for an Australian organisation, but CVA protocols and health and safety procedures work to a comparable European standard. Leaders are first-aid trained, there is a 24-hour duty manager system and emergency evacuation plans are in place.

Personal accident insurance is provided for volunteers and safety advice is also available in Japanese and Korean as well as simplified Chinese, German and French.

Demonstrable achievements

For such a well-run organisation they make a surprisingly poor effort on writing up field progress reports and detailing their conservation achievements. Their impact is clear, but this is not related to conservation gains:

- They have planted more than one million trees for habitat and land restoration.
- They have collected over 1,000 tons of native seed for revegetation and reforestation projects.
- They have built and restored over 300km of walking tracks and boardwalks that reduce erosion and animal disturbance.
- They have installed more than 80km of conservation fencing to protect vulnerable areas and preserve native species.
- They have completed 500 wildlife and biodiversity surveys to assist with threatened species management.
- They have established a carbon forest site at the W James Whyte Island Reserve comprising over 200ha and situated approximately 50km west of Melbourne. During 2007 they planted over 45,000 trees, shrubs and grasses, resulting in approximately 5,500 tonnes of carbon being stored in the native vegetation.

Post-trip follow up

All volunteers complete evaluation questionnaires and there is an 88.6% satisfaction score. Monthly newsletters and a bi-annual magazine are distributed to ex-volunteers and there are Christmas barbecues at local offices. There are lots of local post-project programmes for ex-volunteers to join, including the Green corps, Better Earth and Green gym, and overseas volunteers are also eligible to enter the twice yearly CVA awards scheme.

EARTHWATCH INSTITUTE

☎ 01865 318838; 🖰 www.earthwatch.org. It also has offices in America, Australia and Japan.

They are a registered international environmental charity and limited company arranging and running conservation research projects in partnership with academic institutions and research scientists. Conservation proposals for projects are submitted to Earthwatch and evaluated by a team of expert peers and only the most scientifically significant are accepted. Local and international scientists lead 130 research projects in 40 countries departing annually to Africa, Madagascar, Seychelles, Canada, North, Central and South America, Caribbean, China, Mongolia, Australia, New Zealand, Thailand, Malaya, Sri Lanka, Iceland, Europe and UK.

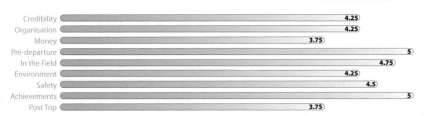

Credibility	4.25
Organisation	4.25
Money	3.75
Pre-departure	5
In the Field	4.75
Environment	4.25
Safety	4.5
Achievements	5
Post Trip	3.75

Background

Earthwatch was founded in Boston, Massachusetts, in 1971 by scientists from the Smithsonian Institute and 39 volunteers. Its aim was to create a new funding model for scientific research due to dwindling government funding and an increased urgency for scientific information and action to promote sustainable environments. In 1990 Earthwatch opened its European office in Oxford and started recruiting 'European' volunteers.

Credibility

Projects are peer-reviewed to ensure they make an effective scientific contribution to sustainable environments. The National Geographic Society has previously awarded them for being the best voluntourism organisation and they have extensive media coverage in *The Independent*, *Daily Telegraph*, *BBC Wildlife* magazine and many others.

They collaborate with 50 other conservation organisations (ie: WWF, Kew) and are supported by 40 corporate partners including HSBC, DuPont, Cadbury/Schweppes and Rio Tinto. Funding comes from a variety of sources, including volunteer fees, governments, universities, foundations, trusts and donations.

Projects run from year to year focusing on environmental issues, sustainable conservation solutions to human/wildlife conflicts, maintaining biodiversity, assessing management and conservation practices, endangered habitats, threatened species and climate change.

Organisation

Earthwatch accept corporate responsibility for expeditions and hold open days, pre-field days, lectures and opportunities to meet past volunteers. There are 20,000 global members and 4,300 volunteers go on projects each year. In 2007 the European office (Oxford) sent 1,200 volunteers. Activities are all very scientific and include biodiversity surveys, reef diving, observing and recording behaviour, mapping distribution, radio tracking, camera trapping, laboratory work, climate study as well as other scientific research activities.

Expedition groups average 12–14 members with, a minimum age of 18 and an average age of mid-40s. Team lists are circulated before departure so volunteers can make joint travel plans. A few more structured and highly facilitated family and teen expeditions are arranged each year. A very useful complimentary access to the Wexas Travel service is provided to assist volunteers with their travel plans.

Where the money goes

Expedition fees are considered charitable donations; two-week expeditions typically costs from £900 to £1,900. A £200 deposit is required which is refundable up to 60 days before departure (minus a £50 administration fee), when the full balance is due. All fees are forfeit if cancellation is after 60 days. It is possible to transfer between expeditions up to 60 days before departure without penalties.

Fees include a welcome pack, 30-page expedition briefing, health assessment form, medical insurance, project transport, academic and field staff, emergency medical evacuation and carbon offset payment for flights with ClimateCare.

Around 66% of a volunteer's contribution is spent on and around conservation projects.

There are grants for students and teachers to participate in expeditions and since 1998 440 teachers in Europe have been awarded Earthwatch Environmental Awards and joined 70 field expeditions.

Pre-departure preparation

Explicit scientific aims and objectives for each expedition are provided before departure. A designated Earthwatch leader accompanies all teams working with in-country partners, eg: academics, NGOs, governments, etc. A written job specification is provided with the expedition research brief detailing the type and amount of activity.

Optional pre-field days are organised for volunteers to develop travel writing or photographic skills. Guidelines for individual preparation and detailed schedules of in-country training are provided for each expedition.

Expedition briefing includes details of the environmental field conditions and anticipated activity levels. Volunteers are screened to match fitness with project requirements along with a compulsory check-up with their GP.

In the field

The intended conservation purpose is clear and all projects are long-term investigations. Accommodation ranges from safari camps, village houses, thatched rondavels, riverboats, ranches, hotels and family stays, which may be located in the wilderness, villages or towns. Local cooks and support staff are normally employed, but some expeditions require limited assistance with domestic chores. These are scientific expeditions, not holidays, so expect a regular and sometimes demanding work schedule. Relaxation time is set aside each day, along with rest days to enjoy the unique features of the local environment.

Environment & culture

In-country expedition energy consumption and volunteers' international flights are carbon-offset with ClimateCare. There is good advice about how volunteers can minimise their impact on the local environment, but there is not much information on cultural orientation before departure.

Safety

Currently they are working towards BS8848:2007; some projects are already compliant, others will be in the near future. The planning and risk assessments are carried out by Earthwatch field staff and available for inspection before departure. Field conditions, risks and hazards are very detailed in the expedition briefing. There is an in-country crisis management team and medical evacuation plans are in place including air ambulance. Field staff are trained in emergency procedures and qualified nursing staff are usually on site. Emergency assistance from dedicated field-management staff is available 24/7.

Demonstrable achievements

All projects are written up and many scientific research papers are published from the results. Scientific outcomes are detailed on the website, in publications and lectures. Just a few examples include:
- In 2004 resolved hippo/human conflict in Ghana by creating sustainable livelihoods.
- Secured RAMSAR protected status for Kenyan wetlands around Lake Elmenteita in September 2005.
- Achieved the diversion of shipping lanes in Spain to aid dolphin conservation in November 2006.

Post-trip follow up

Evaluation forms are completed. Specialist volunteer liaison staff keep volunteers in touch with projects; they also organise events, lectures and produce a volunteer newsletter. Research findings are widely publicised and brought to the attention of key decision makers. Advice and some funds are available for ex-volunteers to start their own local 'community action environmental project'.

ECOTEER
✉ contact@ecoteer.com; 🖰 www.ecoteer.com

This is an internet directory to specific conservation volunteer projects around the globe; it does not organise volunteer projects. It facilitates and enables overseas projects with a low income to have a web presence for free and puts volunteers directly in touch with specific projects.

Volunteers pay £10 to register as a member, which gives them access to a searchable internet database of 216 projects, it also allows them to post a request for a specific type of placement. There is no middle person and volunteers make their own arrangements directly with the projects.

Background
Ecoteer was founded by Daniel Quilter in 2005 after a difficult experience trying to arrange a year's volunteering in Asia without paying large sums of money to placement companies. He spent six months in Saba, Borneo, and was given food and accommodation in return for his work at an eco-lodge. On his return home he set up Ecoteer to promote projects that required volunteers, including those that do not require a fee.

Where the money goes
Ecoteer provides listing space to organisations, institutions, eco lodges and charities that would like to advertise their volunteering opportunities. It sees itself as more ethical and responsible than most other volunteer companies because it bypasses the middle person. Over 50% of projects are free, and if there is a fee volunteers give it directly to the project and as a result 100% of a volunteer's fee is spent on the project compared with as little as 30% by some placement organisations. The only money Ecoteer makes is from each volunteer's £10 membership fee and website advertising commission from accommodation, flight bookers and travel insurance.

Organisation and volunteer opportunities
Out of the 216 projects available only 60 are specifically conservation oriented (28%) and each year around 250–350 volunteers book their trips this way. Project vetting is elementary and takes the form of contacting two past volunteers and receiving positive feedback. Most volunteers are university students or recent graduates looking to gain some work experience in the eco-travel industry.

Ecoteer has a more interactive website than Green Volunteers and it is possible to get advice and first-hand comments from past volunteers. It is also possible for volunteers to advertise on the site for a specific placement and for eco-lodges to advertise for volunteers to fill specific roles, eg: guide, chef, boat crew, language skills, etc.

There are also YouTube clips and some eco-style employment opportunities are offered that might be better described as internships (working for free in return for board, lodging and work experience). New projects are regularly posted and they never list projects sold by placement agencies.

Ecoteer does not endorse or validate any listings posted on its website; it does make an effort to only include accurate placement details, but it does not accept responsible for the content of these listings.

Examples of projects
Seychelles Conservation Project
It costs around £750 for eight weeks and runs all year round. The project is based on Silhouette Island and volunteers work with conservation scientists on a range of biodiversity studies, removing invasive plants and helping with the giant tortoise reintroduction project. Undergraduate research studies are especially welcome.

Guatemalan Wildlife Preservation Organisation
It costs around £60 per week, which covers dormitory or homestay-style board and lodging and runs year-round (but only Sept–May for turtle-nesting activities). It is a rescue centre caring for and rehabilitating a wide range of rainforest animals confiscated on the black market by the Guatemalan government. Volunteers help looking after the animals, conducting surveys and releasing animals into the wild.

Malaysia Rainforest Lodge
Most of the time accommodation and food are free, but there is a minimum contract of three months and volunteers learn to work as river cruise guides, chefs or general workers. The project is based in Borneo and preference is given to people with relevant degrees or experiences. Runs year round.

Great Baikal Trail Project, Russia
It costs around £150–180 for a minimum of two weeks and includes a pick-up from either Irkutsk or Ulan-Ude airport. Also provided is a visa invitation letter, meals, tented accommodation, assistance with official registration, translation and finding accommodation. The work is hard and involves building a 1,300-mile circum-Baikal hiking trail around the world's largest and deepest lake in Siberia. Volunteers come from all over Russia as well as 20 different countries around the globe. Runs from June to September.

ECOVOLUNTEER

This small operation prefers contact via its wide range of international agents, so has no postal or telephone contact details; an email link is available via the website ✑www.ecovolunteer.org. If no suitable local agent exists bookings can be made directly with Ecovolunteer via its website. Currently, there are no agents in the UK.

Ecovolunteer is a placement service which links people with conservation projects. Project destinations include Europe, Africa, Asia, North, Central and South America. Most projects are run by local wildlife and nature conservation NGOs, who also operate as the incoming tour operator for Ecovolunteer. There are a number of unique projects not offered by any other placement service.

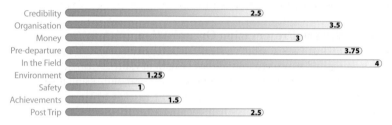

Credibility	2.5
Organisation	3.5
Money	3
Pre-departure	3.75
In the Field	4
Environment	1.25
Safety	1
Achievements	1.5
Post Trip	2.5

Background

Ecovolunteer is a small Dutch-registered tour operator run by Roel Cosijn who set up the company in 1992 as an independent, privately financed organisation. He is a biologist motivated by conservation ideals and sees the Ecovolunteer programme as a meaningful opportunity to contribute. He says the wildlife, conservation and research activities always come first; these are not tourism enterprises and volunteers should consider their participation to be a privilege.

Credibility

Local scientists and conservationists run many projects, but it varies from project to project. Ecovolunteer has no marketing strategy, has never entered for any awards, and doesn't bother to keep press clippings. It has a good fair trade policy that prioritises the benefits to projects over those of volunteers. It is a member of the Dutch Rhino Foundation and the Preservation and Protection of the Przewalski's Horse. It accepts no external sponsorship.

Organisation

They offer a range of 30 species-specific projects, many of which are unique to Ecovolunteer. Activities include rescue centres, game reserves, animal tracking, anti-poaching patrols, outreach education, animal surveys, laboratory work and sustainable development. Project leaders are not detailed on briefing sheets, but past volunteers can be contacted for comments.

Its small scale and global recruitment make open days unrealistic. Many projects have small numbers of volunteers coming from a wide mix of Western backgrounds and typically they are more mature than typical gap-year placements. The average age is 20–35, but with an increasing number of 40–50 year olds.

Each project has a news section on the website that goes back several years and provides a good feel for how projects are developing. The website also has a unique search function for conservation projects by destination, species, or by month of travel.

Where the money goes

A two-week project costs from £140–1,200. Generally the fee includes accommodation, project activity, food, and sometimes an airport pick-up, but the cheapest may require you to find your own way from the airport to an obscure destination and buy your own food.

Cancellation penalties depend on which international booking agent is used; expect to pay a 10% deposit, which becomes non-refundable 120 days or less before departure. Cancellation penalties have a sliding scale until all fees are forfeited one week before departure, but different booking agents may apply different booking conditions. A minimum of 77% of the recommended retail price is transferred to the conservation organisations that operate Ecovolunteer projects.

Pre-departure preparation

There are no training events, but detailed project files are available on the web prior to booking along with photographs, local news and better-than-average volunteer comments. In-country training is entirely the responsibility of each local NGO.

There are well thought through aims and objectives and often clear weekly work plans, but volunteers are warned that they are not allowed to specify the jobs they want to do, but are expected to adapt completely to the needs of the project.

Environmental conditions and fitness requirements are specified by many projects and there is usually a good kit list, but travel directions vary from 'get a bus' to being met at the airport.

In the field

Projects are very hands-on and as far away from a tourist experience as you could imagine; volunteers are there to work for the projects' priorities – end of story. The intended conservation benefits are usually very clear.

Accommodation is invariably basic, such as a biological field station, a locally rented home, a cabin on a research vessel, or occasionally a tent. Expect to share a room, kitchen, toilets, bathroom and other facilities with other eco-volunteers and assist with cleaning and shopping as part of your daily duties.Projects are staffed entirely by local people, the work is hard, and there is no sense of providing entertainment for volunteers.

Environment & culture

There is no clear carbon offsetting strategy on the website, although some booking agents do promote carbon offsetting. Ecovolunteer is working with Trees for Travel and does aim to become carbon neutral in the near future.

There is little information about how volunteers could minimise their impact on the local environment, but often there is detailed cultural advice about local communities and traditions.

Safety

General safety standards are unspecified and basically down to each individual project; British Standards Institute BS8848:2007 is not used in Holland. Ecovolunteer do not carry out or require risk assessment or crisis management procedures to be carried out by projects. First-aid equipment is expected to be in place, but volunteers are likely to have to fall back on their travel insurance in cases of emergency.

Demonstrable achievements

Documented conservation outcomes and achievements are surprisingly weak for an organisation led by a biologist. There is plenty of information about conservation activity, but no analysis about its ultimate impact. Some local NGOs have produced research papers on their specific activities.

Post-trip follow up

All volunteers are asked to complete evaluation questionnaires, although only a small number actually do. Almost uniquely Ecovolunteer publish all questionnaire responses on their website (under testimonials) in the form of narrative comments.

EDGE OF AFRICA
+27 44 3820122; ✉ info@edgeofafrica.com; 🖱 www.edgeofafrica.com

Edge of Africa is a small new South Africa-based company. They aim to assist valid, scientifically based conservation activities and research using volunteers. They are not simply a placement agent, but work alongside volunteers with wildlife researchers, conservation organisations and communities in various regions of southern Africa.

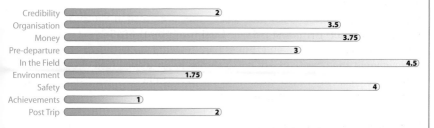

Credibility	2
Organisation	3.5
Money	3.75
Pre-departure	3
In the Field	4.5
Environment	1.75
Safety	4
Achievements	1
Post Trip	2

Background
Edge of Africa is the new branding for ConservationCo originally founded by Dayne Davey and Mark Slatter in 2006. Both have degrees in zoology and have grounded the company with scientific roots. Through their research experience, volunteer programmes, conservation education and links with local scientists, they saw a need for linking up conservation efforts with scientists and volunteer helpers.

Credibility
There is a good science base to their conservation projects, but they are too fresh and new to have received awards or had much media coverage beyond the local newspapers. They take an ethical stance and have established good working links with the South African National Park, the Environmental Observation Network and Venda University.

Organisation
Edge of Africa is a South African specialist working with projects along the Garden Route. They run five conservation projects and have around 150 volunteers per year, coming from a wide age spectrum and they work in small groups of six to ten. Projects focus on cheetah tracking, reforestation, removing invasive species, a Rastafarian eco-project, wildlife monitoring and various species studies, eg: Knysna grass owl, blue duiket. Some projects include a community or a schoolwork element.

A booked place is assured, group leaders accompany volunteers, and some projects are led by local academics. Research for thesis study is possible and prospective volunteers can make contact with previous volunteers.

Where the money goes
A two-week project costs around £500–650; all costs are covered from the

assembly point onwards. A 25% non-refundable booking fee is required, but cancellation penalties are generous. The balance is not due until 14 days before departure and 50% of the fee is refundable on cancellation. Alterations are possible without incurring penalty charges. Around 75% of the fee is spent on and around the project except when bookings are made via a third-party placement agent, in which case a 35% fee has to be paid to them; 10% is earmarked to support ongoing work at each project.

Pre-departure preparation
Pre-departure training is not practical as they are based in South Africa, but their in-country training isn't detailed either until arrival. Environmental conditions and fitness requirements are outlined, but specific aims and objectives are not. Volunteers get a good idea of their general tasks, but little guidance on kit requirements.

In the field
The conservation issues are quite clear, although the anticipated outcomes are less detailed. Accommodation is usually on site; some locations have private rooms while others require sharing (three max). Some volunteers stay in rustic farm cottages that require sleeping bags. One of the aims is to introduce aspects of local culture and people. Even though Edge of Africa is a relatively new organisation some projects have a well-established research track record. Projects run for a full working week and volunteers may have to shop for groceries themselves using an allowance.

Environment & culture
Volunteers are encouraged to carbon offset their flights and one expedition involves indigenous reforestation along the South African coast. No advice is provided about minimising the impact on the local environment, but there is a good cultural briefing for the Rastafarian eco-project.

Safety
British Standards Institute BS8848:2007 is not applicable in South Africa, but they do carry out risk assessments and have emergency planning protocols in place. There are full first-aid kits at each site and these are taken by project co-ordinators, along with telecoms equipment, whenever volunteers are working in the field.

Demonstrable achievements
Achievements are a weak area, primarily because they are new, but field scientists have written papers about some of the project sites and species databases are being compiled.

Post-trip follow up
Volunteers complete evaluation forms and a newsletter is provided, which covers project updates and now has a mailing list of 2,000.

ELEPHANT HUMAN RELATIONS AID (EHRA)

☏ +264 64 402501; M +264 812332148; ✉ elephant@iway.na;
🖰 www.desertelephant.org

EHRA is a Namibian-registered non-profit organisation that assists the Ministry of Environment and Tourism and local NGOs in promoting a mutually beneficial relationship between the humans and the expanding population of desert-adapted elephants in the northwestern regions of the Namibian Desert.

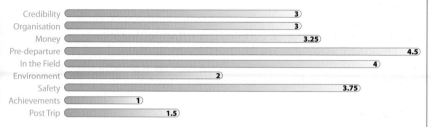

Credibility	3
Organisation	3
Money	3.25
Pre-departure	4.5
In the Field	4
Environment	2
Safety	3.75
Achievements	1
Post Trip	1.5

Background

South African EHRA founder, Johannes Haasbroek, studied political science, development studies and anthropology, later moving on to nature conservation. He has worked on various conservation projects in southern Africa and Namibia, including game reserve management, professional hunting, tour guiding, reserve development, anti poaching, guide training and rural development. While working with Save the Rhino Trust in Namibia, he developed systems to facilitate conservation without the aid of outside funding and became aware that elephant populations were expanding south. Recognising a need for a multi-angled approach to help solve the problem he founded EHRA.

Credibility

This small niche project works to help local people as well as the elephants. Its roots are practical, rather than scientific, and it has had good media coverage in *The Independent* and the *New York Times*. Operating since 2001, its main partner is the Namibia Ministry of Environment and Tourism. There is no official responsible travel policy, but the project serves local people, creates employment, operates in a very low-tech, eco-friendly way and has forged working links between Namibian, British and American schools.

Organisation

The project works exclusively in Namibia and with its elephants. The key tasks are tracking and monitoring the herds to compile identikits of local herds and especially bulls; mapping their movement patterns; and working with the local communities to build structures to protect vulnerable water supplies from damage.

Around 100 volunteers work with EHRA each year and groups tend to be small. A booked placement is assured and names, photographs and a brief biography of project leaders are on the website. An excellent video, which really captures the essence of the project and its locality, is on the website and on YouTube. Volunteers come from all walks of life, but share a similar passion and interest. Contact lists are circulated beforehand and previous volunteers can be contacted for personal comments.

Where the money goes
A standard period of two weeks costs £480 if booked directly with EHRA but could be considerably more if booked through a placement agency. The fee includes food, camping-style accommodation, pick-up from Swakopmund, local transport, expedition briefing and a health assessment form for your GP. Cancellation penalties are of the least onerous type, with no deposit required and full payment due 30 days before departure. It is not until ten days before departure that all the fee is forfeited if cancelled.

The in-country spend is more or less 100%, as fees cover the cost of running the organisation, the volunteer trips and the salaries to the Namibians who work for EHRA.

Pre-departure preparation
There is obviously no UK-based pre-departure training, but the in-country training is explained and the project's aims and objectives are very clear. The environmental field conditions and fitness requirements are spelt out and the video on the website makes the conditions very clear. Volunteers know what their tasks will be. They get a good kit list and clear travel directions.

In the field
The intended conservation benefits of the project are well explained; it is a long-term commitment to the people and elephants of Namibia. Accommodation is a basic tented camp or sleeping under the stars when out tracking. The work is hard with weekends off and all participants must contribute towards camp duties. Lots of local people work on the project and volunteers work with local village communities.

The EHRA project is a perfect opportunity for people to really return to basic levels of living, learn simple camp-craft and survival skills, and get back in touch with nature.

Environment & culture
There is no carbon offsetting provision, but they are very focused on environmental solutions for energy generation and the camp is very eco-friendly. It is built to use water efficiently, dispose of waste effectively, and generate its own power. They are experimenting with bio-diesel and aim to design eco-friendly solutions that local people can also use, eg: composting toilets made from oil drums using only materials accessible for local communities.

Safety

BS8848:2007 does not apply in Namibia, but staff have first-aid skills and are present 24/7. There is first-aid equipment and permanent telecoms systems. Staff carry out site risk assessments and there is an emergency contract with SOS (🖰 *www.internationalsos.com*), which can provide air evacuation in emergencies and there are details of how to reach medical facilities.

Demonstrable achievements

As a small practical conservation project, its achievements are not well documented. Data mapping of elephant herd movement is recorded on the web and is useful for understanding which water resources are being used. Biological samples from dead elephants are sometimes collected for other research projects.

Post-trip follow up

Most volunteers come through placement agencies so they get little feedback. They have established an EHRA group on Facebook and have a regular project news section on the website as well as producing a newsletter.

FRONTIER AKA **THE SOCIETY FOR ENVIRONMENTAL EXPLORATION**

☏ +44 (0)20 7613 2422; ✉ info@frontier.ac.uk; 🖰 www.frontier.ac.uk

Frontier is a registered company and a not-for-profit organisation that undertakes field research into environmental issues, implements practical conservation projects and builds sustainable livelihoods in developing countries. They lead their own scientific expeditions, as well as offering a wide range of overseas placements. Key destinations are Madagascar, Cambodia, Fiji and Australia, Central and South America, Africa, southeast Asia, China and Sri Lanka. It works extensively with overseas academic institutions and also offers a number of conservation and educational placements with local NGOs and eco-adventures.

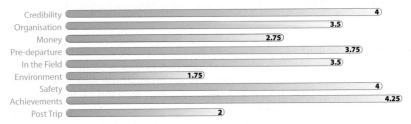

Credibility	4
Organisation	3.5
Money	2.75
Pre-departure	3.75
In the Field	3.5
Environment	1.75
Safety	4
Achievements	4.25
Post Trip	2

Background

The Society for Environmental Exploration is the original not-for-profit NGO and 'Frontier' is now a banner name, used to represent its collaboration within different countries, eg: Frontier Tanzania is a collaboration between the Society and the University of Dar Es Salaam. After working for Raleigh International, Eibleis Fanning founded Frontier in 1989 when she saw an opportunity for volunteers to provide manpower and funding for conservation research projects, as opposed to the team- and character-building expedition style of many other organisations.

Credibility

Advisory groups in the UK and all host countries guide each Frontier work programme. There are ten Frontier-led science projects and five ethical travel trails (with conservation/community elements). In-country staff are based at each regional HQ to supervise in-country placements.

They see themselves as a scientific organisation so don't compete for awards, but have received professional recognition by securing over US$3.3m for over 30 projects from organisations such as WWF and CARE International.

They have good media coverage in newspapers, magazines and journals, including *Real Travel*, *Sport Diver*, *Geographical*, *The Guardian* and the *African Journal of Ecology* and they are members of the World Conservation Union. Work is supported by business donations and grants from HSBC, Cable and Wireless, BP, National Lottery, Darwin Initiative (DEFRA) and Conservation International (CEPF).

Organisation

Of 164 projects, 35% (57) focus on conservation, others include community, teaching, management and journalism. Activities include tropical habitat conservation, wildlife tracking, biodiversity monitoring, mangrove reforestation, sustainable development of medicinal plants, sanctuaries and breeding centres and game ranger courses.

Twice-monthly open days are held in London and at various exhibitions around the country. Volunteers are interviewed before a place is offered and can contact other team members after booking via the online client area or social networking sites. Short write-ups of past projects are available on the web along with quarterly technical reports. Training courses and dissertation opportunities are available and postgraduate students can get a 50% discount off expeditions if their thesis relates to ongoing research activities.

Where the money goes

Project costs average around £1,100–1,495 for four weeks, with options to stay for up to 12 weeks; fees include pre-departure training and in-country transport. A £200 non-refundable deposit is required, with the balance due in two instalments at eight and four weeks before departure. Cancellation after the first instalment is due forfeits that instalment; similarly after the due date for the second instalment. If Frontier cancels the trip a refund is made (minus the deposit) and the deferment of a booked trip may be possible in special circumstances.

The proportion of a volunteer's fee spent in-country varies, but can be up to 75%.

Pre-departure preparation

Telephone interviews are standard and volunteers have to pass a written medical test and produce a signed medical form from their GP confirming that recommended vaccinations and malaria prophylaxis have been complied with.

Science expeditions have a UK briefing weekend six weeks before departure to meet fellow volunteers names, photographs and biographies of field staff are on their website, but not for placement projects.

Some project information is surprisingly florid on the website, but after booking it hardens up with good practical advice and information. More background is provided for Frontier's own expeditions than for volunteers on placement projects.

In the field

Although there are aims and objectives for every project they are generally more detailed on Frontier-led research expeditions compared with placement projects. Outlines are provided on the website, but it's not until a volunteer signs up that more detailed information is provided.

Accommodation is invariably basic, usually tents, longhouses (constructed by the volunteers) or *bandas* (locally built huts made from palm leaves) and volunteers can expect to help at meal times. No provision can be made for special diets.

All programmes are long-term collaborations between host-country institutions such as universities and government ministries. Local people are widely employed, including drivers, cooks, guards, game guides and boat crew.

A word of caution to any budding writers or photographers: Frontier, unusually, claim to 'retain all copyright in, and editorial control over, works, including literary, film and photographic works, which participants may create or contribute to during their participation on Frontier's projects or thereafter'. A Frontier spokesperson told me, "while we retain copyright over all material produced on our projects, I am not aware of Frontier ever literally claiming copyright over volunteers' personal photos'. Nevertheless volunteers are expected to assign copyright of their writing and photographs to Frontier.

Environment & culture
Carbon offsetting is encouraged, but no contribution is made towards international flights or in-country generated emissions. They are developing their own carbon offset programme of reforestation in Sumatra which volunteers can make their carbon offset payments to. There is no special emphasis on minimising the environmental impact, but there is good cultural guidance on Islam and some basic language guidance.

Safety
BS8848:2007 is expected to be fully implemented by summer 2008 on a self-declared basis. Staff are available 24/7 on their field expeditions and good risk assessment protocols are in place, but not necessarily on placement projects. Volunteers need a confirmation letter from their GP indicating they are fit and healthy for their chosen project.

In the event of an emergency there is an established medical procedure. There are no medical or nursing staff on site, but first-aid equipment is available and there are established links with local doctors and hospitals. Comprehensive evacuation and medical plans are in place and there is support from permanently staffed country headquarters, which are in radio or telephone contact 24 hours a day with the field camps and London HQ.

Demonstrable achievements
There are exceptionally well-written-up field reports about Frontier-led expeditions; project reports appear in the in-house Frontier technical report series, magazine articles and scientific journals. All technical reports (and many peer-reviewed articles) are available on the website. Practical conservation achievements include:
- Tanzania's first multi-user marine park at Mafia Island was

established following management recommendations and data from Frontier surveys. The marine park warden and technical adviser are ex-Frontier staff.

- Quirimbas National Park, the first national marine park to be designated since Mozambiquan independence, was founded using information and recommendations from Frontier's survey work.
- The Southern Mikea region of Madagascar has recently been listed as a protected area based on Frontier's comprehensive research reports on the area.
- The Montagne de Français is another area in Madagascar that has recently been incorporated into the Ramena complex of protected areas based on Frontier's research work in the region. Frontier continues to be involved with the planning, monitoring and management of this area.
- A Frontier medicinal plant income-generating project in Sa Pa, Vietnam, has led to a ten-fold increase in income for participating farmers.

Post-trip follow up

There is an in-country debriefing and feedback at the end of projects and on return home a system for written feedback directly to the Frontier London office.

An annual newsletter is produced outlining recent work and achievements. Volunteer teams arrange reunions, set up their own Facebook groups and meet on MSN. There are also opportunities to assist Frontier in the London office with open days, at careers fairs or at pre-departure events.

GAP YEAR
It is not a contact service; everything is accessed via ⌐www.gapyear.com

This is an internet directory of conservation (and other) projects around the globe. They do not organise or offer trips, but list 270 operators who cater predominantly for the young gap-year market. The website has over 100,000 pages, including a travel buddy link-up service, chatroom, blogs, photo journals, travel planning and a travel shop providing a host of travellers' add-on requirements.

Background
Founded by Tom Griffiths and Peter Pedrick in 1998 and listed in *The Times* 100 best travel websites and awarded the Britain Youth Travel Award for best website in 2007. It is really a general-purpose backpackers or gap-year community website and has a lot of useful information and contact networks and claims over one million annual users.

Volunteer opportunities
The conservation volunteer projects advertised on the website provide a general overview of the project including price and, unusually, they include details of the specific project placement provider. You contact the project provider directly not Gap Year.

Examples of projects
Desert Elephants in Damaraland, Namibia
It costs £1,299 for four weeks and includes airport pick-up, food and tented accommodation. The project has two phases: the first is working with villagers to help build stone walls to protect water supplies from elephants, and the second is tracking and monitoring the movements of desert elephants. Real Gap are listed as offering this version of Desert Elephants in Damaraland, but many other companies also offer this project as well as the local NGO itself – EHRA, see page 81.

Sea Turtle Conservation, Sri Lanka
It costs £1,295 for four weeks and includes airport pick-up, food and accommodation with a host family along with a few other volunteers. The project involves helping with patrolling the beach, guarding nests and protecting them from poachers and predators. It aims to minimise human interference, so turtles can breed under natural conditions. Projects Abroad are listed as offering this project, see page 113.

Community and Marine Conservation Project, Honduras
It costs £2,495 for six weeks and includes airport pick-up, visa, food and shared accommodation. The project supports ongoing conservation and research work helping to collect data and the dissemination of information to protect the coral reefs. The cost also includes all dives, dive training and dive equipment. Quest Overseas are listed as offering this project, see page 116.

GLOBAL VISION INTERNATIONAL (GVI)

📞 01727 250 250; ✉ info@gvi.co.uk; 🖱 www.gvi.co.uk. It also has offices in America, Australia and Ireland.

They lead their own expeditions and also offer a range of overseas placements with an emphasis on sustainable development through long-term local partnerships. Key expedition destinations include Madagascar, Seychelles, Africa, Central and South America. Work is primarily with charities, not-for-profit and government organisations. It runs ten major expeditions along with a series of placements – some with world-renowned scientists.

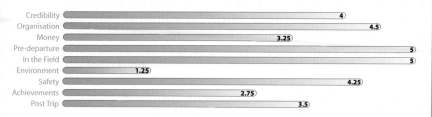

Credibility	4
Organisation	4.5
Money	3.25
Pre-departure	5
In the Field	5
Environment	1.25
Safety	4.25
Achievements	2.75
Post Trip	3.5

Background

GVI is a limited company founded in 1998; there is also a GVI Charitable Trust. Co-founder Richard Walton is a Fellow of the Royal Geographical Society and is largely responsible for the development of Global Vision International from its early days on an island off the coast of Honduras. He has lived and worked overseas for many years as a volunteer and expedition leader and continues to be involved in all aspects of the day-to-day running of the company.

Credibility

Scientific guidance comes from prominent conservation organisations such as the Dian Fossey Gorilla Fund, the Jane Goodall Institute and Rainforest Concern. They also work in partnership with overseas universities, national parks and government agencies. They have won awards from Project Aware for their marine parks work and have a good media profile in *The Guardian*, *The Times*, *BBC Wildlife* and have featured on Sky TV and the BBC *Holiday* programme. They are members of a number of ecotourism and volunteer organisations and get sponsorship support from some overseas government environmental agencies.

Organisation

Project activities include reef monitoring, biodiversity surveys, turtle protection, population monitoring, game parks, animal tracking, animal sanctuaries and small-scale infrastructure developments to support ecotourism.

About 55% of projects are conservation programmes and 45% involve teaching, community or development work.

A booked placement is generally assured and they retain full responsibility for volunteers; leaders accompany all expeditions and field staff support volunteers on placements.

Conservation-related BTEC qualifications are possible on five- and ten-week training courses and PADI diving qualifications are integral for some projects. There are regular open days and some projects have genuine opportunities to follow up volunteering with unpaid internships potentially leading on to paid leadership roles.

Where the money goes

Fees range from £1,100–1,500 and projects from four to ten weeks. All standard costs are covered, which usually includes airport pick-up and first-aid training. A £250 non-refundable deposit is required on booking and the balance is due 12 weeks before departure (projects longer than 120 days have different rules), after which no refunds are possible. Project alterations are possible, but incur a £150 administration fee if less than 12 weeks before departure. On average 70% of a volunteer's fee is spent in and around projects although it varies between individual projects.

Pre-departure preparation

There are no residential pre-departure courses, but preparation includes free online wildlife courses and a detailed 25-page field manual where in-country training is specified. Project aims and objectives are detailed in the planning guides along with environmental field conditions and anticipated activity levels. Video clips give a clear idea of tasks and activities, while project blogs and news reports give a feel for daily activities. There is good kit and travel advice in the field manual.

In the field

The intended conservation benefits are clear and all projects are long-term partnerships with overseas agencies. Accommodation is usually basic, but can have showers, a bar and some social amenities; it could be homestay, shared flats, bush bungalows, dormitories or tented camps. Local staff are integral to all projects and Seychellois nationals have the opportunity to participate in a GVI National Scholarship Programme for skill development and can attend some projects for free. Scientific training on expedition projects is very rigorous and volunteers must meet minimum standards before being deployed on field activities.

Environment & culture

Volunteers are encouraged to carbon offset their flights and some project activities act as carbon offsetting initiatives. There is little emphasis on the volunteers' impact on the local environment and little in the way of cultural preparation.

Safety

They expect to self-certificate to the new BS8848:2007 standard by late 2008. Risk assessment protocols are in place and are carried out by GVI staff on their own expeditions and by trained staff on placement projects. Emergency planning is clear and covers accidents, kidnapping and other hazards; 24-hour emergency contact numbers are issued to volunteers and first-aid kits are provided. GVI's insurance cover provides emergency assistance from Specialty Assistance (⁕ *www.specialty-group.com/ assistance.html*).

Demonstrable achievements

Detailed written project reports of field activities are gathered, but not always posted on the website. Most project research data is collected for local government or conservation agencies to use, but conservation achievements are not well documented. However, practical conservation outcomes do include:

- In 2005 established Mexico's first zoned, multi-user, marine protected area with a lagoon and reef-based buoy scheme, reducing reef damage caused by divers and anchor damage from boat traffic.
- In the two years that GVI Amazon has been established and operating, a full-time field research station has been built in the Yachana Reserve, Ecuador; expedition members and staff have documented 500+ species.
- GVI is working to help families to build energy-efficient stoves, which use up to 75% less firewood and dramatically reduce home respiratory problems and damage to local forests.
- In South Africa GVI has collected seven years of data on the full predator suite and elephants at the Karongwe Game Reserve, contributing to seven annual reports for the reserve management and landowners, enabling all management decisions made on the reserve to be well informed.

Post-trip follow up

Questionnaires are completed and expedition field representatives are elected to ensure staff know what volunteers think and feel about the project. Feedback is also regularly made to the organisers of placement projects. Monthly newsletters and quarterly expedition updates are posted on the website and there are plans to work with charity and conservation organisations back in the UK.

GLOBALXPERIENCE
☎ 0800 881 8888; ✉ via weblink only; 🖥 www.globalxperience.com

GlobalXperience are a limited company and an ABTA-bonded tour operator offering a wide range of overseas placements with a strong emphasis on sports coaching and general community projects as well as many conservation projects. Destinations include South and Central America, Australia, Africa and Southeast Asia.

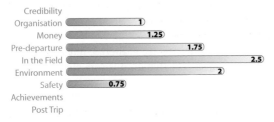

Credibility
Organisation — 1
Money — 1.25
Pre-departure — 1.75
In the Field — 2.5
Environment — 2
Safety — 0.75
Achievements
Post Trip

Background
GlobalXperience are part of the Ethical Travel Group Limited.

Credibility
The company did not wish to divulge any information about itself or its operation beyond that which is available on its website. However, not much of the information used to assess credibility is available on the website, so it has been difficult to assess them on the same level as other organisations. A number of 'conservation' project descriptions read more like tourist trips rather than hands-on conservation activities.

Organisation
They offer around 250 programmes across the globe, although less than 25% are conservation related and some are only vaguely conservation-minded. Projects include work in zoos, wildlife sanctuaries, monitoring wildlife, sustainable tourism projects, animal welfare and conservation education.

They accept responsibility if you suffer injury or your contracted arrangements are not provided as promised or prove deficient as a result of the failure of GX, their employees, agents or suppliers.

If you are not accepted onto your chosen programme a suitable alternative will be offered. There are no details about open days or who the in-country representatives are. No details are available about past project activities or ex-volunteers contacts.

Where the money goes
Two-week projects range from £350–890, but pricing is not always clear. One turtle project is advertised at £275 per week, but is actually £665 for a minimum of four weeks.

A non-refundable booking deposit of £150 is required. If you don't receive the placement you booked your fee (minus deposit) is refunded, unless they find you a suitable alternative placement. If you cancel within 30 days of departure all fees are forfeited. Amendments to a booking are possible for an administration fee of £50–£100. An unspecified contribution is made to each project.

Pre-departure preparation
There are pre-departure factsheets and courses on safety and gap-year advice can be booked as extras; a non-specific in-country orientation is also provided. Project aims and objectives are vague and are set by the local project, so there is no clear job brief. Good general packing advice is provided, as well as a brief overview of environmental conditions, but nothing about fitness requirements.

In the field
A website fact-file provides a very general overview of projects, which are usually ongoing. Accommodation varies from farm lodges, shared rooms, guesthouses or tented camps and help with domestic duties may be required. You will work with local people and the working week varies from half to full days.

Environment & culture
They claim each trip will be 100% carbon neutral, but don't provide any details of how this is achieved. Cultural advice is briefly touched on, but in no depth.

Safety
No information about their BS 8848:2007 status is available or details about risk assessment or on-site safety procedures. A 'Red 24' contact telephone number enables volunteers to access security and safety advice and an action response service can be purchased for an additional £150.

Demonstrable achievements
No records of conservation achievements are available and there is no written evidence about the effectiveness of specific projects.

Post-trip follow up
No information is available about evaluation or post-project follow-up.

GREENFORCE

☏ 020 7470 8888; ✉ info@greenforce.org; 🖰 www.greenforce.org. They also have an office in America.

This not-for-profit organisation has been operating since 1992, providing a range of conservation projects with a strong adventure and fun element. Core conservation expedition destinations include the Bahamas, Fiji, Tanzania and Ecuador. They work alongside local people to develop long-term sustainable action plans rather than one-off projects. Longer programmes always include TEFL, sports and community projects along with conservation and paid employment arrangements in Australia, Spain and Ecuador.

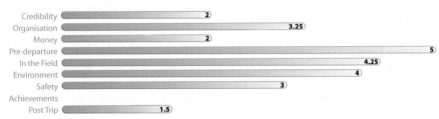

Credibility	2
Organisation	3.25
Money	2
Pre-departure	5
In the Field	4.25
Environment	4
Safety	3
Achievements	
Post Trip	1.5

Background

The inspiration for Greenforce came from the Earth Summit held in Rio de Janeiro in 1992 when the 168 signatories of the convention on biodiversity were required to undertake baseline surveys of their at-risk regions. A group of Ugandan scientists asked Marcus Watts to come and assist them and this experience later led him to found Greenforce.

In 2008 Greenforce merged with Trekforce (see page 133); they are both now owned by Marcus Watts, but intend to maintain their individual identities.

Credibility

For their core projects they employ their own scientists and base them on site for at least a year, although this is not the case with project placements. They have no awards and little by way of media coverage and are working on a responsible travel policy.

They are members of key conservation and volunteering organisations, including the Marine Conservation Society, World Conservation Union (IUCN), National Council for Voluntary Organisations and the International Volunteer Programs Association. They have no sponsorship, so all work is funded solely by volunteer contributions.

Organisation

They run around 18 expeditions with approximately 350 volunteers per year and around 60% of projects have a conservation focus. In addition to core expedition destinations there are placements in South Africa, South America, Nepal, India and China that focus on reef diving, penguin rescue, great white shark monitoring, tracking and biodiversity studies, reforestation, sustainable development along with other projects on TEFL, sports and community projects.

Project bookings are assured unless the original one becomes unsafe or insufficient numbers are recruited.

There are four open days per year plus a presence at key exhibitions and people can attend the office for one-to-one briefings. Names and details of scientists and project leaders are not provided until the pre-departure training day where volunteers also meet other project members. There are no written details about the progress of previous projects, but it is possible to talk to previous volunteers.

Where the money goes

Most core conservation expeditions are ten-week projects averaging £2,400 although there is a three-week Tanzania option for £1,300 and a four-week great white shark project for £1,400. The only two-week trips are adventure holidays. Fees include pre-departure training, airport pick-up and in-country transportation. Unqualified divers on marine projects will need to pay £300 for a PADI diving course.

A £200 non-refundable deposit is required at booking and the full balance is due two months before to departure. Cancellation less than three months before departure incurs a 50% penalty; if it is less than one month all fees are forfeited.

Around 64% of each volunteer's fee gets spent in or around the project (based on audited accounts of 2006–07).

Pre-departure preparation

A one-day pre-departure training event, to meet the team, is held in London for volunteers departing on core expedition projects. In-country training is detailed in the project information packs, which also include the aims and objectives of each project. A typical working day is outlined along with study materials such as species identification sheets.

There is clear advice on environmental conditions and health issues such as immunisations and guidance on malaria. There is a planning checklist, full packing and equipment guidance along with visa advice. Arrival information is good and includes pre-project accommodation advice and full transfer details.

In the field

The intended conservation benefits are clearly described in pre-departure packs. Greenforce works alongside local people and local or scientific NGOs to develop long-term sustainable action plans so that when it leaves the future of that region will continue in balance between nature and human needs.

Accommodation is of reasonable comfort although there will usually be little choice but different projects may be housed in hostels, rural village houses or traditional communal grass *bures* and volunteers can expect to take turns cooking for the group. Projects operate a standard five-day week from nine to five or its equivalent.

Local people are involved on every project, but to differing extents, including labour, scientific guidance, assistant leaders, in-country co-ordinators and of course suppliers.Creating an effective protected habitat must involve the local community, as external aid cannot be relied upon. Development plans therefore incorporate an income element to support the local infrastructure.

On core projects an exceptional volunteer may be invited to stay on as a trainee after the project has finished.

Environment & culture

They do not encourage volunteers to use commercial carbon offsetting as it is considered to be overpriced and Greenforce have established their own volunteer credit scheme and offset more carbon than is produced by volunteers. On some projects volunteers participate in these carbon offset schemes.

There is little information about how volunteers can minimise their environmental impact at their project site, but issues are covered in the training day.

Each information pack contains good detail about the country visited, culture, geography, terrain, language and in-the-field time is allocated specifically to meeting and getting to know people in local villages.

Safety

They are compliant with BS8848:2007 on a self-declared basis. Risk assessment protocols are in place at their expedition sites and at project placements.

Greenforce staff live on site at their core expedition sites 24/7; there are no professional medical facilities, but staff have wilderness medical training. Placement projects are managed by local partners and organise their own safety procedures. There are comprehensive first-aid kits on site and oxygen kits at dive locations.Greenforce have links with local organisations to assist with field emergencies, but no written emergency protocols were available for inspection.

Demonstrable achievements

All data and reports are considered to be the property of the host-country partners and Greenforce are unable to publish any details.

Post-trip follow up

Volunteers complete evaluation forms and an annual reunion party is held every December. Bi-monthly newsletters are distributed to ex-volunteers, but they are not available on the web.

GREEN VOLUNTEERS
☏F 01767 262560; ✉ green@greenvolunteers.org;
🖰 www.greenvolunteers.org. It also has offices in America and Italy.

This is a conservation volunteer listing service in the form of a book and an internet directory, which form an information network detailing opportunities around the globe. The Green Volunteers book costs £12, which also gives free access to a searchable internet database of the book's content. It puts volunteers directly in touch with conservation NGOs and charities, but does not act as a booking agent.

Background
Fabio Ausenda is the pioneer of putting small conservation projects on the world stage. He started on a small scale in 1989 with Europe Conservation, a non-profit organisation providing volunteers for conservation projects in developing countries. Its success led to the publication of *Green Volunteers* in 1999. As a result of the internet boom it is now available as a book and a searchable internet database. He has published other volunteering guides to humanitarian and development and archaeological and heritage volunteering.

Organisation and volunteer opportunities
Green Volunteers does not organise or offer trips, but is a comprehensive conservation volunteer information source listing around 500 NGOs, charities and organisations on five continents around the globe. It is focused on conservation and does not list ecotourism or adventure projects.

For each project there is background information, web links (where available) and direct contact details. Volunteers make all their own arrangements by contacting and booking directly with their chosen overseas project.

This is an invaluable information source if you are looking for a DIY placement and do not want to book an expensive 'package' with a UK provider. In some cases you could end up on the same project as volunteers who have booked a UK or USA package costing considerably more.

Examples of projects
Hebridean Whale and Dolphin Trust
No cost, but volunteers must pay for their own accommodation and living expenses. Six weeks minimum March–October. Work involves welcoming tourists into the centre, explaining about the local marine life, helping visitors identify what they have seen, promoting membership schemes, manning the small shop and helping with fundraising.

Hawaiian Forest Preservation Project
No cost, rustic accommodation; volunteers must pay for own food and will need to rent a car to reach the project site. It runs all year round. Work primarily involves removing invasive weeds and replanting native trees.

INTERNATIONAL VOLUNTARY SERVICE

☏ +44 (0)131 243 2745; ✉ scotland@ivsgb.org; 🖱 www.ivsgb.org/info

IVS-GB is a charity and the British branch of Service Civil International (SCI), a worldwide network of partner organisations supporting sustainable projects of direct benefit to local communities. IVS differentiates itself from the wide range of other commercial volunteer organisations by being entirely value-based, as opposed to income based. It runs on a shoestring and is probably the cheapest source for an overseas volunteer placement. Projects don't involve attractive flagship animal species, but focus on environmental improvements and sustainable development for local communities. A unique feature of IVS is that volunteer teams are never a clique of people from the same country, but are always a wide international mix.

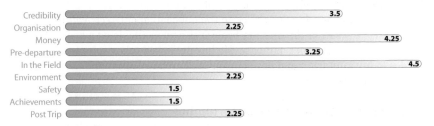

Credibility	3.5
Organisation	2.25
Money	4.25
Pre-departure	3.25
In the Field	4.5
Environment	2.25
Safety	1.5
Achievements	1.5
Post Trip	2.25

Background
In 1921 a group of French and German volunteers worked together to repair a French village that had been destroyed during the First World War. The project was led by Pierre Ceresole, who then set up Service Civil International to further the aims of peace, justice and understanding in war-torn Europe. The first international project in Great Britain was to build a swimming pool for the colliery town of Bryn Mawr, Wales, in 1931. This was the beginning of International Voluntary Service.

Credibility
This very low-profile organisation has a refreshing absence of commercialism, which might create a poor first impression if compared with the state-of-the-art websites that are now so standard. They spend next to nothing on advertising and promotion, but have been around for over 75 years. They have good media coverage and are members of a host of volunteer and international organisations. They receive additional funding from central government, the Scottish government, British Council, Lottery Fund, as well as Lloyds TSB and a number of private trusts. They have a good responsible travel policy.

Organisation
Project hosts abroad are always charities or not-for-profit organisations and they plan and implement projects and provide food and accommodation. Destinations are too numerous to list; projects are available in over 100

countries on every continent around the globe. Of the 983 projects (referred to as camps), 327 are environment- or conservation-focused although they are not available all year round.

All projects have a people element and emphasise sustainable development, eg: building for ecotourism, creating nature trails, animal care, botanical gardens, river and beach cleaning, recycling projects, reforestation, removing invasive plants, African game sanctuaries, etc.

Project places are limited because they mix teams and volunteers come from a range of different countries. As a result, a place is not guaranteed until finally booked. This also means you will not know who the other volunteers are until you arrive at the project. Contact details with the host organisation are available before booking and there is no upper age limit, but the vast majority of volunteers are aged between 18 and 26 and more females than males apply.

Previous projects are not written up, but volunteers are encouraged to talk to previous volunteers about the work. There are no open days, but they do attend many university and volunteer exhibitions throughout the year.

Where the money goes
Volunteers must become a member of IVS-GB at the time of booking and pay a set fee for each project. In addition, you need to cover your travel costs. A few host organisations in poor economic circumstances may require an additional modest contribution towards board and lodgings.

A non-refundable membership fee (£35, or £15 unwaged) is required and the fee is a flat rate for each overseas project (£150, or £130 unwaged); UK-based projects cost about half this fee. The fee is the same regardless of whether the project is two weeks or one year.

If volunteers cancel, the membership fee is non-refundable. There is no refund if cancellation is not for a valid reason; but 100% may be refundable, minus £15 administration fee, if cancellation is due to serious and unavoidable circumstances, but this is at IVS-GB's discretion.

Around 80% of the total income is spent on the organisation's charitable activities. Financial records are publicly available and detailed in the annual review.

Pre-departure preparation
Project information packs are written by each country's host organisation so they are variable and inconsistent, some being far more detailed than others.

Volunteers applying for projects in the south (Africa, Asia and South America) must be over 21 and preferably have already completed a short-term project in Europe or had similar experience.

There are pre-departure training days in June, but there is not much information about in-country training. General project aims are clear, but specific objectives are often left vague; this is in part to do with involving volunteers in the project planning process.

Information packs give packing advice which usually suggests bringing a sleeping bag, mat, work clothes, gloves, work boots, etc. Good travel information is provided although some projects may need you to arrive at a pick-up point while others expect you make your own way to the project location.

In the field

The conservation benefits are usually clear although invariably couched in terms of people rather than wildlife. The host organisation is responsible for volunteers, so you need to be clear about their health and safety regulations when you arrive.

Some projects are long term and ongoing, but they could also be one-off activities. The host is responsible for providing food and accommodation for the volunteers and accommodation is always very basic ranging from mattresses in a school hall, to camping, to dormitories in a youth hostel or residential centre. There will be basic washing and cooking facilities and volunteers must share cooking and cleaning tasks on a rota basis. Work is usually on a five-day week from 09.00 to mid-afternoon. Everything is run by local people; this supports one of the cornerstones of all IVS projects – meeting, working and socialising with people from another country.

Environment & culture

Volunteers are encouraged to carbon offset their travel, but no contribution is made by IVS-GB. There is little information about how volunteers can minimise their impact on the local environment, but they are urged to respect local customs and knowledge. Respect for local cultures is very high on the agenda and volunteers are encouraged to be aware of their role as 'learner' rather than just 'giver'. A key priority is bringing together a mix of international volunteers to encourage international understanding and inter-cultural co-operation.

Safety

They are not currently working towards BS8848:2007 and safety and emergency procedures are vague because they are the responsibility of the overseas host organisation. Nevertheless, risk assessment procedures were evident for UK projects and overseas hosts are expected to maintain similar standards. Inevitably procedures will vary from country to country, but IVS-GB is part of a scheme (Service Civil International) that provides basic third-party and personal accident insurance cover for the duration of the volunteer project. Nevertheless full personal insurance is also required.

Demonstrable achievements

There are no written records or field reports and outcomes are not routinely assessed or publicised. Some general examples of environmental outcomes from official documentation include:

- A fishermen's federation was established in Senegal to improve life

conditions of its members concerning production, trade, materials'
purchase, accessing funds and health care, education work on reducing
inequality in villages between rich and poor and stopping the
migration to big cities.

- A sustainable farming project was established in Lesotho.
- A training and demonstration herbal farm project was developed in
  India to find a water-intensive yet marketable crop.
- An environment and reforestation project was established in Nepal
  focusing on garbage management, anti-plastic and awareness
  raising campaign.

Post-trip follow up

Evaluation questionnaires are gathered from all volunteers and there are
follow-up events to meet up with other volunteers. Newsletters are
circulated to members and post-project groups are encouraged to engage in
awareness raising, publicity and fundraising, as well as supporting new
volunteers going out to developing countries.

INTI WARA YASSI

☏ +591 44 136572; ✉ intiwarayassi@gmail.com; 🖰 www.intiwarayassi.org

Comunidad Inti Wara Yassi is a grassroots Bolivian NGO founded by Juan Carlos Antezana in 1992 after he took street children on a trip to explore their country and observed the terrible impact that man was having on nature (deforestation and animal abuse). The wildlife refuge was founded in the grounds of Parque Machía, near Villa Tunari, to house and rehabilitate wild animals, taken from unsuitable or illegal captive environments and rehabilitate them so they can be released back into the wild. When this is not possible the refuge provides animals with the respect they deserve and works to ensure the utmost freedom for each individual. Tania Baltazar (Nena) runs the refuge now with a small team of permanent Bolivian volunteers helped by innumerable overseas volunteers. Their philosophy is that no wild animal should be abused or kept as a pet.

Volunteer opportunities

It is not necessary to book in advance; potential volunteers can visit as a day tourist and then sign up for a two-week placement, as there is always more work than hands to do it. Long-term volunteers are more than welcome, but this can be arranged while you are there. The main refuge is at Parque Machía and a new development has opened at Parque Ambue Ari; they are in the middle of nowhere, which is perfect for the animals, but a little inconvenient for visitors.

In the field

The work is hard. Days start at 07.00–07.30 and end around 17.00–18.00, with an hour lunch break and a day off every 15 days. The work varies greatly and could involve tending sick monkeys or dealing with newcomers, who need a lot of attention and security before they can trust people or other monkeys. Many of the animals are of endangered species. They house about 300 monkeys of various species (spider, capuchin, squirrel, titi, howler and tamarin) along with hundreds of birds from toucans to hawks to the big macaws, as well as coatis, turtles, snakes and a few wild cats (ocelots, pumas and a jaguar).

Volunteers working in the aviary will be preparing birds for their return to the wild or simply enriching the lives of those that have suffered cruelty and may never to fly again. Others could work on the raptor release programme, training them to hunt and fly on their own.

Monkey cages need to be cleaned and beddings washed; big cats are walked daily and need one or two volunteers to be with them at all times. Volunteers may also guide visitors, explain about the animals and the importance of wildlife and habitat preservation. In addition, at the newer Parque Ambue Ari refuge there is maintenance and construction work to be done, such as cutting new cat trails or building new enclosures.

Where the money goes

Volunteering (including accommodation, kitchen facilities, hot shower, etc) costs £73–90 at Parque Machía (food is extra, approx US$2.50 per day) or £80 at Parque Ambue Ari (food included) for the first 14 days. After the first 14 days the daily fee will be around £4 per night. Accommodation is onsite in dormitories with bunk beds, although some volunteers stay in nearby villages.

Demonstrable achievements

This is a well-respected animal refuge that has no government or external funding and relies entirely on volunteer fees and donations to continue its work. Inti Wara Yassi has been operating for 15 years, there is no hint of commercialism and the animals always come first. It might not live up to the standards of a relatively wealthy organisation like the RSPCA because it is working in a third world economy, but that just makes the work even more valuable.

Jane Goodall chose Juan Carlos Antezana, founder and president of Comunidad Inti Wara Yassi, as one of her heroes and he featured with others on her *Heroes* programme on the Discovery Channel in August 2006.

i-to-i

☎ 0800 011 1156; ✉ sales@i-to-i.com; 🖰 www.i-to-i.com. They have additional offices in America, Canada and Australia.

A UK limited company providing a placement service that matches volunteers with projects overseas. It is one of the largest, high-profile, volunteer placement agents in the UK. Conservation destinations include Africa, Central and South America, Asia and Australia.

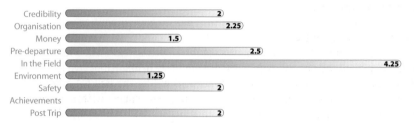

Credibility	2
Organisation	2.25
Money	1.5
Pre-departure	2.5
In the Field	4.25
Environment	1.25
Safety	2
Achievements	
Post Trip	2

Background

Founded in a Leeds bedsit in 1994 by Deirdre Bounds after she returned from teaching and travelling abroad. In 2007 it was sold in a multi-million pound deal to First Choice holidays, which is now part of the corporate travel giant TUI.

Credibility

All projects are operated by overseas organisations and the quality of the conservation work is unspecified as i-to-i do not control the projects and see this as the responsibility of their overseas project partners. They have received no awards, but have a high media presence with features in the *Daily Telegraph*, *The Independent* and *The Guardian*. It is a commercial enterprise so there are no third-party sponsors and its main links are with trade organisations rather than with conservation bodies. The ethical travel policy is not very specific and is not externally audited.

Organisation

It's a large organisation with around 350 projects, sending 5,000 volunteers. Although only about 16% are actually conservation projects that's still more than some specialist companies. Most projects are TEFL and gap adventure-style trips.

Project work includes eco-parks, animal rescue and rehabilitation, reforestation, fuel-efficient projects, animal monitoring, surveys, beach cleaning and turtle protection, but volunteers may be asked by some project organisers to do other tasks, eg: teach some English or transport animals.

The volunteers remain the responsibility of i-to-i throughout their stay at the project. In-country co-ordinators are hired by i-to-i, but they and their staff are not employees therefore i-to-i cannot exercise direct control over them or be responsible for their actions. In-country co-ordinators vet or visit each project, but have no direct control over the projects.

Specific placements are not guaranteed – volunteers choose the provisional location of their placement on booking and are able to view the final details of the placement on the website not less than seven days before arrival.

Regular open days are held around the country and it's possible to contact previous volunteers. There's a chat room on the website, but no written details about the work of previous volunteers. It primarily caters for the younger traveller.

Where the money goes
Fees range from £395–1,495 for a two–four-week placement and a non-refundable booking deposit of £150 is required. If you don't receive the placement you booked, your fee (minus deposit) will be refunded – unless they find you a suitable alternative placement. If you cancel within 30 days of departure all monies are forfeited. Amendments to a booking may be possible for an administration fee of £40–75.

Around 30% of the booking fee is spent in country and no financial contribution is made towards projects.

There is a good welcome pack including a CD, airport meet-and-greet service, food is usually included, but there may be no transport after the initial drop-off.

Pre-departure preparation
Pre-departure training is restricted to the welcome pack that includes an excellent CD. In-country training is unspecified and consists of an 'orientation' by the local co-ordinator and whatever the project subsequently provides. Project aims and objectives are vague and set by the local project, so there is no clear job brief.

Health, safety and equipment issues are discussed in considerable depth on the welcome-pack CD.

In the field
A website fact-file provides a good overview of specific projects which are usually ongoing. Accommodation varies from family homestay, volunteer houses, dormitories, guesthouses or tented camps; private room upgrades are sometimes available. Volunteers will work with local people and be expected to complete a five-day working week.

Environment & culture
There are no carbon offsetting arrangements and little guidance on how volunteers can minimise their impact on the local environment, but there is a good general discussion about local cultures on the welcome CD.

Safety
There are no plans to implement BS8848:2007, but sound risk assessment

procedures are completed by in-country co-ordinators covering transport, accommodation and project sites. Volunteers are issued with a 24/7 UK-based emergency number and the local co-ordinators' contact details. They have their own safety and security procedures called Venturesafe, but will soon adopt the corporate procedures of their new owners TUI. A safety kit is usually in place, but is the responsibility of individual projects. The primary emergency response involves contacting relevant travel insurance providers.

Demonstrable achievements

There is no information about conservation achievements because i-to-i do not set up or run the projects. Projects run themselves and are responsible for deciding the work that volunteers do, so it is considered to be their responsibility to keep written documents of how the work is progressing, their achievements and their goals.

Post-trip follow up

Volunteers complete electronic evaluation questionnaires and many subscribe to the e-newsletter to keep up to date with company news.

OPERATION WALLACEA

☎ +44 (0)1790 763194; ✉ info@opwall.com; 🖰 www.opwall.com. It also has offices in America and Canada.

Operation Wallacea uses teams of university academics to run biological and conservation research programmes in remote locations across the world. Key project destinations include Indonesia, Honduras, Egypt, Cuba, South Africa, Mozambique and Peru. These expeditions are designed with specific wildlife conservation aims in mind, from identifying areas needing protection, through to implementing and assessing conservation management programmes.

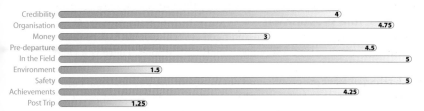

Credibility	4
Organisation	4.75
Money	3
Pre-departure	4.5
In the Field	5
Environment	1.5
Safety	5
Achievements	4.25
Post Trip	1.25

Background
Operation Wallacea Trust is a UK-registered charity established in 2000 in order to support activities that directly contribute towards the conservation of biodiversity. It is entirely independent of Operation Wallacea the limited company founded in 1995, which is the business arm that volunteers actually book their place with.

Credibility
Projects are science driven and led by international academics from around the world. They have won a British Airways award for Best Project in a National Park, an ASEAN Tourism Organisation Best Project award and a British Guild of Travel Writers award. They work with innumerable universities and conservation-focused organisations in overseas localities. Although not high profile, they have media coverage in *National Geographic*, university newsletters, a number of internet sites and have received substantial project funding from the Darwin Initiative and the World Bank.

Organisation
They are marine and rainforest specialists and volunteers work as scientific assistants with ongoing research studies, which are ideal for dissertations and medical electives. Volunteers tend to have a strong interest in science and research courses and PADI training may be available.

Past projects are written up as annual reports, but may not always be on the website. Previous volunteers can be contacted informally on a number of Facebook groups. Recruitment is mainly at universities and sixth-form presentations, so most volunteers tend to be of student age.

Where the money goes

Fees are around £950 for two weeks, £2,800 for eight weeks; all costs are covered from the expedition assembly point and include transport, dive and jungle training and possibly dissertation supervision. There may be additional costs for dive equipment hire and national park entrance fees.

A 10% deposit is refundable until 26 weeks before departure, or if your university will not allow participation. Transfer to a subsequent project may be possible, but would be on a case-by-case basis. All fees are forfeited from 28 days before departure and 60% of each volunteer's fee is spent in and around project activities.

Pre-departure preparation

Pre-departure training days are arranged several months before departure and there is good liaison with educational institutions. There is a clear description of each project on the website, including fitness requirements, description of local geography and environment, as well as some cultural issues.

The aims and objectives of the scientific research are very clear although the specific tasks of individual volunteers are not. Packing, travelling and general preparation are well thought through and well documented.

In the field

All projects are long term and involve a detailed assessment procedure, initial assessment of the biological value of the site, ecosystem monitoring, and monitoring socio-economic change in adjacent communities. Funding applications are then submitted for conservation management and progress is monitored on an ongoing basis. Accommodation is basic homestays or tented camps in relatively isolated locations. Local academics, guides and general helpers work at project locations and project organisation and responsibility is shared with local organisations.

Environment & culture

Carbon offsetting is not included in the fee. There is some advice about how volunteers can minimise their impact on the local environment, but very little background or detailed information about local cultures.

Safety

They already work to most of the BS8848:2007 standards and expect to fully certified by late 2008. Good risk assessment protocols are in place and high-priority emergency evacuations, normally by helicopter but in some cases in conjunction with overland routes, have been developed for each location. Project leaders are on site 24/7, as well as a qualified medical officer with medical supplies and good telecoms equipment.

Demonstrable achievements

There is a surfeit of scientific documentation and research papers on field activities. Practical conservation achievements include:

- Persuaded the Indonesian government to establish the Wakatobi Marine National Park in southeast Sulawesi, Indonesia, which has substantially reducing illegal fishing.
- Established a best practice example of sustainable reef fishing around the Kaledupa reefs, Indonesia, involving registration, small business payments in exchange and a weekly fisheries monitoring.
- Succeeded in stopping the clear-felling of the Lambusango forests, Indonesia, against a background where 2% of the forests on Buton Island (location of the Lambusango forests) was clear-felled in the previous decade.
- Developed a new ethical fair trade scheme called Wildlife Conservation Products in Indonesia, reducing logging, hunting and encroachment of the forest–farm boundary.
- Reported on the state of the Cusuco Cloud Forest National Park, Honduras, identifying how the diversity and forest cover are changing. Introduced the Wildlife Conservation Products scheme to buffer-zone communities for supply of coffee at enhanced prices. Increased involvement of local communities in delivery of the expeditions and handed over management of the expeditions to a wholly locally owned company called Expedicionesy Servicios Ambientales.

Post-trip follow up

All students are interviewed at the end of their expeditions rather than using a standard questionnaire and the results are recorded into an end-of-season report.

PERSONAL OVERSEAS DEVELOPMENT

☎ 01242 250 901; ✉ info@thepodsite.co.uk; ⬆ www.thepodsite.co.uk

They are a small registered company with a very hands-on approach and a non-profit ethic that primarily provides development/educational placements in schools, care homes, disadvantaged communities, but with several animal welfare and conservation opportunities. Around 450 volunteers travel with them each year to 15 general placements, four of which are conservation projects in Peru, Thailand, Belize and Cambodia.

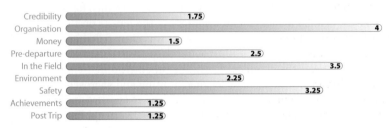

Credibility	1.75
Organisation	4
Money	1.5
Pre-departure	2.5
In the Field	3.5
Environment	2.25
Safety	3.25
Achievements	1.25
Post Trip	1.25

Background

Mike Beecham, Alex Tarrant and Rachel Smith founded PoD in 2001. Their aim was to use their previous experience of leading expeditions and doing voluntary work to provide a link between small charities and other organisations in less developed countries and people in the UK wishing to do something worthwhile abroad.

Credibility

This small registered company works on a very personal level with individual volunteers and schools parties. It has not won any awards, but has some media coverage in *Green Pulse*, a top-ten listing in *The Independent* and major television coverage of one of its partners (Belize Zoo). In addition to conservation it organises community and English-teaching placements as well as some adventure add-ons. It has a good responsible travel policy.

Organisation

Conservation projects include an elephant rescue centre, gibbon rehabilitation centre, dog rescue, bear rescue, rainforest research, zookeeper assistant work and coral reef diving. Volunteers are interviewed by phone to ensure they get the right placement; PoD retains contractual responsibility although placement partners are primarily responsible for co-ordinating day-to-day activities whilst on the programme.

Occasionally changes may need to be made for reasons which may include: the requirements of the local community, PoD partners or volunteer safety and well-being.

There are no formal open days, but they do attend a variety of travel exhibitions.

Unusually for a placement provider they share details of the NGO or charity that volunteers will be placed with, so it is possible to look at their websites and get a better understanding of the organisation.

Dissertation studies may be available in Peru and PADI certification in Belize.

There are no past project reports available, but contact with ex-volunteers can be provided for further discussion. UK staff personally visit and assess each new project before volunteers are placed and again during project placements. Amazingly, PoD are small enough to know every volunteer by name.

Where the money goes

A two-week project fee is around £850 and most costs are covered from the assembly point onwards, but you need to make your own way there from the international airport.

A £200–300 non-refundable deposit is required at booking and the balance is due eight weeks before departure. After eight weeks all fees are forfeited. It may be possible to transfer a project booking to another person, but this would incur a £100 administration fee.

Around 64% of a volunteer's booking fee gets spent in and around the project.

Pre-departure preparation

A telephone interview is standard, but there is no pre-departure training for individual volunteers and in-country training is not specified. Pre-departure training courses are arranged for school parties, which are accompanied by an expedition leader.

The clarity of the job brief is variable with some projects providing more details than others.

The kit advice is useful and includes suggestions of what is best to buy there (cheaper and helps local economy) instead of before you go. Arrival information is very detailed, including local background, taxis, hotels, getting cash, communications, personal security and onward travel information. Health guidance is useful, but there is nothing on the fitness requirements of the project.

In the field

The intended conservation benefits are generally well laid out, but it is emphasised that the needs of the project dictate what needs to be done and when.

Most projects are well established and ongoing, but they are not idyllic, easy-going holidays; the work can be quite draining and can be six-day weeks. Accommodation is basic and likely to be dormitory style; bedding and mosquito nets are usually provided.

European or American staff direct most of their projects, but local people run the operational aspects.

Environment & culture
Volunteers are encouraged to carbon offset their international flights, but it is not included in the fee. Good advice is provided about how volunteers can minimise their impact on the local environment. Useful cultural advice is provided in the project information packs.

Safety
They are in a position to self-certify for BS8848:2007 compliance and are in the process of being audited by an external health and safety specialist and expect to complete the assessment by early 2009.

The risk assessment procedures are comprehensively thought through; company staff are not on site (except with school parties), but the company owners visit and assess each project before and during placements.

Safety equipment is the responsibility of local projects so may vary, but generally includes first aid, telecoms and transport provision.
There are emergency response plans for dealing with major incidents that cover civil disorder, evacuation and moving injured personnel to hospital.

Demonstrable achievements
They do not have any written reports of their own, but one project NGO report was available. Placement partners sometimes report on their work, which PoD volunteers have contributed towards, including the following:

- Involvement with the construction of an observation shelter for the Mascoitania clay-lick, and nearly all tourism companies that visit the clay-lick are using it.
- Involvement with the planting of 4,000 seedlings in recent months in the Aguanos community and Salvacion community. A further 3,000 seedlings will be planted within the next few months.
- Involvement with the first phase of the project and the MLC Biogarden has produced a first yield. They are now systematising the data and analysing the best soil mixture.

Post-trip follow up
Evaluation questionnaires are sent to all volunteers to assess their experience and project work.

PROJECTS ABROAD

+44 (0)1903 708300; ✉ info@projects-abroad.co.uk; 🖰 www.projects-abroad.co.uk. They also have offices in Australia, USA, Canada, France, Denmark, Germany, Italy and the Netherlands.

They are a registered company with over 150 trained staff at overseas destinations and offer over 100 placements. The overseas staff are more involved in local projects than many other placement organisations. Their key destinations are Africa, eastern Europe, Asia, Central and South America. The company's main focus is on sending university students for work experience in teaching, medicine and sports as well as conservation. But an increasing number of their volunteers are people taking time out on academic- or career-related breaks.

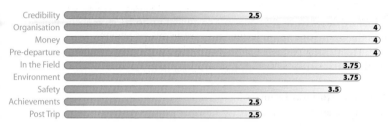

Credibility	2.5
Organisation	4
Money	4
Pre-departure	4
In the Field	3.75
Environment	3.75
Safety	3.5
Achievements	2.5
Post Trip	2.5

Background

Established in 1992 by Peter Slowe, who still runs the company. Originally it was a small enterprise called Teaching and Projects Abroad, primarily focusing on English teaching placements. Since 1997 it has grown and diversified into other volunteering sectors being added, so that in 2008 it changed its name to Projects Abroad to reflect its more generic role.

Credibility

Projects Abroad work in partnerships with local organisations and local scientists usually lead conservation projects, although no biographical details are provided. They have never competed for any conservation awards and do not receive any sponsorship or external funding. There is a good media profile in the nationals, including *The Times* and *The Independent* and volunteers have featured on local and national radio and television.

Organisation

They are a general-purpose volunteer organisation with 2,500 volunteers travelling with them each year and around 20% (12) of projects are conservation or animal-care focused. Most volunteers are under 25, but there are an increasing number of older career breakers.

Conservation projects include rainforest protection in national parks, protecting turtles and crocodiles, sustainable development, coral reef research, mangrove replanting, animal tracking and monitoring in game reserves and environmental protection. There are also veterinary and animal-care projects working with domestic and wild animals in rural and city areas.

Full responsibility is accepted for volunteers and because Projects Abroad run many of their own projects booked places are normally assured. Regular open days are offered and it is possible to contact previous volunteers. Details of recent project activities are included in regular newsletters, dissertations are possible and three-month placements can earn Bath Spa University credits (CATS).

Where the money goes

A two-week project costs around £995; all costs are covered after arrival, including visa, medical insurance and an airport pick-up. A £195 non-refundable deposit is required at booking and the balance is due three months before departure. It is possible to cancel up to three months before departure incurring an administration fee of £65; cancellation penalties apply less than three months before departure on a sliding scale until one month before departure, when all fees are forfeited.

Pre-departure preparation

A dedicated web page gives access to detailed project information and explores individual volunteer motivation and future plans. Good handbooks are provided with all the necessary information as well as a Spanish-language guide for Latin country volunteers. A general framework for daily activities is outlined, but specific aims and objectives are left vague.

Bi-monthly newsletters from each country are posted on the website and give a useful insight to the destination, the volunteers working there and local activities.

Environmental field conditions and general health and safety issues are well covered along with detailed packing advice. There is excellent official arrivals information, but limited travel details because you will be collected from the airport.

In the field

The project purpose and tasks are clearly outlined, although the proposed conservation outcomes are less specific. Local company staff are usually on-site or involved in some aspect of project organisation and volunteers are expected to work a five day week. Accommodation consists mainly of homestays with local families, but there are some shared dormitory rooms or tented camps.

New projects are always being added, so there is a mixture of long-term and developing projects; local people are heavily involved at a senior level in organising and managing projects as well as all other aspects of field activity.

Environment & culture
Carbon offsetting is not included in the volunteer fee, but they do offset their own staff's flights and in-country activity. They address cultural issues and how volunteers can minimise their environmental impact whilst abroad, but more significantly they employ local people in senior positions in all countries.

Safety
They have no plans to implement the British Standards Institute BS8848:2007, but they have a good risk assessment procedures and first-aid equipment at key locations. Experienced local field staff are available to deal with local problems and the company's travel insurance (Endsleigh Insurance) covers medical emergencies and repatriation if necessary.

Demonstrable achievements
Volunteer activity and project progress is not regularly written up, but over the years clear conservation achievements have been made:
- A model farm has been established in the southern province of Tamil Nadu, India, creating a small ecological reserve for birds and insects.
- The survival rate of young olive ridley turtles has been increased 80-fold on the 20km of Pacific coast in Mexico where they run a wildlife reserve.
- Their ecological reserve at Taricaya in the Amazonas of southern Peru has been recognised by the Peruvian government as leading the way in animal release back into the rainforest.
- Volunteers have been restoring the bushvelt by removing alien plants and old fencing on the Botswana–South African border, both of which were associated with the former use of the reserve as a cattle range
- New mangroves have been planted at Ao Nang in Thailand following devastation caused by intensive shrimp farming and the 2004 tsunami.

Post-trip follow up
All volunteers complete evaluation forms and newsletters are distributed to past volunteers and an alumni network has been established.

QUEST OVERSEAS

☏ 01444 474744; ✉(Africa) beth@experiencequest.com; (Latin America) helen@experiencequest.com; (diving) chris@questunderseas.com; ⌨www.questoverseas.com

They lead their own projects and offer a range of additional overseas placements. It is a UK limited company organising long- and short-term humanitarian and conservation volunteering, as well as eco-friendly holidays for 18–24 year olds and older career breakers. Key destinations include Africa, Central and South America, the Mediterranean and the Galapagos Islands.

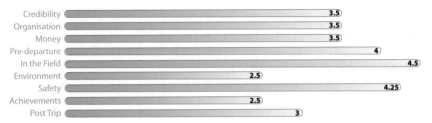

Credibility	3.5
Organisation	3.5
Money	3.5
Pre-departure	4
In the Field	4.5
Environment	2.5
Safety	4.25
Achievements	2.5
Post Trip	3

Background

Michael Amphlet, a Fellow of the Royal Geographical Society, founded Quest in 1996. Being a nomadic, outdoor type he joined the British army but was expelled from Sandhurst for having 'an attitude problem'. After leading an expedition to South America he found his army 'attitude problem' was a perfect match for conservation volunteering.

Credibility

Local organisations lead the scientific and conservation agenda using expertise from universities and government departments. It has been short-listed and highly commended for Virgin Holidays Responsible Tourism Awards – Best Volunteering Organisation in 2005, 2006 and 2007. It has in-depth media coverage in the *New York Times*, *Mail on Sunday* and the *Daily Telegraph* and has received some sponsorship funding for specific targeted projects.

Organisation

Project activities include work in game parks, animal sanctuaries, rainforest conservation, reef diving, conservation and sustainable development. Many projects are conservation oriented, along with adventure, TEFL and community projects, but no written progress reports are available.

Quest leaders lead some of the projects, whilst others are placements with local projects with on-site Quest supervision.

Volunteers are mainly aged 18–25. You can speak with past volunteers and conduct thesis studies (topics suggested), or take PADI diving courses.

Regular open days are held at their office, as well as online interactive project seminars.

Where the money goes

A typical three-week project may cost £1,195 and is broken down into £720 fee plus £475 specific project donation (paid separately); around 42% of the total fee is spent overseas plus the 19% donation, which makes a 60% in-country spend.

Fees include pre-departure training, airport pick-up and national park entrance fees.

A non-refundable (but exchangeable) deposit of £250 is payable and the balance plus the donation is due 60 days before departure. Cancellation charges are on a sliding scale until 30 days before departure, when all fees are forfeited.

Pre-departure preparation

Volunteers are interviewed to ensure the project is right for them. A good countdown-planning framework is provided along with pre-departure training (for projects over three weeks) and a team-building weekend. The weekend includes team briefings on personal kit, project expectations, health and safety, risk assessment, cultural awareness, responsible travel and onward travel suggestions. Volunteers have the opportunity to meet project leaders and fellow volunteers and an optional wilderness-training course is available.

Some projects are clearly outlined, but others have considerably less detail.

In the field

Projects are long term (five years) and the intended benefit of each is clearly stated, but only general aims are provided and no specific project objectives. Only locally owned accommodation is used, which is invariably basic with little or no choice and varies from project to project. They always employ local people, buy local food and support local businesses to enhance their impact on the community.

Environment & culture

Carbon offsetting is strongly promoted and a £20 charge for international flights is added to the fee and paid to Climate Care; a further £20 is encouraged to offset project activities. Cultural and responsible travel issues are explored in depth in the pre-departure training event.

Safety

The British Standards Institute BS8848:2007 is expected to be implemented by late 2008. There is a good protocol for on-site risk assessments, comprehensive first-aid kits are available, as well as mobile phones onsite. Quest-led projects have leaders on site 24/7, whereas placements have in-country co-ordinators who meet up with volunteers and liaise with project managers. Emergency planning and crisis management is well documented with named UK senior staff and includes air evacuation provisions.

Demonstrable achievements

Professionally written scientific papers and field records of conservation volunteer activity are shared with overseas projects and scientists and are available to volunteers on request.

- The Ecuador Amazon Project has financially sponsored Rainforest Concern in planting 1,000 acres of trees.
- The Bolivia Animal Sanctuary Project is involved in preparing animals for rehabilitation and has funded the purchase of a new piece of land as a sanctuary and halfway house for animals due to be released. The land known as 'Ambue Ari' is some 800ha and Quest donations went towards buying about 50% of that (around US$30,000).
- The Brazil Coastal Rainforest Project teams plant endangered tree species working with local NGO Amainan to regenerate the forest. So far they have sent four teams to the project and have planted in excess of 2,000 trees.

Post-trip follow up

All volunteers complete evaluation forms and summary statistics are available on request.

There is a welcome home pack for 18–22 year olds, a meeting or phone interview with placement volunteers, newsletters for all with project updates, and project updates are also found on the charity website.

RALEIGH INTERNATIONAL
☏ +44 (0)20 7183 1270; ✉ info@raleigh.org.uk; 🖥 www.raleigh.org.uk

Raleigh is a UK-based youth development charity, providing volunteers with the opportunity to take part in either five- or ten-week projects that are part community development, part environmental and part adventure expeditions. Key destinations include India, Costa Rica, Nicaragua, Malaysia and Namibia. Projects are aimed at young volunteers (17–24), but also more mature career breakers as volunteer managers (25+). There is a more structured personal development element and generally a higher level of support and supervision than on most other projects.

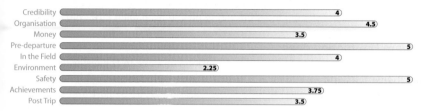

Credibility	4
Organisation	4.5
Money	3.5
Pre-departure	5
In the Field	4
Environment	2.25
Safety	5
Achievements	3.75
Post Trip	3.5

Background
Raleigh International has its origins in Operation Drake which was launched in 1978 by HRH Prince Charles and Colonel John Blashford-Snell, with the aim of running youth projects from ships circumnavigating the globe. Today it is a multi-national organisation with a broader range of destinations, mainly focusing on disadvantaged parts of the world.

Credibility
Science directors oversee the planning and implementation of the scientific components of projects along with local partner organisations and international scientific bodies.

They have no conservation awards although they have received a Millennium volunteering award. It has a good media profile in *The Times*, *The Independent*, the *Daily Express*, *BBC Wildlife*, lots of Chilean newspaper coverage and a television documentary on rhino preservation in Namibia.

An environmental policy is in place and they are members of WWF and the Royal Geographical Society. Additional funds come from commercial and government agencies including Deloitte, Jardine Lloyd Thompson, Capgemini, HSBC, IBM, Barclays and Deutsche Bank, Darwin Initiative and the EU.

Organisation
There are ten core expeditions annually, plus tailor-made schools and corporate expeditions. Around 750 young volunteers go on Raleigh expeditions each year plus around 300 older volunteer managers.

There is a community development and adventure aspect to all projects, but sustainable development and some conservation is also core. Conservation elements include tracking endangered species, trail creation and maintenance, eco-infrastructure building, wildlife and plant surveys.

A couple of open days are held each month and volunteers usually get to meet project leaders at residential courses. There is an alumni section on the website with 3,000 registered ex-Raleigh volunteers on it. New and past volunteers use it as a forum to talk to each other. There is also a Facebook forum for new volunteers to get in touch with alumni. In 2009 there will be a mentoring scheme with alumni and new volunteers.

An excellent social-inclusion dimension is that 20% of volunteers are young people from disadvantaged backgrounds on scholarships. Also all projects have scholarship places for young people from each host country.

Where the money goes

Fees are considered to be charitable donations and are in the order of £1,500 for four weeks and £2,995 for ten weeks, which includes medical insurance, a three-day UK residential training event, in-country transport and a welcome CD.

A £200 non-refundable deposit is required at booking and the balance is due two months before departure. Generally cancellation forfeits all funds although it may be possible to defer a trip until a later date.

Around 61% of the donation is spent in and around projects although specific donations are deemed to be for the charity as a whole. A full set of audited accounts is available in the annual report and on the website.

Pre-departure preparation

There are separate residential weekends for volunteers and volunteer leaders, usually six weeks prior to the expedition. They cover safety briefings, risk assessment, casualty evacuation, training in the correct use of tools, and camping and safety equipment, including radios. Additional information is provided about what day-to-day life on a Raleigh expedition is like, the kit that will be required and more details about the project purpose. Quite a bit of time is spent on team building.

The in-country training is equally detailed. Clear aims and objectives are detailed in project briefing sheets and the welcome CD has good county-focused advice. There is a comprehensive overview of all potential environmental and health risks along with fitness requirements and getting fit. The medical co-ordinator attends each residential event to deliver a medical presentation, health forms need to be completed and detailed vaccination requirements are checked. Good arrivals and travel advice is provided along with recommended overnight accommodation for early arrivals.

In the field

The intended conservation benefits are well laid out and clearly linked to community development and sustainable living, but there is also a strong personal development element on all projects. All projects are long term, are not holidays and are hard work, but only a third of the time will specifically involve conservation or environmental work.

Accommodation is usually dormitory style and beds may be mats on the floor; mosquito nets should be brought and facilities are likely to be basic.

There is a strong local community involvement, in addition to local young people participating on all programmes. There is a no-alcohol policy as well as the normal no-drugs policy.

Environment & culture

Volunteers are encouraged to carbon offset their travel, but it is not included in the fee.

Volunteers are encouraged to minimise their environmental footprint and pre-departure events provide a background to the destination country and an introduction to some cultural issues. An impressive booklet on cross-cultural issues is provided for all volunteers.

Safety

They are self-certified to the new BS8848:2007 standard for overseas fieldwork expeditions and will be seeking an independent assessment to ratify compliance.

Comprehensive risk assessment procedures are in place for all projects. Head office also provides 24-hour emergency cover and support for each expedition and there are always qualified doctors and nurses on each programme. All necessary safety equipment including buoyancy aids, helmets, protective goggles, GPS receivers, flares and communications equipment are provided. A network of HF radio communications enabling field base to have a 24-hour radio watch and project sites call in twice daily. A comprehensive crisis management plan is in place, including air casualty evacuation. Emergency plans are produced for each overseas programme and for every project site. A medical and personal accident insurance policy covers all participants and also, when necessary, participants are repatriated on medical or compassionate grounds.

Demonstrable achievements

There are good summary documents and highly detailed publications about their conservation and development work. The website also has a University of Edinburgh research paper reviewing the effectiveness and impact of Raleigh expeditions. Specific achievements have included:

- In 2007 established the infrastructure for an eco camp on the Kinabatangan River in Malaysia. The MESCOT (Model for Environmentally Sustainable Community Tourism) project is providing a sustainable source of income and employment for the community. The alternate income source through the development and promotion of ecotourism has reduced illegal logging and hunting activities in the area.

- Worked with the International Tropical Conservation Foundation to help create a marine reserve, which is part of the UNESCO World Heritage sites in Bacalar Chico National Park and Marine Reserve, Belize. A ranger's headquarters with dock and lookout tower was built and the development of ecotourism in the area was supported by constructing overnight accommodation for visitors.
- Built composting toilets at local villages in Hosekersunda, India, to decrease pollution of the water supply by sewage. The eco-sanitation units require no water to operate and provide families with rich compost to improve both yields and the nutritional value of produce from their own organic vegetable gardens to make a saleable commodity through which to increase their income.
- At Imbak Canyon, Sabah, Borneo, they have been recording baseline biological and mapping data and feasibility studies for a field centre base camp, helicopter landing sites and trail networks. Also helped establish a primary conservation area including constructing a base camp of kitchen, toilet and sleeping areas for the rangers and visitors.
- At Danum Valley Conservation Area, Sabah, Borneo, they have landscaped an area for a gazebo, cut nature trails, mapped the area and accompanied scientists with various forest research projects. An 800m trail and a plant nursery have been built and areas of the rainforest mapped. In addition, data was collected on seedlings planted in an area that had previously been logged.

Post-trip follow up

All volunteers complete an end-of-project evaluation questionnaire and volunteer managers have a one-to-one debriefing. In addition there is a follow-up electronic questionnaire after one month, which is more open ended and often produces more insightful comments.

Once back home volunteers are directed to UK organisations that have short- and long-term volunteering opportunities; currently they are with the National Trust, Groundwork, People and Planet and BTCV. There is an informal reunion three months after each expedition.

REAL GAP EXPERIENCE AND GAP YEAR FOR GROWN UPS

☎ 01892 516164; ✉ info@realgap.co.uk; 🖰 www.realgap.co.uk

These two organisations are essentially the same company but with a different age focus. It has a wide selection of volunteering opportunities includingcommunity work, conservation, teaching English, adventure travel, sports and expeditions and around 60 of them are conservation-related projects. Projects are available in Africa, Australia, New Zealand, the Far East, Mongolia, China, North, Central and South America. They also provide a range of other travel service options.

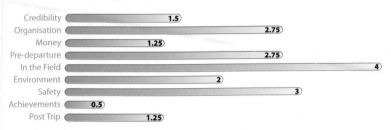

Credibility	1.5
Organisation	2.75
Money	1.25
Pre-departure	2.75
In the Field	4
Environment	2
Safety	3
Achievements	0.5
Post Trip	1.25

Background

Real Gap is part of Real Travel Ltd, which started life as the Work and Travel Company set up by David Stitt, who is still the current managing director. It has been in operation since 2000 and started offering gap-year travel in 2003. The sister company called Gap Year For Grown Ups (🖰 *www.gapyearfor grownups.co.uk*) is a more recent innovation and their focus is self-evident.

Credibility

The scientific and conservation aspects of projects are the responsibility of each individual project rather than Real Gap and it's not known if any have gained awards.

There is a responsible travel policy and a responsible travellers code on the website. They are not members of any conservation organisation and receive no funding from outside sources.

Organisation

They send around 8,000 volunteers on gap-year trips, of which around 1,000 are on conservation projects. Volunteers tend to be adventurous 18–24 year olds. Tasks include rescue and rehabilitation of wildlife, turtle protection, coral reef research surveys, rainforest conservation, marine mammal surveys by boat, African game reserves, field guide training, national park maintenance, surveying and monitoring. PADI courses are also available.

There are no written details of previous project activities or who the local project co-ordinators are. Some previous volunteers can be contacted depending on whether they have opted in to share contact details with other volunteers.

The company doesn't have many open days, but makes regular school presentations as part of its recruitment programme and prospective volunteers can visit their Kent office for a chat.

Where the money goes

A two-week project costs around £550–850, which sometimes includes internal transfers, but not always, and there may be additional pre- and post-project accommodation costs. A non-refundable deposit of £195 is required; fees minus deposit will be refunded up to 12 weeks before departure after which cancellation charges operate on a sliding scale down to two weeks, after which all fees are forfeited. It is possible to postpone a trip, for a £35 administration fee, if notification is made ten weeks before departure.

No details are available about what portion of a volunteer's fee gets spent in and around projects.

Pre-departure preparation

No pre-departure training is available, but there are project profiles on the website and further destination and project factsheets after booking. They provide a general indication of project activity although specific tasks are agreed on site. Quite a few projects have video clips, which are very informative. Dive projects require medical certification, but there is little else about fitness requirements or the environmental conditions at project locations.

Equipment lists are generic rather than specific and an optional gap-year safety course is available for £150.

In the field

Conservation benefits are generally alluded to but not with any clarity. Most projects appear to be long term although this is not under the control of Real Gap. Accommodation is variable, including tented research camp, caravans, dormitories and local homestays. Projects are mainly work oriented, but there is an emphasis on having fun. Local people organise and run all projects.

Environment & culture

Carbon offsetting is not included in the fee, but volunteers are encouraged to pay to offset the carbon emissions from their international flights. There is a good ethical travel section but little focused information on how volunteers can minimise their environmental impact whilst on the project.

Safety

They do not currently comply with BS8848:2007, but plan to do so at some point in the near future. Risk assessment procedures are in place for all projects and there are emergency protocols to deal with any on site crisis. Volunteers are issued with a local co-ordinator's telephone number and a 24-hour emergency contact number should they need to contact UK staff.

Demonstrable achievements

There are no published reports about the activities or achievements of previous projects and assessing the conservation outcomes is considered to be the prerogative of local projects rather than Real Gap. However, details were provided about:

- A Costa Rica turtle protection project that has helped to reduce nest poaching, cutting it from 95% to 10% thus offsetting a significant future population crash of endangered leatherback and hawksbill turtles.

Post-trip follow up

All volunteers are asked to complete feedback forms on their experience. The newsletters circulated are primarily about offers, deals and promotions rather than project achievements or conservation outcomes.

RESPONSIBLE TRAVEL.COM

℡ 01273 600030; ✉ amelia@responsibletravel.com;
🖱 www.responsibletravel.com

This is an online travel directory providing an overview for prospective volunteers seeking information about what is out there in the marketplace; essentially they are a recruitment service for placement organisers and other eco-friendly travel services. It lists hand-picked, pre-screened volunteer opportunities and holidays that maximise the economic benefits of tourism to local people, whilst minimising negative cultural or environmental impacts on the destinations. They do not organise or offer trips, but list 270 operators and accommodation providers who do. The website also includes unedited reviews of holiday experiences and it is free to the user.

Background
In 2001 Justin Francis sat down with Anita Roddick, the founder of Body Shop, and explained his business idea. She got him to write on one side of the paper all the negatives associated with the worst forms of tourism. On the other side were ideas which reconnect tourists with local people, cultures and environments in a mutually respectful and beneficial way and Responsibletravel.com was born.

Organisation
This directory works differently from Green Volunteers and Ecoteer by providing a free website with more information about specific projects, but nothing about the actual project providers themselves.

Responsibletravel.com visitors get referred, via the website, to specific project providers that might be local tour services, eco-lodges, or one of the big placement organisers referred to elsewhere in this book. It is a useful resource for scanning a wide range of project opportunities offered by hundreds of different organisations; visitors can then focus in and contact a specific provider for further information and then get in touch by email. To be listed on Responsibletravel.com organisations have to demonstrate policy and practices that meet the following minimum standards:

Policy and procedure
This includes written confirmation that the company has a procedure for responding to traveller's complaints and suggestions concerning responsible travel practices.

Environmental policy
This includes evidence of water conservation, waste management practice of suppliers and minimising damage to the environment, wildlife and marine ecosystems. They should promote destination visits to appropriate local projects with direct or indirect environmental benefits.

Social policy

This includes accurate pre-trip information on the social and political situation in each destination and ways to minimise negative impacts on local cultures.

Economic policy

This includes evidence that the company policy requests destination suppliers to employ local people wherever possible, make use of local produce, manufacturers and other services and suggestions of local services that provide local community benefits (eg: restaurants, guides, shops, craft markets).

Examples of projects

Big cat conservation, Botswana and Namibia

It costs £1,390 for two weeks, which includes local transport, food and own room in rustic reed buildings. The project involves surveying general prey species and top predators by capture, collar and radio tracking methods. It aims to study how to minimise human/predator conflicts and so aid top predator conservation. Unspecified placement provider.

Dolphin conservation, Greece

It costs £550–700 for six days, which includes food, accommodation, insurance, lectures and scientific supervision in small groups. The project involves working side by side with researchers spotting and recording dolphin activity. It aims to document the main threats to the animals, prevent ecosystem damage and facilitate common dolphin recovery. Unspecified placement provider.

Elephant conservation, Thailand

It costs £285–595 for one to three weeks, which includes food and accommodation. The project provides refuge for domesticated elephants that have been roaming the streets of Bangkok and other cities and volunteers help care for them. It aims to give refuge to elephants in a safe environment as close to nature as possible. Unspecified placement provider.

STARFISH VENTURES

✆/F 0800 1974817; ✉ enquiries@starfishventures.co.uk;
🖱 www.starfishventures.co.uk

This is a small, limited company based in Thailand with some part-time staff also based in the UK. It specialises in supporting development projects in Thailand through the placement of foreign volunteers, providing financial aid, expertise and project management. It is an introductory service providing volunteer and gap-year placements in Thailand.

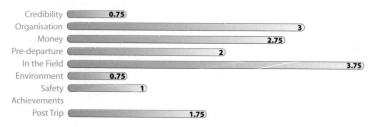

Credibility	0.75
Organisation	3
Money	2.75
Pre-departure	2
In the Field	3.75
Environment	0.75
Safety	1
Achievements	
Post Trip	1.75

Background
Dan Moore, the director and founder, set up Starfish in November 2003 following a career break in Thailand where he met a director of schools in Surin and ended up stayed for six months assisting schools and camps with their language education. Although not a registered 'not for profit' organisation Starfish has not made a profit in three years but Dan says, 'that is not the purpose of Starfish'.

Credibility
This small organisation only operates in Thailand and works on a perceived need rather than a scientific basis. It has received project funding from Rotary International, but being so small and new it has not achieved the profile of larger enterprises and does not go in for PR or advertising promotions.

Organisation
It is a Thai specialist with only four (25%) conservation-related projects covering animal welfare, dog rescue, gibbons, turtle conservation and an elephant sanctuary. The company is too small to run open days. Around 100–150 volunteers travel with them each year. There are no previous project activity reports, but previous volunteers can be contacted for their opinion. The in-country co-ordinators are named and volunteers are put in touch with each other before departure.

Where the money goes
Fees range from £700–900 for two weeks, which includes medical insurance for EU residents, airport pick-up and overnight accommodation in Bangkok, but food is not provided. A £300 non-refundable deposit is required and the

balance is due four weeks before departure. Cancellations get a refund (minus deposit) up to four weeks before departure, after which all fees are forfeited. Around 60% of fees are spent in and around projects.

Pre-departure preparation
There are no pre-departure training events and general preparation is limited, but includes some information on health, equipment requirements and travel plans. Project briefs and in-country training are not very detailed.

In the field
The intended conservation benefits are not explored, but the purpose of wildlife sanctuary activities is fairly self-evident. Accommodation is simple and basic with single or shared rooms and volunteers will have to arrange their own meals. The work schedules vary from a four-day week to six shorter days. All projects are organised and run by local people and Starfish have given a long-term commitment to all projects.

Environment & culture
There is no written information about environmental issues or any detailed cultural preparation.

Safety
There are no plans to implement BS8848:2007. No formal risk assessment of locations is carried out and no explicit emergency planning was evident, but they do provide medical insurance cover for volunteers from EU countries.

Demonstrable achievements
There are no written records of project activities or examples of practical conservation outcomes or achievements.

Post-trip follow up
Volunteers complete evaluation questionnaires and are kept in touch with project developments after returning home and there is a Facebook discussion group.

TRAVELLERS WORLDWIDE
☎ 01903 502595; ✉ info@travellersworldwide.com;
🖰 www.travellersworldwide.com

Travellers Worldwide is the trading name of TravelQuest Limited, a UK-registered company. Since 1994 Travellers Worldwide has grown into a major international provider of various volunteer placements offering over 300 projects and sending international volunteers all over the world. Destinations include Africa, South America, Australia, Brunei (Borneo), China, Cuba, India, Malaysia, Russia and Sri Lanka.

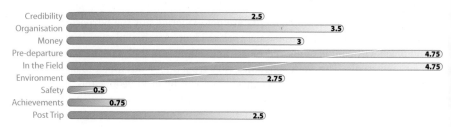

Credibility	2.5
Organisation	3.5
Money	3
Pre-departure	4.75
In the Field	4.75
Environment	2.75
Safety	0.5
Achievements	0.75
Post Trip	2.5

Background
Phil and Jennifer Perkes established Travellers Worldwide in 1994 to enable people from all over the world to experience living and working in foreign countries. Having travelled extensively and worked in various countries, they believe that everyone should have the opportunity to meet and live with different races and ethnic groups and gain experiences and memories that will stay with them for the rest of their lives.

Credibility
The scientific and conservation guidance comes from in-country sources, sometimes universities, government departments or local NGOs.

They have no awards, but do have good national and local media coverage in *The Independent*, *National Geographic*, *Eve* magazine and a range of regional newspapers. They have a responsible travel policy and they don't receive financial support from other sources.

Organisation
They offer 250 projects although only 12% (30) are conservation focused, and specialise in sports and coaching placements. Conservation activities include rescue and rehabilitation of wildlife, coral reef research surveys, rainforest conservation, marine mammal surveys by boat, African game reserves, field assistant work for great white shark conservation, national park maintenance, bush survival skills and assistant zookeeper work. They also offer an eight-week training course for a certificate from African Global Conservation Academy; there are also some undergraduate-level research opportunities.

Volunteers include gappers plus career breakers, and specific placement requests are matched up after booking so specific projects are not guaranteed when booking.

Names, photographs and contact numbers of country co-ordinators that look after volunteers and liaise with partner organisations are posted on the website. Volunteers are provided with the contact details of other volunteers so that they can contact each other prior to departure although little information about the progress of past projects is available. There are no regular open-day events.

Where the money goes

Fees for two-week projects range from £675–1,295 and up to £2,295 for four weeks. This includes electronic booklets on the placement, the country, project and safety, as well as an airport pick-up, a company ID card with local and UK contact details and in most cases food and accommodation.

A partially non-refundable deposit of £190 is required at booking, but is refunded along with any fees if your project choice is unavailable or no acceptable alternative can be provided (less £90 administration fee). The outstanding balance is due three months before the departure date. Cancellation charges are on a sliding scale from a full refund (minus deposit) up to three months before departure down to 21 days, after which all payments are forfeited. Placement alterations are possible but not guaranteed and would incur a £40 administration fee. Around 60% of each volunteer's fee is spent in and around the project.

Pre-departure preparation

There is no pre-departure training, but there is excellent documentation covering advice on planning, travel, safety on the ground, cultural differences and etiquette, along with country information, packing, climate preparation and fitness requirements. The job brief is clearly laid out in separate booklets but some are more detailed than others. There is especially good local contact information including accommodation and telephone contact details.

In the field

The conservation benefits of projects are clearly outlined and local co-ordinators assist with liaison in the field. Most accommodation is with local families and occasionally school residences, hostels or guesthouses. On arrival volunteers get an induction to their new country including transport, banks, safety issues, cultural issues and places to visit. Projects are run entirely by local people and a useful cost-of-living outline is provided.

Environment & culture

Carbon offsetting is encouraged, but no contribution is made to international flights or locally generated carbon emissions. Useful advice is provided on minimising environmental damage and understanding cultural differences. A very good guide about captive-animal welfare is provided for relevant projects.

Safety
Travellers Worldwide have not implemented BS8848:2007, but they aim to incorporate it in the future. Where they have control, they try to ensure that first-aid equipment is on site, but this is not always possible. No details of risk assessment or emergency protocols were available for inspection.

Demonstrable achievements
There is little written detail of conservation achievements arising from project placements. Although, since 2003 they have been working with the Greater St Lucia Wetland Park Authority in South Africa to update information on the less charismatic, yet equally important, rare, threatened and endemic species found within the park.

Post-trip follow up
All volunteers are sent a debriefing questionnaire at the end of their project but probably a more useful device is their innovative live volunteer 'a day in the life' feedback sheet sent to HQ whilst the trip is still under way.

TREKFORCE WORLDWIDE

☏ 0845 241 308; ✉ info@trekforceworldwide.com; 🖳 www.trekforce.org.uk

Trekforce Worldwide is a limited company that focuses on conservation, teaching and challenging expeditions for gappers (two–five months), career breakers, company groups (social responsibility) and media work with television/film crews. Key destinations include Belize, Guyana, Borneo and Papua New Guinea. Their emphasis is on projects in remote places, and adventure with some extensive jungle training on every project.

Credibility	3
Organisation	4
Money	3
Pre-departure	5
In the Field	3.5
Environment	4
Safety	4.75
Achievements	3
Post Trip	2

Background

The International Scientific Support Trust, founded by the explorer Wandy Swales, developed into Trekforce in 1990. Initially it was formed as the conservation charity Trekforce Expeditions and now it operates as the registered company Trekforce Worldwide. In 2008 it merged with Greenforce (see page 94), but both organisations are currently retaining their individual identities.

Credibility

Projects are designed in partnership with local communities and sometimes they are able to access international development funds for projects. They have some local and internet media coverage and provided the expedition expertise for BBC and Sky TV extreme adventure programmes with Bruce Parry, Ben Fogle and Jack Osbourne. They have previously received project-funding support from UK government and EU coffers.

Organisation

They run their own projects, in partnership with local NGOs, so bookings are for pre-planned projects. They are rainforest and jungle specialists, but they also offer some add-on teaching and diving placements. The majority of activities are practical infrastructure building or creating tracks to support ecotourism. These projects are often in national parks and are usually connected to the developmental needs of ranger patrols and scientific research. Some rapid assessment biodiversity surveys are also conducted. Most projects have three distinct components – practical jungle training, conservation activities and an extended jungle trek. Adding on a diving or teaching placement can extend the project length up to five months.

The project plans are clear and they use their own leaders whose biographies and photographs are detailed on the website. Monthly open days to meet staff and past volunteers are organised and ex-volunteers can be contacted. Written details of past project activity are available on request.

Where the money goes
Project fees range from £1,200–4,000 for three weeks to five months and include a UK pre-departure training course, carbon offsetting, park entry fees and an on-site medic. A £200 (£350 for extreme adventures) non-refundable deposit is required and the balance is due six weeks before departure. A sliding scale of cancellation charges applies but unusually 25% is refundable even for last minute cancellations and volunteers can transfer departure dates if they have a serious problem.

Around 56–60% of each volunteer's fee is spent in and around the project.

Pre-departure preparation
A residential pre-departure orientation and team-building course is included and excellent acclimatisation and jungle training is provided on arrival. Each project's aims are well laid out and there are excellent destination and project briefings. Essential health and vaccination information is provided and there is a useful guide to getting fit before you go. The planning documentation is also excellent and there is extremely detailed and very practical guidance on packing and kit requirements.

In the field
The intended conservation benefits are clear and there are usually five- to ten-year development plans for projects. Accommodation is invariably basic and involves sleeping in the open during the jungle trek. A good deal of project time (about 50%) is spent on wilderness training, adventure activities and the jungle trek. There are good links with the local community and plenty of time for the adventure side of the trip.

Environment & culture
Carbon offset costs are built into project prices and it covers international flights and all in-country project activities. Excellent guidelines are provided about environmental protection but only an outline of local cultural issues.

Safety
They are BS8848:2007 self-certified for overseas fieldwork expeditions. Good risk assessment protocols are in place and there are telecoms and first-aid equipment on-site. A field leader and a medic are on site 24/7 and there are clear emergency evacuation procedures.

Demonstrable achievements
There are annual updates of all project activities on the website and details of practical conservation achievements are available but with little evidence of publication.

- Responsible for influencing the creation of a number of national parks including the Elijio Panti National Park in Belize, including jaguar protection.
- to help protect Chiqubul National Park – recently completed a ranger station for the Forestry Department in southern Belize to monitor the illegal Xateroe farmers crossing from Guatemala to strip the forest of saleable products .
- Completed a number of visitor and research centres that are now being used as research facilities (eg: the ranger station at the northern end of Iwokrama National Park, Guyana).
- Built a community centre in Rancho Dolores, Belize; helped set up a sustainable gibnut or paca (beaver-like rodent) farm (Royal Rat) as an alternative to peccary hunting.
- Planted 250,000 diptocarp trees in the Danum Valley, Borneo, as part of a Royal Society biodiversity project in 2006.

Post-trip follow up

Feedback is gathered from all volunteers and on return home reunions are arranged, newsletters are distributed and ex-volunteers help out at briefing events and on recruitment programmes.

VOLUNTARY SERVICE OVERSEAS (VSO)

☏ +44 (0)20 8780 7200; ✉ enquiry@vso.org.uk; 🖳 www.vso.org.uk. There are additional offices in Ireland, Canada, Netherlands, India, Kenya, Uganda and the Philippines.

This international charity is now in its 50th year and is unique because it pays volunteers a living wage. Although VSO specialises in development work there are a number of environment- and conservation-related opportunities. A major difference from most other organisations is that they seek skilled and professionally competent volunteers – often, but not always, graduates. Projects are 'specialist assignments', which usually last one to two years; volunteers do not normally work as part of a group of volunteers.

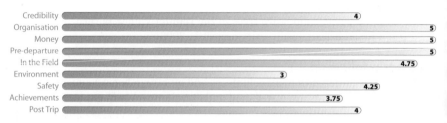

Credibility	4
Organisation	5
Money	5
Pre-departure	5
In the Field	4.75
Environment	3
Safety	4.25
Achievements	3.75
Post Trip	4

Background
Alec and Mora Dickson founded VSO with the backing of Inter Church Aid (now Christian Aid) and the late Bishop of Portsmouth. In 1958 the first VSO volunteers left the UK to give a year's voluntary service in Ghana, Nigeria, Northern Rhodesia (Zambia) and Sarawak. Since then over 30,000 volunteers have worked in over 70 countries.

Credibility
Volunteers are likely to take the relevant professional expertise to the project they are working on. VSO was voted top international development charity in the International Aid and Development category at the Charity Awards 2004. They have a good media profile, their views are regularly sought by the media and recent stories have appeared in the *Daily Express*, *The Guardian*, *The Times* and the *Times Educational Supplement*.

VSO are members of the National Council of Voluntary Organisations, British Overseas NGOs for Development (BOND), the British Volunteer Agencies Liaison Group and the Tropical Agriculture Association. They also work with innumerable government and university environment departments. Many projects are supported by the World Bank along with sponsorship from commercial organisations such as Randstad, BAA, Accenture, IBM and MSD (Merck).

Organisation
VSO currently works in 34 countries in the developing world primarily tackling poverty, but there are conservation and sustainable living

opportunities in Malawi, Papua New Guinea, Uganda, Mozambique, Guyana and the Philippines. In 2008 the range of opportunities included agriculturalist, livestock worker/vet, irrigation engineer, horticulturalist, geologist, forester, fisheries and coastal manager, ecotourism adviser, environmentalist, natural resource manager and new opportunities continually become available.

There are regular open days, but they are usually focused on specific skill areas and only professionally qualified or specifically competent volunteers are accepted for VSO. The website has a video library that gives a flavour of volunteer activity, but as the projects are often one-offs they may not be directly relevant. There are also updated 'newsroom' stories about 'live' VSO project activity and prospective volunteers are strongly encouraged to talk to previous volunteers.

Where the money goes

VSO is different from all other organisations in this book because they pay volunteers, rather than charge them. Volunteers receive a monthly allowance appropriate to the placement country and three weeks annual leave. VSO also cover the cost of flights, holiday pay, grants on arrival and return home, insurance as well as medical expenses, personal liability, life insurance and motor insurance for VSO vehicles. VSO also pays for relevant vaccinations and provides guidelines as to those which are necessary.

There is a transparent record of cash flow in the annual report.

Pre-departure preparation

All long-term volunteers (six months plus) take a range of UK-based courses, including preparing to volunteer, health and security workshops, and workshops outlining the skills for working in development. Volunteers (under six months) take a two-and-a-half-day course that enables them to consider the benefits and constraints of short-term placements and introduces VSO's way of working.

There are incredibly detailed in-country briefings and clear aims and objectives, which the volunteers work is assessed against with reports at six, 12 and 18 months.

Volunteers are given a medical examination before departure by qualified medical staff and given details on the climate, political situation of the area where they will be working, and essential kit advice.

When volunteers arrive in country they are met by a VSO driver and taken to their accommodation. The first few days or weeks include in-country training, which may include language training along with visits to the community and their placement employer.

In the field

Each VSO placement, whether in the area of environment or elsewhere, focuses on outcomes that impact on the local community. Volunteer placements often include an element of training colleagues so that work continues after the volunteer leaves. Work is usually long term (one or two years), although there are also a number of specialist short-term assignments.

In terms of accommodation, volunteers live like any other local although they usually have their own room. They work a standard working week and essentially work with and for local community organisations rather than VSO.

Environment & culture
No specific carbon offsetting arrangements are in place and nor is there information about how volunteers can minimise their impact on the local environment. All volunteers receive a handbook and a country briefing tailored to the country they will be working in. It covers the history of the country, the context of VSO's work, cultural norms, and packing advice with suggestions from previous volunteers.

Safety
BS8848:2007 is not considered relevant to VSO as volunteers are working overseas for long periods and not engaged in dangerous activities. Each programme office assesses each volunteer employer before volunteers start work. As volunteers are usually not in daily contact with VSO it is their day-to-day responsibility to ensure their own health and safety, except in emergency situations. Every country has developed individual detailed risk assessment and evacuation plans as part of their comprehensive security protocols. All were updated in late 2007 and tested in early 2008.

An emergency phone number to a dedicated local medical adviser is provided along with free first-aid kit and other safety essentials, as required, eg: mosquito net, cold weather clothing allowance, etc. Emergency evacuation plans are well thought through, whether it is to the local hospital or repatriation home.

Demonstrable achievements
Professional position papers are available on a range VSO issues as well as volunteer accounts of their experience in the field, although they are not always that detailed. Outcomes identified from volunteer 'end of project reports' include:

- A natural resource manager in the Philippines brought together otherwise unconnected people and groups to draw out their knowledge and expertise and produced policies for the least destructive frequency and methods of harvesting. This led to lucrative community-based livelihoods.
- A Philippines project surveyed and defined the characteristics of the water catchment of the Andanan River, and developed a management plan to conserve and protect the area. The placement contributed to the adoption of sustainable natural resource management practices by local government units and NGOs, and raised community awareness of the

need for environmental protection and the conservation of resources. The placement also contributed to more sustainable livelihoods for the residents of the area.

- A team of volunteers supported Cambodia's community fisheries stakeholders. Empowerment has been enhanced by training and support to resolve problems in the community by sharing their ideas, and the patrollers and authorities controlling the illegal activities have been escorted. This has resulted in reducing river pollution and stopping four cases of illegal fishing, as well as the seizure of 27 illegal fishing nets. Sustainability has been enhanced and four of the conservation sites began to produce a larger variety of fish.

Post-trip follow up

Before volunteers return to the UK an exit interview is held with a member of the programme staff.

There is a dedicated debriefing team offering careers advice, a resettlement pack with leavers' advice and a weekend meeting for returned volunteers is held. Local groups and ex-volunteer networks are set up across the UK and a life-changer's newsletter is produced.

Way Out Experiences (WOX)

☎ + 44 (0)845 371 3070; headquarters in Kuala Lumpur, Malaysia; ☎ +60
(0)3 7724 2272 ✉ orangutan@w-o-x.com; 🖰 www.orangutanproject.com

WOX is a UK- and Malaysia-based limited company that organises the Great Orang-utan Project (GOP). This is a collection of orang-utan conservation projects in both peninsular Malaysia and Malaysian Borneo, funded by volunteer contributions and coordinated by conservationists employed by Way Out Experiences.

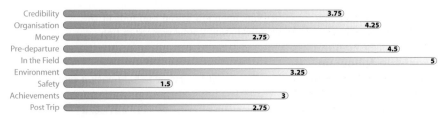

Credibility	3.75
Organisation	4.25
Money	2.75
Pre-departure	4.5
In the Field	5
Environment	3.25
Safety	1.5
Achievements	3
Post Trip	2.75

Background

Founded in 2003 by two environmentalists, Guillaume Feldman and Afzaal Mauthoor, Way Out Experiences (WOX) is an international tourism company with over 50 years combined experience in environment and animal conservation. It is based in the UK, Kuala Lumpur and Kuching (Sarawak, Malaysian Borneo) and it aims to contribute to conservation issues by using the principles of business for social and environmental outcomes.

Credibility

GOP staff have degrees in zoology, environmental policy, environmental science, environmental law, conservation and biochemistry and previous experience of working in government, marketing and ecotourism in UK, Malaysia and Mauritius. The website has a comprehensive set of policies on responsible volunteering.

They have won a local Malaysian award called Wild Asia and have had several local UK press stories, mostly about the first cataract operation on a blind orang-utan called Aman. They work in partnership with Sarawak Forestry Corporation (SFC), Zoo Negara, Zoo Taiping, Batang Ai National Park and have sponsorship through University of Sarawak, Malaysia, Malaysian Airlines, Tourism Malaysia and Tourism Sarawak.

Organisation

Their key focus is on Malaysian Borneo. The Great orang-utan Project (GOP) is a combination of three components: Batang Ai (wild orang-utan populations), the Matang Wildlife Centre (rehabilitation and release) and three Malaysian zoos (captive breeding and education) and a separate turtle protection project. There are only four focused projects whose work includes, cleaning, feeding, painting, building, trekking and protecting turtle nesting locations.

There are no open days, but prospective volunteers are welcome to call in at the UK offices for an informal meeting to chat over plans for the future. The names, biographies and photographs of project staff are on the website. About 80% of volunteers are aged between 25 and 45; most are independent female travellers, working in professional or clerical jobs in South East England. People are set up with buddies before departure and there are dialogue groups on Facebook and MySpace where The Great Orang-utan Project group hosts previous volunteers who post photographs and talk about their experiences.

There are good project outlines and some useful video clips give a feel for the projects in action. An excellent 'reality check' section lets volunteers know exactly what to expect when volunteering.

Where the money goes

Fees range from £999 for two weeks to £1,299 for four weeks and include an overnight stay in Kuching. There is a clear cash breakdown of expenditure in the 'Before you Go' document.

A £550 non-refundable deposit is payable within 14 days of booking. Cancellation penalties are on a sliding scale, with a 95% penalty within 59 days of departure and all fees forfeit within seven days before departure. Amendments may be made up to eight weeks before departure with a fee of £40 per alteration per person.

Around 44% of each volunteer's fee is spent in and around the project.

Pre-departure preparation

UK pre-departure training is not really practical as the main office is in Malaysia, but there is good background documentation about the work of GOP, plus videos of work in action.

There is orientation and health and safety training on arrival. The first week of on-site training focuses on equipment, familiarity of animals and their habits, team building, supervision rules and conservation talks. It could take a week of training to get to a point where volunteers are well versed with working conditions.

Aims and objectives are well laid out in the 'Before You Go' documentation and health risks are outlined. It is made clear that the work is physical and temperatures high, so volunteers need a reasonable level of fitness. The terrain is hilly in places and the weather is hot and humid; volunteers unable to cope with this environment and terrain are not permitted to join fieldwork expeditions.

The key tasks are clearly explained although not on a daily basis. Good packing advice is provided and there are excellent arrival details with telephone contact numbers and directions if things go wrong.

In the field

The aim is to release orang-utans back into the wild and generate ecotourism for local people. Work with the orang-utans is based exclusively on what is in their best interests and not what volunteers might like to do, so there is no touching or cuddling of animals. All projects are long term and ongoing.

Volunteers will live in a rainforest area 50 minutes from the city of Kuching and accommodation is based in a jungle chalet amongst the staff quarters. There are separate bedrooms, fan, lounge and dining area, simple kitchen and bathroom with cold showers. This is jungle living with considerable comfort, but volunteers should not expect luxury and need to bring their own mosquito net. A food allowance is provided and volunteers are taken to the shops to buy food for the self-catering meal arrangements. The work is demanding, usually from 08.00 to 17.00 Monday to Saturday possibly working some Sundays, but there is a degree of flexibility so volunteers can take time-off to visit other parts of Sarawak.

A major emphasis is that local communities benefit from GOP activities and that all organisational responsibility is eventually transferred to Malaysian people. GOP employs 15 members of staff, which are a mixture of UK and Malaysian nationals.

Environment & culture
They do not routinely endorse commercial carbon offsetting schemes, but have established voluntary credit schemes in India and Borneo where volunteers may be able to plant trees or install energy saving technology to offset their project carbon footprint. Schemes are currently being evaluated and details are expected to be on the website by 2009.

There is a well-documented policy about how volunteers should minimise their impact on the local environment and a good introduction to how life in Malaysian Borneo is different from what volunteers may be used to.

Safety
They expect to be BS8848:2007 self-certified by the end of 2008. Company staff are on site 24/7 and some first-aid equipment is available, although unspecified. Risk assessment and emergency procedure plans were not available for inspection.

Demonstrable achievements
There are no written reports, but there are good video clips of the animals at various centres. In partnership with the Sarawak forestry research team, data is used to ascertain the behaviour and health of the orang-utan population. The data is collated, processed and published with cooperation from the University of Malaysia. Specific outcomes include:

- Pulling together a comprehensive education and information internet resource for orang-utan protection and conservation. This involves the Sarawak Forestry Corporation leading on the rehabilitation centre, the local Iban communities leading on sustainable development within their community and UNIMAS leading on research.

- They have rebuilt existing orang-utan enclosures to improve the quality of life for resident animals.
- They have carried out the first cataract eye surgery on a partially blind orang-utan.
- They have created sustainable working opportunities for local communities.

Post-trip follow up

Volunteers complete a pre-evaluation survey prior to applying for a placement, which is used to assess the suitability of candidates. A post project evaluation form is completed on site and there are plans to set up a post experience evaluation after volunteers arrive back home.

There is an ongoing 'latest news' section on the website for volunteers to keep in touch with project activities and a diary of life at the project so they can see their work being continued.

WORLDWIDE OPPORTUNITIES ON ORGANIC FARMS (WWOOF)

✉ contact is via the website; 🖱 www.wwoof.org. It has 50 relatively independent branches around the world: see 🖱 www.wwoofinternational.org.

Free food and accommodation almost anywhere in the world! That's what's on offer with World Wide Opportunities on Organic Farms (WWOOF) in return for five to six hours work a day for five or six days a week.

This novel internet directory to working on organic farms around the globe is an opportunity for travellers to experience a sustainable and environmentally friendly way of living. It might not be everybody's idea of 'hard core' conservation but you will get hands-on experience of organic growing, country living and an insight into ecologically sound lifestyles.

Background

WWOOF hosts may be located on large or small farms, small-holdings, houses with large gardens or woods and all variations in between. The sites are either growing organically or in conversion and the deal is that volunteers help their hosts in exchange for food and accommodation.

The organisation was set up in 1971 by London-based secretary Sue Coppard because she wanted to get out into the countryside, and has gone global. There are now 24 national WWOOF organisations, listing thousands of hosts around the world. Hosts in countries with no national organisation are listed as WWOOF Independents, which currently lists 900 hosts in over 50 countries. Destinations include, UK, Europe, North, Central and South America, Africa, Asia, Australia and New Zealand.

The activities will be wide and variable, including sowing, making compost, gardening, planting, cutting wood, weeding, making mud-bricks, harvesting, fencing, building, typing, packing, milking or feeding animals.

Volunteering

Volunteers need to become a member of the national organisation where they want to travel to which usually costs around £20. You then search the list for hosts that interest you and then make direct contact with them to arrange a stay. You negotiate with your host, before you arrive, concerning the needs and expectations of both parties. Stays can be from one week to a couple of months.

Volunteers need to be genuinely interested in learning about organic growing, farming, country living or ecologically sound lifestyles and give the agreed hours of help in return for food and accommodation. Accommodation is, in essence, a homestay arrangement so volunteers will be living in someone's home and sharing their life.

Examples of projects
Wildlife shelter, Australia
The shelter sits in the middle of Stanley Forest between Beechworth and Yackandandah townships in Victoria, Australia. They care for and rehabilitate orphaned and injured native wildlife, including birds, with many native animals visiting the property as a safe haven, especially in the evenings. WWOOFers must have a devotion to caring for animals. Work includes feeding baby wildlife, exercising young wildlife, collecting gum leaves for possums and koalas, cleaning cages, fixing and building cages. At any one time there are at least 15 animals requiring two–four-hourly bottle-feeding. Opportunities will also arise to go out on calls to rescue or collect distressed wildlife. There is accommodation for one–two people in a caravan or shed but no children; mixed diet and no alcohol.

Rural farm, Mexico
Five acres of land on the outskirts of a small, friendly village, 3kms from a beautiful beach on the Pacific coast of Mexico. There are over 100 coconut palms, lots of other fruit trees, a small vegetable garden and a big old house. They require one or two WWOOFers to help with projects like building a solar collector for hot water, a compost privy, a drip irrigation system, pruning fruit trees, weeding, watering, etc.

There are two rooms for rent, and if they're not occupied WWOOFers can stay in them, otherwise its camping out. There is internet connection at the main house. The mail to Mexico can be slow, so email contact is preferable. No smokers allowed!

School gardens, Sierra Leone
General gardening skills are required for this project, which has helped to start food gardens at several schools and children's homes. The children and staff eat from the gardens and the students sell the surplus to help cover school fees and other facility costs. Meanwhile, the children learn valuable gardening and business skills.

UK AND IRELAND CONSERVATION VOLUNTEER OPPORTUNITIES

It is not necessary to save or fundraise thousands of pounds or travel halfway around the globe to engage in meaningful conservation volunteering. Here are a few UK- and Ireland-based organisations dealing with local issues:

CENTRE FOR ALTERNATIVE TECHNOLOGY
☏ 01654 705953; ✉ courses@cat.org.uk; 🖰 www.cat.org.uk

The Centre for Alternative Technology (CAT) is part registered charity, part public limited company that aims to inform, inspire and enable positive environmental change. CAT is a pioneering research and demonstration centre that has established a worldwide reputation for demonstrating ecological technologies and lifestyles as well as running courses, publishing books, teaching at all levels and providing information and environmental consultancies.

Background
It was originally a community – founded by Gerard Morgan-Grenville in 1973 – dedicated to eco-friendly principles and a 'test bed' for new ideas and technologies. It has developed into a cutting-edge scientific organisation working with academics from all over the world.

Volunteer opportunities
Long-term volunteers work at CAT for six months, usually in a specific department gaining skills and experience in one area. Several CAT departments take on volunteers in areas which include engineering, building, information, biology and media. They run general courses on sustainable development, renewable energy, ecology, botany and wildlife, nature's larder and wilderness skills.

During summer and spring CAT runs a short-term volunteer programme where volunteers come for a week and experience life at the centre, usually working in the gardens and around the visitor centre with an emphasis on organic growing and sustainable woodlands.

Professionals such as electricians and plumbers come to CAT for week-long installers' courses on renewable energy. These include installing woodburners, photovoltaic systems, domestic solar heating, hydro-electricity, building a wind turbine, converting to bio-diesel, heat pumps and a host of eco-friendly building courses. They also run a number of postgraduate MSc courses covering renewable energy, environmental building and architecture.

Daily entry costs £6.40–8.40 with an eco-friendly 50% discount if you arrive by train. Every course is priced differently, so it depends on whether participants are high waged, waged or non-waged and whether it is a course for professional installers. A full-board weekend course costs around £140 (£60 tuition only), a week-long course around £500–800.

Demonstrable achievements

CAT's achievements include the creation of a centre for alternative technology long before it became fashionable, educating and training special groups, and opening up the whole issue of renewable resources to the public in an accessible way. As well as raising the research to an academic level, it also addresses the practical issues of applying knowledge by training professional installers in the practical methodology. It has produced dozens of scientific 'How to ...' books based on work at the centre.

CAT is open on a daily basis for visitors, there are also regular special event days and education officers provide tuition, discussion and tours so that visitors can make the most of their visit.

FLAT HOLM PROJECT

029 2035 3917; flatholmproject@cardiff.gov.uk; www.cardiff.gov.uk/flatholm

Flat Holm is an island off the Welsh coast and is a Site of Special Scientific Interest and a local nature reserve. It was established as a nature reserve in 1982, is a haven for wildlife including shelduck and slow worms, and home to one of the largest colonies of lesser black-backed gulls in Wales. Spring and summer bring a profusion of rare and interesting wild flowers.

Volunteer opportunities

The project employs a full-time warden (based on the island all year), two seasonal assistant wardens, two boat crew, an administrator and a project officer. There are opportunities for up to six volunteers at any one time on short-term placements of a few weeks, but a commitment of six months is ideal though not essential. Undergraduates can volunteer for up to a year as part of their university placement. There is no fee and volunteers get free board and basic accommodation as well as help with travel expenses and external training.

Volunteers get involved in all aspects of the day-to-day running of the island, including recording and monitoring wildlife, practical habitat management, stock care and control, leading guided tours for visitors, maintaining listed buildings, leading volunteer work parties and delivering education to school groups.

If full-time volunteering is too big a commitment, it is possible to become a member of the voluntary group – the Flat Holm Society – which is involved in many areas of the island's work including helping conduct guided tours and practical conservation work.

Demonstrable achievements

- The depleted maritime grassland home a host of rare species has been restored and protected on the northern side of the island, whilst the gull colony has been allowed to develop on the southern side.
- A number of other wildlife monitoring schemes have been developed

over the years including slow worm, butterfly (including canopy trapping), birds (including ringing), rabbits, invertebrates and shelduck.

- A renewable energy project was completed in 2006 including the installation of a wind turbine and two photovoltaic systems that now provide electricity for the main island buildings. In addition, solar water heating and biomass boiler systems were installed at both the farmhouse and Fog Horn Cottage, in preparation for its renovation and use. These new systems have reduced the reliance on diesel generators, which are now only used as a back-up.

IRISH SEAL SANCTUARY

☏ +35318354370; ✉ info@irishsealsanctuary.ie; ⌨ www.irishsealsanctuary.ie. The sanctuary is scheduled to move to new premises at the National Marine Conservation and Education Centre at Bremor, Bath Rd, Balbriggan, Co Dublin in late 2009, so check the website to see if the contact details have changed after this date.

The Irish Seal Sanctuary is Ireland's only full-time, wildlife rescue and rehabilitation facility covering all coastal areas. It is an NGO that primarily deals with sick or injured seals, but also assists with cetaceans and oil-spill-impaired seabirds. They are able to provide veterinary care for around 70–80 seals and they have an active programme of research and education.

Background
In 1987 Brendan and Mary Price started the Irish Seal Sanctuary in their back garden after regularly discovering foundling seals on their doorstep. Their belief is that before you can solve the big world problems such as climate change you must first respond to the problems on your own doorstep.

Volunteer opportunities
The sanctuary aims to recruit a minimum of four full-time resident volunteers per pupping season. There are two seasons per year, one starting in June (common seal) and the other in October (grey seal); both can last three–four months or longer.

A minimum of three months' commitment is ideal, but there are also places for 20 additional day volunteers. Previous experience of working with animals is preferable, but not essential. Volunteers will need their own transport; room and board can be arranged, but essentially volunteers need to be self-funded. Volunteers get involved in all aspects of the sanctuary's work including collecting sick animals, repair and maintenance, talking to the public, feeding duties and the high-profile seal releases. The Sanctuary's seal releases back into the wild have become one of Ireland's largest wildlife events, creating considerable media interest and providing a great opportunity to generate public support.

Demonstrable achievements

In total the sanctuary has been involved with the rescue and rehabilitation of around 700 seals. They are active campaigners for the protection of seals and other marine life and have recently employed an education officer to promote their work in schools and with the public.

NATIONAL TRUST

☏ 01793 817632; ✉ volunteers@nationaltrust.org.uk;
🖰 www.nationaltrust.org.uk/volunteering and www.nationaltrust.org.uk/

The National Trust is an independent charity established in 1895 because of concern about the impact of uncontrolled development and industrialisation. Then, as today, the trust acts as a guardian for the nation in the acquisition and protection of threatened coastline, countryside and buildings. Its preservation and protection work in England, Wales and Northern Ireland is carried out through practical caring and conservation, through learning and discovery and through encouraging visitors to enjoy their national heritage.

The National Trust for Scotland was established as an independent entity in 1931, but it operates on the same principles and purpose of its parent organisation. It is the largest conservation charity in Scotland.

Volunteer opportunities

There is a range of different types of volunteer opportunity and you can search for volunteering opportunities on both National Trust websites.

The National Trust runs around 450 working holidays at 100 locations every year throughout England, Wales and Northern Ireland as well as Scotland. Venues include coastal, woodland, countryside, farmland and historic buildings. They range from two to seven days and from £60 a week, which includes food and hostel-type accommodation, and domestic chores are always undertaken as a group.

There are full-time volunteering placements that assist wardens in a range of activities, including conserving properties, working on the land, and helping people to enjoy and understand them. This type of placement often suits countryside conservation, environmental or horticultural students. Depending on the location, this role could include woodland work, drystone walling, fence and gate building, working with volunteers and education groups, liaising with tenants, farmers, local communities and local authorities, conducting guided walks, erosion management and improving access for disabled visitors.

There are around 53,000 active volunteers that participate at every level of the Trust including room stewards and garden guides, as well as getting involved in different areas of practical conservation work, eg: scrub clearance, litter picking, clearing brambles, fencing, etc.

Demonstrable achievements

This multi-million pound charity is in a league of its own; massive in scale, wide ranging in its brief and with over a hundred years of experience, it is one of the most influential conservation organisations in the UK. It is the largest non-governmental landowner in the UK, managing over 250,000ha, of which approximately 80% is farmed. But unlike many other landowners, National Trust land is held in perpetuity for the benefit of the nation.

It looks at the big picture with campaigns on a range of issues and produces reports and comments at public inquiries and on white papers about proposals that could damage the natural environment. But it also organises innumerable practical projects like restoring the damaged peat resources of the High Peak by planting 7,000 cotton grass plants, which will help conserve a vital carbon store.

ROYAL BOTANIC GARDENS KEW
www.kew.org/aboutus/volunteers

Kew is the most renowned botanical garden in the world; it has one of the world's greatest collections of plants and houses over 35,000 specimens. Their scientific research includes developing a plant DNA barcode, a world seed bank, plants of economic and medical importance, and the promotion of biodiversity. It is a registered charity that relies on volunteers for a range of vital activities, including gardening, guiding, education and welcoming visitors.

Volunteer opportunities

Kew does not have long-term volunteering opportunities, but there are daily volunteers who work on a regular basis.

Kew regularly recruit volunteers to their horticultural volunteer programme which supports the work of gardens by helping with basic horticultural maintenance tasks such as planting, pruning, weeding and propagation. Opportunities are available from Monday to Friday, both outdoors and in the glasshouses.

Volunteers who are interested in plants but also want to work with people are especially welcome to help with plant maintenance and answer general visitor enquiries in the plant shop at Victoria Gate. Opportunities are available every day.

There are also other opportunities to work with school groups and disabled visitors. A new facility called Climbers and Creepers is a play area devoted to encouraging young children to become interested in plant/human relationships. A volunteer application form is available on the Kew website.

Demonstrable achievements

Kew's achievements are legion and include creating a globally significant seed bank with over a billion seeds aimed at preserving the planet's biodiversity. The massive gardens have become the most diverse concentration of plant species in the world.

It employs hundreds of scientists, many of which are still travelling the world looking for new species or monitoring the status of endangered habitats. Scientists are active in 40 different countries at any one time.

ROYAL SOCIETY OF THE PROTECTION OF BIRDS (RSPB)

☏ 01767 680551; ✉ (general enquiries) volunteers@rspb.org.uk, (residential bookings) vwsbookings@rspb.org.uk; ⦿ www.rspb.org.uk

The RSPB works for the conservation of biodiversity, especially wild birds and their habitats, as well as tackling the wider problems that threaten our environment. They are the largest wildlife conservation charity in Europe. Over 20,000 volunteers are involved in managing nature reserves, administration, scientific research and leading community-based adult and youth groups.

Volunteer opportunities

They have more than one million members, over 12,200 volunteers, 1,300 staff, 170 nature reserves, ten regional offices, four country offices and one vision – to work for a better environment rich in birds and wildlife. They run 200 nature reserves covering almost 130,000ha and home to 80% of our rarest and most threatened bird species.

It is possible to join one of the teams of volunteers that work all over the UK and help to create, manage and monitor habitats for birds and other wildlife. You could get involved in building stock fences and new hides, clearing paths for visitors, creating ponds for natterjack toads or dragonflies, planting hedges to attract nesting songbirds, putting up and monitoring nestboxes, guarding endangered species, animal surveys or helping in a visitors centre.

There is no fee for volunteering although overseas volunteers must register (£25) before applying. The RSPB provide volunteer accommodation and will reimburse any necessary expenses incurred while working on the reserve, but not transport to and from the site. The accommodation will be fairly basic but will have all the normal facilities, and volunteers must provide and cook their own food. Accident and liability insurance cover is provided whilst engaged in RSPB work. Volunteer placements can be for two weeks or more and there are also student or work experience placements of six months.

Alternatively, if you do not live near one of their nature reserves you can get involved in monitoring birds in your local area; either way contact ✉ volunteers@rspb.org.uk for further information.

Demonstrable achievements

- Completion of major land habitat deals and acquisitions in Lancashire, Scottish Highlands, north Wales, Kent and salt marshes on the River Dee.
- They were major players in stopping legal logging in Harapan Forest, Sumatra, Indonesia.

- Their 'Wildlife for All' project, with the Royal Parks, won an important National Charity Award.

Examples of projects

Wales

Ospreys are annual visitors to Wales on their migration from Africa. Records show they had never nested there until 2004, when a pair chose to nest near Porthmadog in the Glasyn Valley. Volunteers get involved with a 24-hour nest protection scheme operating during the breeding season, in three shifts of two people, and helping staff and volunteers talk to visitors, recruit members and interpret footage from the nest cameras.

Orkney

The farmland, wetlands and shoreline on the Orkney island of Egilsay is managed for corncrakes, waders and farmland birds. Another moorland reserve on the island of Rousay is managed for hen harriers, merlins and red-throated divers. Volunteers assist with survey work in spring and summer on both islands. Note that corncrake surveys take place at night. There will be lots of hands-on practical work on habitat management and estate work. Both work and weather can be tough.

Essex

The reserve at Old Hall Marshes, Maldon, Essex, is a working farm and one of the largest remaining coastal grazing marshes in the east. Its reedbeds and saltmarsh provide a refuge for breeding and wintering waders and wildfowl. Volunteers assist with physical management, livestock-related tasks as well as bird and non-avian monitoring.

TREES FOR LIFE

0845 6027386; rosie@treesforlife.org.uk; www.treesforlife.org.uk

Trees for Life is an award-winning Scottish charity working to restore the Caledonian Forest. The distinctive Caledonian Forest habitat, dominated by Scots pine, is substantially depleted and fragmented. Only 1% of the original forest remains and overgrazing by sheep and deer prevents its natural regeneration. These remnants need special care and protection; beyond this, the forest needs to be allowed to expand in area to secure this rich ecosystem for the future. They are planting around 100,000 trees every year and have a target of one million by 2010.

Volunteer opportunities

Each working week consists of ten volunteers aged 18 and over, with no upper age limit. The work can be physically challenging; sometimes reaching work sites can require long walks over rough terrain, so volunteers need to have a reasonable level of fitness to take part. However, volunteers usually find a pace of work they can cope with. There is also a gentler volunteer nursery week, located at the field base, for those who feel the regular working week may be too much for them.

Every work group is led by Trees for Life staff or trained volunteers. As well as tree planting, volunteers also get involved with removing old fences, cutting down non-native trees, survey work, seed collection and potting up saplings.

Transport is provided to and from Inverness at the start and end of the week and accommodation and food, including vegetarian and vegan options, is provided. Cooking and other chores are carried out on a voluntary rota basis. The week starts with a walk to introduce the volunteers to the forest and then on Sunday the work begins. Most working days run from around 09.00 to 17.00.

Fees start at £50 per week for an unwaged member to £100, although additional donations are encouraged if people can afford it. Volunteers are covered for public liability and limited personal accident cover. There are two tree-planting seasons, one from March to May and the other September to November.

Demonstrable achievements
To date they have planted over 700,000 trees, and have fostered the growth of many thousands more naturally regenerating seedlings.

A series of research papers have been written about some of the scientific work of the Caledonian reforestation project and many are available on their website.

Working in effective partnerships with organisations such as the RSPB and the Forestry Commission Scotland, Trees For Life invite volunteers to help deliver their programme of practical woodland regeneration, restoring a unique part of the UK's natural heritage.

URBAN CONSERVATION

Conservation in exotic locations has a whole host of attractions, but it is not necessary to go abroad or spend lots on money to engage in meaningful projects. There are many opportunities within the UK and Ireland for conservation, and usually it's not even necessary to go elsewhere within the UK. Very often there is a conservation issue that could be addressed within several hundred yards of where you live. It could be restoring derelict land, saving endangered green-field sites, growing organic food on an allotment in a wildlife-friendly way, or working on an organised urban regeneration project. Here are a few urban-based organisations that volunteers can engage with on their home turf.

FEDERATION OF CITY FARMS AND COMMUNITY GARDENS
℡ 0117 9231 800; ✉ admin@farmgarden.org.uk; 🖱 www.farmgarden.org.uk

City Farms and Community Gardens are locally based projects working with people, animals and plants. This is not a national organisation; each one is unique and they are, or aim to become, community led and managed projects that work with a sustainable ethos. Most are dependent on volunteers for their survival and development, as they often only have a few, if any, paid staff.

They would suit city based volunteers who do not have the time to run their own allotment, but would like to get in touch with the natural world and work with other people on a communal project. For a list of local city farms check the website or call the number above.

GROUNDWORK
℡ 0121 236 8565; ✉ info@groundwork.org.uk; 🖱 www.groundwork.org.uk

Groundwork started in the late 1970s when the Countryside Commission was looking for ways to improve the physical environment of the urban fringe – the 'no man's land' on the edge of towns and cities that was often overlooked and tended to become run-down and derelict.

Groundwork (formerly Groundwork Foundation) has become a leading environmental regeneration charity that works in every region of the UK from small community schemes to major regional and national programmes. Their network of over 40 local trusts works in partnership with local people, local authorities and businesses to promote economic and social regeneration by improving the local environment.

Groundwork trusts regularly involve volunteers, especially people seeking work experience before moving into full-time paid employment. The type of volunteering opportunities available will depend on the types of projects being run by individual trusts. Identify your local branch from the central website and contact them about local opportunities.

NATIONAL SOCIETY OF ALLOTMENT AND LEISURE GARDENERS

www.nsalg.org.uk

The National Society of Allotment and Leisure Gardeners aims to protect, promote and preserve allotment gardening.

Urban allotments are potentially much more than pottering about in the garden. They have a long tradition of self-sufficiency, some lead the way on organic growing and in some urban areas they may be a rare green space that has become a major habitat or a crucial transit route for native wildlife.

Allotments are major targets for building developers, and councils often see them as 'wasted space' that can bring in some easy cash. It is vital that people take up available allotments in their area to prevent them becoming part of our asphalt and concrete jungle. They provide city-dwellers with great opportunities to learn about nature and sample food that is fresher than anything found in the supermarket.

WILDLIFE TRUSTS

☎ 0870 036 7711; ✉ volunteer@wildlife-trusts.cix.co.uk;
🖰 www.wildlifetrusts.org

The network of 47 Wildlife Trusts work together with local communities to protect wildlife in all types of habitat across the UK, including towns, countryside, wetlands and coastal waters.

Volunteer opportunities

The Wildlife Trusts are a membership organisation whose volunteers carry out a wide range of tasks, including developing and maintaining community gardens, biodiversity surveys, focused species protection, practical and scientific work in nature reserves, and running Wildlife Watch groups to enable young people to discover and explore their local environment.

Opportunities don't always have to be outdoors; Trusts also need volunteers to assist with general organisation, computers, finance and administrative work. Volunteers are the foundation upon which the Wildlife Trust movement has been built and people's time is an integral part of the partnership's success. There are 765,000 Wildlife Trust members, each has a large number of regular and casual volunteers, equating to more than 24,000 active volunteers across the whole of the Wildlife Trust Partnership.

Demonstrable achievements

They are very proactive in preserving all aspects of the natural world and are now responsible for 2,200 nature reserves across the UK; some of these they own and some they manage for others. They regularly hold fundraising initiatives to help purchase additional wildlife-rich land that comes onto the market, especially if it is at risk of being developed or destroyed.

Their prime purpose in managing reserves is the conservation or restoration of wildlife habitats and they are keen for local people to have the opportunity to share in their beauty. There is no commercialism and nature reserves are considered to be places where wildlife is protected for its own sake, and this often means continuing or restoring the old-time practices, which made them rich in the first place.

In addition to creating more nature reserves the Trusts are also campaigning organisations. Currently my branch is campaigning against a massive new town development at Weston Otmoor, Oxfordshire, which plans to site a park-and-ride scheme for 6,000 cars on a floodplain. It also happens to be an ancient and rare water meadow already listed as a Site of Special Scientific Interest (SSSI).

These Trusts not only help preserve and restore what little is left of our countryside; they are also one of the few voices that can speak out with authority and stand up to developers and government agencies that show little understanding of the future problems they are creating and what they are so keen on destroying. Visit their website to identify your local Wildlife Trust and find out how you can help conserve the nature on your doorstep.

5 WHAT IS LIFE LIKE AS A CONSERVATION VOLUNTEER?

This chapter contains a series of articles about conservation volunteer expeditions that I have been on whilst writing this book. They explore life as a volunteer, working on a range of conservation projects in Greece, England, Namibia, Seychelles and in the rainforest of the Peruvian Amazon.

They highlight the difference between the rose-tinted fantasy while sitting at home browsing through brochures or reading the gushing superlatives on the web and waking up at dawn, stiff after yesterday's work, slipping and sliding through the dripping rainforest looking for secretive animals, or maybe just the telltale signs of their passing.

PROTECTING LOGGERHEAD TURTLES IN GREECE WITH ARCHELON

I arrived in Rethymno, on northern Crete, to find the deserted beaches of the 1970s had become a highly developed tourist area.

This is the same problem that maturing loggerhead turtles are encountering: having hatched on a relatively deserted beach 30 years ago they return to find the same shores lined with hotels, bars and tavernas – not to mention thousands of sunbathers.

Archelon's conservation programme works to protect loggerhead turtles – which are classified as endangered on the IUCN (World Conservation Union) Red List – at all stages of development, but particularly during the hatching season.

At sea, adult turtles are hunted as tourist trophies, deliberately killed by fishermen who think they eat the fish, or accidentally caught in their nets; they are also injured by speedboats, poisoned by pollution, and choked by plastic bags and bottles mistaken for jellyfish. However, it's the threats posed during the early stages of egg laying and hatching that are having the biggest detrimental effect on population numbers.

Normally, each year between June and August female loggerheads crawl ashore at Rethymno to nest, at night, at the same beaches on which they originally hatched. However, between 2000 and 2007 the number of nests on Crete declined from 500

to 162. Researchers believe it's because nesting females arrive to find their path blocked by abandoned sun loungers or are deterred by bright lights, loud music and wandering tourists, and they return to the sea without laying.

Similar problems plague the hatchlings when they emerge from the nests between August and October. Some lack the strength to breakthrough the sand compacted by beach sweepers, and those that do emerge are attracted up the beach towards the lights and music vibrations of the bars and clubs instead of towards the sea. Those that do are often too tired to retrace their steps and subsequently die.

Archelon volunteers help out by

carrying out night patrols during the nesting season, dawn patrols during the hatching season, assisting in the rescue and rehabilitation centre and educating tourists with information and slide shows.

When I and the other 15 volunteers (mainly aged 18–25) arrived, we were instructed to set up our tents and sleeping bags by the project leaders, Simon and Charlotte. Camp was a basic affair:

pungent drop toilets, no electricity and unheated showers. Our dining area was simply a table under a tarp, but the open-air kitchen had running water and bottled gas stove burners. We were all assigned camp chores such as cleaning, shopping and cooking.

Next morning, Simon rattled my tent at 06.15 for my first dawn beach patrol. Eight of us crammed into the old minibus and were dropped off in pairs to survey different sections of the eight-mile beach. It was September, so all nesting had finished; protecting the nests and hatchlings was the main priority.

All known nests were marked with blue and yellow cages and each had to be checked for signs of hatching. New turtle tracks were recorded and followed to see if they reached the sea or had wandered off in the wrong direction; areas between nests were also checked for any unmarked nests.

At 10.00 the teams got together to pool data – which was later entered onto a database – and to debrief the leaders.

On one patrol I discovered a nest surrounded by tourists from a nearby hotel. They were trampling over the nesting area, blinding hatchlings with camera flashlights, blocking their access to the sea and attempting to pick them up – all potentially disastrous.

Our Archelon T-shirts gave us some measure of authority when asking tourists to refrain from interfering with the hatchlings, but it was a constant effort. We urged disorientated hatchlings seawards by pushing sand mounds in front of them until they moved in the right direction. We never touched them and all assistance was by minimising hazards and aiding orientation. As the sun rose we shaded them with beach mats to prevent them overheating. There was a frisson of excitement as each tiny turtle reached the water's edge and swam off; eventually all 18 hatchlings reached the sea under their own steam.

Another important aspect of the work involves increasing awareness about the turtles among tourists and hotel beach workers. Every morning the team visits a different beachside hotel to run an after-breakfast awareness-raising exhibition, and in the evening the team returns to host a follow-up slide show for the guests. We also had to take turns manning the town centre information kiosk.

Evenings were spent arguing about favourite music and films around a scrap-timber campfire, or having a few beers at the local Platanes music bar. Days off were spent exploring nearby villages, taking an afternoon siesta, sunbathing on the beach, or exploring the castle and shops of Rethymno.

Every year Archelon protects over 2,500 nests against human threats and predation; around 300 turtles are tagged and their migration monitored and over 50 injured sea turtles are treated at the rescue centre annually. It's comforting to know that without our efforts many of the hatchlings wouldn't have made it; we really made a difference.

See page 45 for organisation audit.

STRAW-BALE HOUSE BUILDING WITH THE BRITISH TRUST FOR CONSERVATION VOLUNTEERS

The fairytale of the three little pigs has given straw a bad name as a building material of choice. But it turns out that straw-bale houses are not a fairytale, a third-world concept, or a New Age fad, but a product of the industrial revolution developed by 19th-century pioneers in America. The invention of the baling machine meant that prairie grasses could be turned into a good substitute for the Midwest's absence of timber and building stone.

Straw-bale buildings have an incredibly low environmental impact: they can be produced cheaply from renewable resources; have phenomenal insulation properties; require 75% less energy to heat; and are virtually soundproof compared to their modern alternatives. Unlike traditional building materials, which are responsible for producing half of the industrial sector's carbon dioxide output, straw creates a carbon *deficit* by locking carbon dioxide into the fabric of the building.

The British Trust for Conservation Volunteers (BCTV) run eco-house building projects that use these very methods to create an environmentally sustainable building with an extremely low carbon footprint. I joined a project in

North Yorkshire to see what it was all about.

In keeping with the project, our accommodation was a straw-bale building complete with kitchen, shower and hygienic compost toilets. You'd never have known the building was constructed from straw bales if your attention hadn't been drawn to it. The building was large and cosy but lacked residential facilities, so we slept on mattresses or airbeds on the floor. Our two volunteer leaders stocked the kitchen generously with food supplies, but we were still in charge of doing our own catering.

Our work schedule was from 09.00 to 17.00 and after a lecture by architect adviser, Friederike Fuchs, on the building technology and a health and safety talk by the BTCV leaders we donned our boiler suits and trooped over to the building site.

Previous groups had completed most of the building, so we were given the task of constructing the final wall. The timber frame, foundations and a damp-proof membrane were already in place so our task was straightforward wall building using the bales, which had arrived straight from the fields. The process is akin to bricklaying: bales are cut to fit the remaining space at the end of a row and vertical joints are staggered for extra strength.

After five rows the bales are checked for perpendicular accuracy; at this point the wall is pliable and could easily be pushed over. Wooden planks are laid on top and two sets of webbing wrapped around from top to bottom. These are linked with a ratchet and tightened to compress the bales vertically. The planks are screwed into the timber frame to retain the compression and the webbing removed – the wall is now as solid as brick. The compression also squeezes out the air so the bales contain little oxygen and therefore burn less readily.

On the third day, we started the process of sealing the straw walls with lime render.

This part of the process also increases the carbon deficit: the limestone is heated to 900°C which drives out the carbon dioxide leaving calcium oxide, this is then carefully mixed with water to create slaked lime. As the slaked lime dries it takes back carbon dioxide from the atmosphere, releasing water and returning to its original hard limestone form.

Wearing overalls, rubber gloves and goggles we smeared a mixture of sand and the pliable slaked lime onto the walls, working it into the straw so it would provide a strong bond between the straw and subsequent layers of lime mortar. When we were done the building was completely water and fireproof.

The project was an excellent example of how you don't have to travel to far-flung places to make a difference. I found the alternative technology amazing to experience first hand; I hadn't realised how ingenious, yet obvious, it was to lock up carbon within the building process. It seems the first little pig may have been on to something after all.

See page 108 for organisation audit

MARINE CONSERVATION IN THE SEYCHELLES WITH GLOBAL VISION INTERNATIONAL

Standing knee deep in the warm waters of the Indian Ocean off Praslin, I can see Curieuse island, an old leper colony that will soon be home for the next few days.

I'm in the Seychelles on a marine conservation expedition. Along with a team of 20 other international volunteers on either five- or ten-week rotations, I will be measuring the health of the coral, the diversity of fish species in the reefs, tagging turtles and searching for whale sharks. The data is collected for the Seychelles Marine Conservation Society and Seychelles Fisheries Authority, so they can draw up plans for areas that need to be protected.

First, however, we need to undergo training. Most of the project time is spent at Cap Ternay – the main base on Mahé Island. Here volunteers are taught how to dive, take care of our equipment and refill scuba tanks; learn the identification markings that distinguish one species from another so we can accurately identify the key coral and fish species; and attending after-dinner lectures on marine topics. Volunteers are not permitted to collect data until they achieve a 95% accuracy rate in classroom and underwater identification tests.

Diving starts on day one, but it's not until we've all made the grade that we start collecting dive data at various reef locations around Cap Ternay. However, the highlight of the trip is the week spent on

Curieuse Island. Rich, who is the base manager of this satellite camp, has lived on the virtually uninhabited island for almost a year – the only other resident is 'Mama', who has lived there for 23 years.

Rich has converted a ramshackle hut into habitable quarters with a fully functioning kitchen. Rough tree trunks support the veranda roof, reclaimed boards line the new deck and shutters prop open the space where windows might have been. Water is collected from a fast-flowing stream and funnelled to the kitchen taps but has to be boiled before use. Sitting on the veranda later, he reveals his only complaint is that, 'beach holidays are now ruined for me – I'll never find anywhere as perfect as Curieuse'.

Here, in addition to building the fish database and surveying the coral reefs and measuring their recovery from bleaching, we are charged with several other tasks. Depending on the season, volunteers collect plankton samples, monitor populations of octopus, sea cucumbers and crabs, protect the nests of hawksbill, loggerhead and leatherback turtles during nesting season, and going whale shark spotting on the boats to add to the database the Seychelles Marine Conservation Society are compiling on their migration patterns.

Of course it's not all work. One day we go and visit the 250 free-roaming giant tortoises that call Curieuse home. They were hunted to extinction in the mid-19th century, but after the creation of the Curieuse Marine Park in 1979 plans were made to reintroduce them. Breeding pairs were brought from the southern Seychelles atoll of Aldabra and protective pens built so the young don't get eaten by crabs or rats. The population in now building strongly, and was thankfully saved from decimation during the 2004 tsunami. Jason, the island ranger, tells us that on the morning of 24 December 2004 he went down to the beach only to discover all the giant tortoises were missing; they had all moved to high ground. Two days later the tsunami struck.

Another day, we explored the mangrove swamps, hiked across the island to Anse Badamier and spent the afternoon lazing on its pristine beach and drinking fresh coconut milk from husks hacked open using Rich's machete.

Volunteering gives a whole new perspective to nature. You're able to see and touch what tourists miss and contribute in a meaningful way to the preservation of the habitats you visit. Your fee also allows you to give something back long after your stay ends: a percentage of the project fees go towards providing scholarship places for a few young Seychellois on the GVI programme and sponsoring environmental education programmes with local schools.

See page 89 for organisation audit

'Always carry the two-way radio, the poison-bite extraction kit, and two litres of water and you should be alright.' That was the first piece of advice expedition leader Peter Schuette gave on day one of my leopard and cheetah conservation project in Namibia.

Our group of 12 international volunteers had assembled at the attractive Casa Piccolo bed and breakfast in central Windhoek, before being whisked away in a convoy of four Land Rovers to Okomitundu Farm – our home for the next two weeks.

On reaching our base, Peter's words of wisdom became clear: Okomitundu is a 70-square-mile farm located 75 miles northwest of Namibia's capital, Windhoek. It's a vast untamed savanna covered with grass, acacia, thorn trees and dotted with conical hills of crumbling sandstone and dry riverbeds that occasionally flow with flash floods. It's lush during the short rainy season, but arid and harsh during the rest of the year. From October to April it's mainly hot and dry; temperatures average 40°C, but the low humidity makes things bearable.

Facilities on the farm were exceptional: rooms were large and airy twin shares, there was a bathroom with hot showers, and to top it off we had two small swimming pools, a bar and meeting facilities. Breakfast, lunch, afternoon coffee and dinner were prepared by local cooks and eaten al fresco.

Namibia has the world's largest population of cheetahs and it's estimated that 90% of them live in farming areas. The inevitable conflict with humans has resulted in large numbers being captured or shot. They do kill livestock, but the extent of losses and financial damage to the farmers is not really known. The Namibian cheetah is a fascinating flagship species but its ecology is poorly understood and this makes conservation difficult.

Our job, therefore, was to track leopards and cheetahs previously fitted with radio collars, capture new animals, identify and count tracks, and record prey species.

In order to do that we were taught how to identify animal scat (excrement) and recognise spoor (footprints) of the species we were tracking. All this data would then be put towards mapping population density and distribution, as well as recording the animals' health status. Once these factors had been determined it would be easier to develop a new conservation strategy.

Out first task, however, was to learn how to drive off-road in one of the hardy Land Rovers. 'When driving the 4x4 on a dry riverbed use the low stick, never dip the clutch, keep the revs up, and if you get stuck use the diff lock', shouted Peter. It was all very disconcerting at first; driving in old sand ruts was like driving on ice and freshly-blown sand felt like glue beneath the tyres. Before long though we'd mastered the basics and were climbing up 45° hillsides of rock and loose stones with ease.

Now we were ready to be let loose in the field, so at 06.30 the next morning we joined Harald and Brigit Forster, the project scientists (who have been studying big cats in Namibia for the past nine years) and interns for quick cup of tea and a packed breakfast, before loading all the scientific instruments into the 4x4s and barrelling off down the dusty bush tracks.

First of all we had to check the box traps to see if any cats had wandered into them overnight, but all we found were unwanted baboons, warthogs and a small but fearsome honey badger, so after setting them free we moved on to our second task of locating and counting the prey species of the big cats.

However, this was easier said than done. On game farms animals are free to roam at will and because they're not habituated to people or cars they will scatter when disturbed. As we rattled around in the back of the 4x4s trying to look through binoculars and scribble notes on our data sheets, it was invariably the Kalahari Bushman – not us – who spotted the animals first. Piet would just point at a clump of bushes and shout 'kudu' and I would frantically scan the area only to see a rump bounding away through the scrub.

The counts improved as the days

passed. The best was 76 animals when we saw oryx, kudu, hartebeest, wildebeest, warthog, jackal, zebra, springbok, steenbok, mongoose, baboon, snake eagle and a range of lizards. On other days we spotted ostrich and giraffe, but the prize sighting was a leopard sitting on a rock watching us as we drove past. We took the telemetry radio tracking equipment out with us the next day to try and find her again and on our third attempt were able to pinpoint her location; she was hiding near the top of a rocky outcrop and although we couldn't see her we were sure she was watching us.

On other occasions we set out of foot when tracking. Then we relied predominately on the skills of the bushmen. It was enthralling to watch them looking for indicators, such as bent grass, fur or scat, and then guessing the direction the leopard might have taken. Our longest track was over one and a half miles before it was finally lost on a rocky outcrop. I was somewhat relieved that we never actually came across a leopard while on foot.

Another – easier – task was waterhole observation, which involved sitting in a hide or on a rocky outcrop at dawn and dusk and monitoring the animals that came to the waterhole to drink. It was fascinating to observe the behaviour of the various species:
zebra would wait in the bush and then approach in small groups, get spooked, race away and return ten minutes later before repeating the whole process again; baboon troops approached the waterhole like a disciplined group of soldiers, with the large alpha male staying at the back and marshalling the others forward; whilst warthogs were very brazen and approached the water without fear, trotting off when they had drunk their fill.

Towards the end of our stay our scientist, Harald, reiterated the inter-connectedness of the problems associated with cheetah and leopard conservation. 'We can't live in an idealistic bubble,' he told us, as he explained the practical economics of African farming. 'Traditional cattle farmers kill wild game that they see as competitors for limited grazing; they would also kill leopard and cheetah as predators of their herds.'

Game farms permit limited trophy hunting which give native species a value, this in turn encourages game farmers to support wild game by digging watering holes. Harald's explanation seemed unsavoury, but he emphasised that it has resulted in a 70% increase in game species, which has enabled cheetah and leopard populations to return. Any solution to the conservation problem then, also needs to take into account the needs of the local communities.

This trip made it clear to me that conservation is far more complicated than just protecting endangered animals; the reason they are endangered has to be addressed. Local people need to make a living and the really practical solution is to help those in competition with wildlife to make a sustainable living in partnership with their environment. If local people are not intimately involved in any conservation solution it will fail.

See page 52 for organisation audit

AMAZON WILDLIFE CONSERVATION BY RIVERBOAT WITH EARTHWATCH INSTITUTE

There can't be many people who aren't enthralled by the Amazon. There's its vastness, its incomparable and exotic wildlife, the existence of undiscovered tribes, Inca gold and an indefinable magical ambience. It's a place of adventures, mysteries, lost cities, Amazonian warriors, fearsome creatures, magical cures, despotic invaders and greedy businessmen exploiting its people and resources.

Flying is the only way to reach the jungle-locked city of Iquitos – our assembly point for the project – and as we cruise above the rainforest, passengers are treated to an illusory image of film-set tidiness: it looks like a uniformly green carpet that snails have left a

meandering silvery trail across. But then you spot an ugly bald patch and you begin to get some idea of the exploitation of natural resources going on here.

At Iquitos we are met by our science leader, Dr Richard Bodmer, who leads us to our home for the next 16 days – a colonial riverboat named *Ayapua* left over from the rubber-boom era. Together with14 other volunteers, I will survey river dolphins, macaws, caimans, giant otters, monkeys and fish. The dolphins and macaws are used to monitor the health of the aquatic and terrestrial habitats; monkeys, otters, caimans, and fish, are used to monitor the impact of hunting, fishing, logging and recent oil and gas exploration up river; and the fish are being used as key indicator species to determine the success of current conservation initiatives.

The research site is the unmapped conservation concession Lago Preto, 350 miles down the Amazon to Santa Rosa at the Peruvian-Columbian-Brazilian border and then 250 miles up the Yavari River into deepest Amazonia. After four days of puttering down the Amazon's mid-channel – where a constant breeze keeps the mosquitoes at bay – we dock amid clouds of bugs at our destination.

Lago Preto was established after Richard discovered a troop of rare and endangered red uakari monkeys, and it's this species we try to locate on our first foray into the palm swamps by the Yavari River.

The rainforest is hard going. The humidity is close to 90%. Every item of clothing is sopping wet within 15 minutes and rivulets of sweat, unable to evaporate, run down into boots and drip off extremities. Surface tree roots are everywhere: on a slope they are a boon, acting as useful steps in the slippery mud, but on level ground they become a minefield of traps where one careless step can send you sprawling. Vines and lianas hang everywhere. Miniature bogs grip and suck at your boots, making

revolting noises as you struggle to keep them on. I grasp instinctively at trees to balance myself but find super-fine prickles lodged in my palm.

The red uakari monkeys are constantly on the move but we eventually find them. High up in the tree canopy the troop stop to observe us. Some turn their backs and show us their stumpy tails, as if they're mooning; others come down for a closer look and lob a few sticks at us.

Thanks to the added protection their numbers have increased from 150 to several hundred. However, their larger numbers have also made them more brazen and as a result populations of woolly and howler monkeys are in decline because they compete for the same foodstuffs as the red uakari monkeys.

Trekking back to the boat we pass a tree with great buttress roots gouged with jaguar claw marks and a freshly dug Armadillo den. High in the tree canopy, birds squawk amongst epiphytic ferns and bromeliads. Some old rubber trees still have the V-shaped grooves made a century ago by local Indians harvesting the latex.

After trekking through this wild and uninhabited part of the rainforest, arriving back at the boat is a surreal experience. Instead of the usual conservation volunteer base camp – where you only have a damp tent to look forward to and a string of domestic chores that need to be completed before you can eat – the *Ayapua* is like a floating palace in the wilderness. The boat has been fully restored and enhanced as a passenger and research vessel with the charm and splendour more reminiscent of the Orient Express than an Amazonian riverboat. I have my own cabin, with a shower, and the cook has made tea and cakes to welcome us back.

Next morning I sign up for the more leisurely river dolphin survey that involves floating downriver in one of the auxiliary boats and counting the pink and grey river dolphins we encounter, recording their position and behavioural traits. We count six, which is a little disappointing as there were usually a dozen swimming around the *Ayapua*.

The next few days are spent studying the many oxbow lakes found around Largo Preto. They are valuable nursery grounds for river fish because of the lack of predators, they are popular hunting grounds for the local fishermen who come to find the very tasty giant paiche (*Arapaima gigas*) – one of the world's largest freshwater fish, which can grow up to 15ft and weigh 440lb.

A fish research project involves monitoring three lakes: one allows fishing, one is strongly protected and the other allows occasional fishing. Abundance is measured as 'catch per unit effort', ie: how many fish can be caught in one hour.

We canoe out onto the lake and lay nets to see how many and what type of fish are caught in one hour. While we wait our field guide, Philippe, sends me back to the river bank to fish with a 6ft stick, a hook and line.

Every time I cast there is an instantaneous bite and the bait is eaten. My second cast, just 5ft from the shore hooks an eight-inch white piranha and I screech like a child as it swings towards my face. Fortunately our ichthyologist, Mike Walkey, is on hand and expertly takes it off the hook, records the details and returns it to the lake.

Later, we haul in the nets and find three dozen fish of eight different species. Surprisingly our research revealed that in the lakes where no fishing is allowed biodiversity drops because the top predator fish – the paiche – is voraciously eating the smaller species, so it seems that local fishermen actually help maintain the level of biodiversity.

The project combined the rough with the smooth perfectly. I was nervous of roughing it in the jungle and camping in a soggy environment with countless insects for company, but the *Ayapua* provided pampered living conditions whilst allowing me to still experience the rainforest and contribute towards the work of experienced local scientists.

See page 71 for organisation audit.

ASSESSING BIODIVERSITY IN THE AMAZON

Rebecca Joshua

One of the most memorable experiences of my trip to the Peruvian Amazon comes from an activity I wasn't expecting to enjoy. I'd been fascinated by wildlife since childhood but for some reason fish had never managed to capture my imagination, unless they exploded out of the ocean to claw back helpless prey in a blur of jagged jaws. Nonetheless, coaxed by the expectation of piranha, I spent a morning with a team conducting a fish census at Lake Ipiranga.

Completely exposed to the equatorial sun our Peruvian field guide Sergio and I set out by canoe to cast fishing nets. The heat seemed to have subdued even the most attentive insects and I cautiously wondered just how many and what sort of fish were swimming in the still, murky water beneath us. An hour later we returned and found the nets partially shredded – evidence of a covert band of giant river otters in the vicinity. In an attempt to be useful, I took over paddling while Sergio pulled in the catch. Every section of the net Sergio raised was like a street vendor's display of just how varied and intriguing even 'mere fish' can be. There were large whiskered varieties, smaller smooth ones and of course several piranhas. Some unlucky ones had been partially eaten by piranha while caught in the net and one large tiger catfish grunted as it thrashed about in the canoe. We collected over two dozen fish and I found myself surprisingly enchanted by the creatures wriggling at my feet. I was glad, however, to be able to hand the paddle back to Sergio becaue every muscle, from the palms to the nape of my neck, was pulsating with heat and exhaustion.

Back on shore, the whole team carefully identified, measured and weighed the fish, before releasing them back into the water. Completely absorbed in my task of transferring slippery specimens from bucket to weighing basket, I only gradually became aware that the constant chorus of sounds from the surrounding forest had gained a new voice. On the other side of the lake, a group of howler monkeys were making their presence known. As I rinsed my hands in the shallow water at the edge of the lake, I sensed that the pervasive smell of fish, wet mud and the hollow roar of the monkeys were all imprinting themselves on my memory forever.

Rebecca Joshua travelled with the Earthwatch Institute on their Amazon riverboat conservation expedition to Peru

6 FUNDRAISING

By now, you've decided which conservation project you want to participate in, but have perhaps realised you don't have enough funds to finance the trip. This chapter is dedicated entirely to fundraising, and covers how to write the perfect sponsor letter or press release, the rules and regulations of fundraising events, and how to approach the local media for support.

Fundraising can be fun, but it needs organisation, diligence and considerable effort. It's now big business and competition for other people's charitable donations is fierce. You'll be competing with large charities who routinely employ professional fundraisers, so you need to be imaginative (see box on page 176 for ideas).

It's essential to approach fundraising in a professional manner; as well as distinguishing yourself from the competition; you also need to make it clear you're not a scammer, scrounger or racketeer. Make sure you have already raised some of the funding by your own efforts in order to show your personal commitment to the cause.

PLANNING

- Draw up an action plan and discuss it with as many people as possible, especially anyone who has done fundraising before.
- Before doing anything else, first write down exactly what you will be doing, why it is worth doing, when you plan to do it and how much you need to raise. If you are not crystal clear and persuasive no-one will give you a bean (see box on page 174).
- Credibility is important so choose projects run by registered charities or not-for-profit organisations – and always quote their registration number. It may be possible for sponsors to pay donations directly to the conservation organisation on your behalf.
- Clarify the details of what your chosen project has already achieved and produce a leaflet, no bigger than two sides of A4, with the whys and wherefores (see box on page 175).
- Mobilise the internet: Just Giving (*www.justgiving.com*) enables you to set up a charity fundraising account and describe the importance of your project. Include photographs that can bring the project to life. Donors can pay into your fundraising account over the web and see how much has been raised by other donors. Donations may also attract 28% 'Gift Aid' if donors are taxpayers. Email friends and relatives around the globe and direct them to your account. Just Giving charge a 5% service fee on donations, but this is more than offset by their reclaiming the Gift Aid tax concession on your behalf.
- Keep a separate savings account so all project fundraising is clearly accounted for.

DOS AND DON'TS OF FUNDRAISING

DOS

✔ Do start where you are: Who do you already know? Do you know someone who works in a large company that might sponsor you? Could they raise sponsorship from colleagues?

✔ Do be passionate, but above all else be clear and concise in order to generate the best response.

✔ Do be focused with any company you approach. Think: why should they sponsor you? What's in it for them? A furniture company might be more responsive to rainforest projects, pet supplies to animal rescue, etc.

✔ Do try medium-sized local companies (approach the marketing manager or someone dealing with PR or the media). If you have agreed newspaper coverage offer to name them as a sponsor.

✔ Do offer sponsors something in return eg: publicity, a blog for their website, a story for their newsletter, a talk to a staff group.

✔ Do ask for specific donations, but don't stick rigidly to them. Asking for a specific amount will give your donors a helpful benchmark.

DON'TS

✗ Don't cold call big companies and corporations, it is rarely successful; they're likely to have some form of corporate giving scheme already in place.

✗ Don't send out untargeted circulars or emails; there are far too many email scams for anyone to respond to these and they will probably be deleted as spam. Always address people correctly; telephone the receptionist for accurate details. If you get someone's name, title or role wrong you have already reduced your chances of success.

✗ Don't just focus on cash donations; retailers are more likely to donate items as prizes for subsequent fundraising events.

CHARITABLE TRUSTS

There are a number of charitable trusts whose purpose is to give away money to appropriate causes. Most want to fund large enterprises, but a number will potentially fund individuals on a worthy mission. Check out the

Directory of Grant Making Trusts, published by the Charities Aid Foundation and available to consult in many local libraries. Institutions worth approaching are:

Ogden Trust (🖰 *www.ogdentrust.com / news.22.htm*)
Rotary Club (🖰 *www.ribi.org*)
Kirk Fund (🖰 *www.kirkfund.org.uk*)
Overseas Travel Grants (🖰 *www.epsrc.ac.uk*)
Association of Charitable Funds (🖰 *www.acf.org.uk*)
Winston Churchill Memorial Foundation (🖰 *www.wcmt.org.uk*)
Trustfunding (🖰 *www.trustfunding.org.uk*)
Grants on Line (🖰 *www.grantsonline.org.uk*).

You will need to plan well in advance to access these funds and expect to fill out plenty of forms, attend an interview and provide feedback from your trip. You need to target the appropriate fund whose objectives most closely match your plans, make sure your plans are tightly focused and have clear worthy, charitable objectives.

GETTING PUBLICITY IN YOUR LOCAL MEDIA

- Local newspapers often have a community page so write up your project as a story. Be sure to cover what it's about, why it's important, where is it, when is it happening, why you want to do it, etc, then contact a local reporter on the paper and convince them this is an interesting story worth writing about – offer to send an ongoing email diary and photographs.
- Don't send the newspaper a general circular and do not bother the editor. It is more effective to contact a local reporter – let them write it up as their story; this will give them an incentive to push the editor to run it.
- Local radio stations are often keen for something local and different. Plan exactly what you are going to say before telephoning. The more unusual, exciting and interesting you make it sound the more likely they are to be interested. Contact the local news department and explain in no more than one minute exactly what you are doing and what you want. They will want you to follow up with a briefing sheet, so get their specific email address. Include what you hope to achieve, ie: are you asking for sponsorship, publicising a fundraising event, or offering to come in and talk about the project on-air?
- Local television stations might be interested in an extremely wacky fundraising stunt or event especially during the summer 'silly season' when they are looking for newsworthy stories. Bear in mind they are notoriously unreliable for small local stories and will drop you like a stone if a more interesting story crops up.

SPECIMEN LETTER CONTENT

Make your approach letter as personal and as directly relevant to the recipient as possible – if it looks like a mass circulation it's likely to head straight for the bin. Remember that financial scams are now so commonplace that most people are weary of unsolicited correspondence. Scams are characteristically generalised, not directed at named individuals, are mass circulations and exhibit little knowledge about the organisation or person concerned, so make sure you don't fit the scammer's profile. The template below gives you an idea of how to approach it.

Your full address
Telephone number
Email address
Website if available
Date

Recipient's full address

Dear [Title and name of recipient]

Title and purpose of the project

The letter must never run beyond one side of paper.

Opening: two–three lines outlining the conservation issue and why it's important.

A few lines explaining who you are and what it is you are planning to do, eg: tasks you will be doing and the benefits likely to accrue from your volunteering. Include dates of departure and any other deadlines.

Why you believe the project is important. Any relevant experience you have that's related to the project or the issue If you don't have any, then discuss why have you chosen this project. Include additional information about yourself, your background and why you personally want to do this. Does it relate to your future career plans or anything else that will indicate it is not just a one-off jolly?

About four lines of additional background about the project that emphasise its worth. Use some impressive data from a credible source, or a quote, and make it relevant to the recipient.

Include a few lines about how much money are you trying to raise and what efforts you have already made towards your target. What assistance are you seeking? State a cash amount, or suggest a donation of gift items for prizes in a specified fundraising event.

What's in it for them? Explain what their donation will mean for you achieving your overall aim. Reinforce your credibility by offering something in return – putting their logo or a thank you on your website, sharing your diary or blog about the project, maybe writing or sending photographs for a company newsletter.

Thank you for considering my request and I look forward to your reply.

Yours sincerely
Signature

Your name in full
Enc: promotional leaflet

PROMOTIONAL LEAFLET

Think about how you propose to use a promotional leaflet. It is a good idea to make it multi-functional, ie: as content for your website, content for a 'Just Giving' fundraising web page, an attachment to emails, or enclosure with letters requesting a donation. It can also act as a press release when trying to generate local newspaper interest or a wider unspecified audience. This means it needs to be interesting, comprehensive and professional; try to infuse it with your own style and personality. An A5 sheet with printing on both sides is probably sufficient, but if you have lots of photographs and project information it could run to one sheet of A4 – but no bigger. The layout detailed below works well:

FRONT PAGE

1. Don't use small type – 12 point should be the minimum and use 14 point for titles (depending on typeface chosen)
2. Don't smother it with computer smiley faces or irrelevant cartoons and don't overuse exclamation marks!!!!!!!
3. Take advice from anyone you know with design flair or expertise
4. Have a clear title at the top of the front page, perhaps in 18 point
5. A large photograph underneath it of the most compelling image you can find
6. Include some startling facts and figures or a quotation that will catch the attention
7. Elsewhere on the front page include a blurb that encapsulates the essence of the project, what it's about and why it's important to you, or to whoever might be reading the leaflet.

BACK PAGE

This should be more about you; it's an opportunity to enhance your credibility so that readers will want to support your plans.

1. A passport-sized photograph is useful as it identifies you as an individual rather than an anonymous canvasser – and if it features you doing something vaguely relevant to the cause, then all the better.
2. Explain why you want to do the project, why it is important in itself or for the planet as a whole. How will your actions specifically help?
3. Include the names and website details of the organisation arranging the project or details of the overseas organisers.
4. State how much money you have to raise, what progress you have already made towards your target and details of any upcoming fundraising events that you have planned.
5. Make any dates and deadlines very clear.
6. Include the contact details (in a box towards the bottom) that you are happy to have widely circulated, but they should at least include a telephone number and email address.

A–Z OF SPONSORED EVENTS

Stuck for ideas for sponsored events? What about the following:

A Abseiling, aerobics, auctions; a-thons (swim-a-thon, dance-a-thon), arts and crafts sales
B Bring-and-buy sales, bath of baked beans, a summer ball, barbecue, bingo, beard growing, bad-hair day, sponsored bike rides
C Car boot sale, concert, local cinema screening, cake sale, cultural night, car washing, carol singing, Christmas-card making
D Disco, dinner party, dress-down day, dancing, dog walk
E Events, exhibitions, sell unwanted stuff on ebay
F Friends, fêtes, five-a-side football, fashion show, fun run
G Garden plants sale, open-garden weekends, gigs, golf
H Haircutting, heritage walk
I It's-a-knockout competition
J Juggling, joint fundraising, jazz event, jewellery making
K Knobbly knees contest, knitting, karaoke, knock-out pool or darts pub competition
L Literary events, lunchtime activities, limbo
M Marathon running, marathon anything else, market stall, matched funding from your employers, murder mystery party

FUNDRAISING EVENTS

Fundraising events are useful for drawing attention to your project and to why you think it is important. They are primarily aimed at generating sponsorship from individuals, but they can also give publicity to any companies who have already donated to your cause.

Unlike fundraising from the commercial sector these events can be as wacky as you like, but make sure they are fun because they take a considerable amount of organising and the time and effort can sometimes outweigh the cash raised.

It helps to involve as many people as possible at the planning and ideas stage. Get as many other participants as possible so it has an element of competition. Try to plan in partnership with an existing organisation that has an established audience or network, ie: social club, church group, sports club, pub, club, local carnival, workplace, local supermarket, etc.

Make sure all funds raised in this way are precisely accounted for, have another independent person agree the amount raised and make sure that amount is paid into the fundraising account. Send feedback to all the participants and contributors after the event, so they know how much money has been raised and how it will contribute to your goal. For fundraising event ideas see box above.

N   Newspapers, nightclub, nautical activities
O   Organic produce sale, odd-job man, orienteering
P   Promises auction photography competition, photographing, printing, and framing children of friends/relatives, pub, parties, picnic, pet competition
Q   Quiz nights
R   Rich relatives, raffles, rock and roll, radio, rubber duck race, offer a local Rotary club an illustrated talk on your project
S   Sponsored anything, swim, shave, sports day, silly games day (ie: egg and spoon), slave auction for skills and services
T   Treasure hunt, ten-pin bowling, three-legged race, tug of war
U   Ultimate Frisbee (or anything else) competition
V   Vegetarian meals, vegetable stall
W   Write an article for the local paper, worst haircut/dressed competition, welly-boot throwing, 'who is that baby' guessing quiz, wine tasting
X   Xmas party, making xmas cards
Y   Yoga workshop, yo-yo competition, yellow-hair day, yeti costume
Z   Zebra-themed party, zoo

Reproduced with kind permission of Earthwatch Institute (⌘ *www.earthwatch.org*)

LEGAL ISSUES

Remember that professional scammers, scroungers and conmen, as well as legitimate fundraisers, ask for money. If you plan to volunteer with a registered charity it is best to organise the fundraising through them (ie: in their name) and then it is clear that you are not asking for cash for personal use. It is crucial to differentiate yourself from them and to make sure you comply with any legal requirements for raising money. You may need a licence for some sponsored events.

PUBLIC ENTERTAINMENTS LICENCE

If your fundraising event involves two or more people performing in a public place, you will need to get a 'temporary public entertainments' licence from your local authority. If the event is in a social club or church hall they may already have a licence. Holding a paying dance or similar event in a private building may also require a licence.

LIQUOR LICENCE

Selling alcohol at any event, even in your home, requires a liquor licence (giving it away does not). Liquor licences are now the responsibility of local authorities and not magistrates' courts. They are not easy to obtain as many proofs and assurances have to be provided. The most sensible option is to get an existing licensee to apply on your behalf, but then they are responsible for all liquor sales. Events held in licensed pubs or clubs do not need an additional licence provided people buy from the bar.

GAMING BOARD

If you plan to raffle prizes donated by shops remember that raffle tickets must be sold on the day of the raffle; if they are sold in advance they fall under the rules of the Gaming Board, which requires registration. To stop dishonesty raffle tickets must not be discounted and the price, prizes, and when the raffle will be drawn, must be clearly stated.

BLACK-AND-WHITE COLOBUS MONKEYS
Andrew Hayes

Today is another day in the forest. We start out at 05.00, to be at the foot of the 'mountain' by 05.45. It's an isolated hill in the Dzombo Forest Reserve, which we are hoping is still home to some of Kenya's rare Angolan black-and-white colobus monkeys.

We split into our census teams and mark our co-ordinates on the GPS. It starts easy enough, gentle slopes and scattered trees, but the brush and vines begin to thicken as we climb higher and deeper into the forest. We're not following paths, but instead cutting transects to evenly survey the whole forest. The idea is to make as little disturbance as possible, so when we are able to, we crawl under branches and through bushes. It's quite an experience making our own trails; you really get up close and personal with the forest's smaller wildlife.

It's not long before we come across a troop of yellow baboons; we sit as quietly as possible to observe them. There are six, and one is clearly the dominant male. We record their position and move on. There is an abundance of birds, lizards and bugs that I've never seen before and I begin to appreciate why Kenya's coastal forests are classified as a global biodiversity hotspot.

We find our first group of the beautiful colobus after lunch – five adults and one infant. We know the youngster is less than three months old by its white fur. This is the purpose of our census, to find out just how many of this threatened subspecies are left in Kenya and where they live. There are two adult males, with a characteristic white stripe on their undersides, and three females. Most of them are feeding or swinging from the branches.

We finish at 15.30; a long hot day, but very rewarding. There were a few rough parts: getting caught on thorns and dodging army ants, but that's all part of the experience. Getting back to camp we wash and relax, compare notes with the other teams and prepare for tomorrow's assault on the 'mountain'. Dinner has been prepared by a local villager – valuable income for her and welcome down time by the campfire for us – before heading to bed, exhausted.

Andrew Hayes travelled with Global Vision International on an expedition to Kenya

Human encroachment on African elephant territory has
lead to an increase in conflicts. Researchers are trying
to find a way of deterring elephants from entering
human encampments; apparently playing the recorded
sound of angry honey bees is very effective (PL) page 24

above   Volunteers attend a wildlife identification lecture, Namibia (PL)

left   Leopards are anethestised and their eyes covered to protect them from the sun (BE) page 25

below   Authors locating cheetahs using radio signals emitted from their tracking collars (PL) page 23

above Team scientist teaching volunteer how to identify species from their tracks (NR/E)

below Be prepared to get dirty on the job! Volunteers collect poo samples for analysis (EC/E)

above   **Volunteers monitoring a leatherback turtle laying her eggs, Costa Rica** (RS/E) page 27

left   **Loggerhead turtle hatchling, Greece** (PL) page 27

below   **Archelon volunteer erects beach mats to prevent hatchings heading towards the light and sounds echoing from clubs along the seafront** (PL) page 158

above **Volunteers receive their dive briefing before a reef survey, Seychelles** (PL) page 162

right **Volunteers measure coral growth and health, Belize** (JC/E) page 23

below **Camp life: accommodation is basic but idyllic on many projects, Curieuse Island in the Seychelles** (PL) page 162

above Plankton-feeding whale sharks are listed as 'vulnerable' on the ICUN Red List due to the effects of commercial fishing (RD/TIPS) page 28

below Soft healthy corals like this are becoming a rarity; increases in water temperature are leading to widespread coral bleaching (I/TIPS) page 23

above   Orang-utans are being rehabilitated in sanctuaries like Sepilok in Sabah, Borneo (CZ/B) page 26

below   The horn of the critically endangered black rhino is highly prized in traditional Chinese medicine; as a result of illegal poaching there are now only 3,600 individuals left worldwide (AI/TIPS) page 27

Thanks to WWF, the giant panda has become *the* face of wildlife conservation. However, the latest reports suggest there are only 1,590 left in the wild

(HA/NV) page 26

7 BEFORE YOU GO

By now, you've decided where you want to go, which organisation to go with and have set your fundraising plans (if necessary) in motion. All that remains to be organised are the practical details of getting to the country in question. This chapter offers detailed advice on booking tickets, visas, insurance, health and safety, what to take, keeping in touch with home and cultural etiquette, so you can get the most out of your conservation volunteer experience.

BOOKING FLIGHTS

International flights are rarely included in the price of volunteer projects. However, most organisations will have a preferred ticket operator, so it's worth getting a quote from them first – you can at least use it as a baseline against which to compare other quotes.

Cheap airline offers in newspapers and on the web usually refer to a limited number of relatively cheap seats which sell out fast, so booking early tends to work out cheaper but not always.

The ticket price from the same airline to the same destination can vary enormously throughout the week. The most popular days and times command the highest ticket price and are rarely discounted. Weekend flights, the first flights of the day and midsummer are usually more expensive. Flying midweek (Tue–Thurs) is usually cheaper, as are afternoon and evening flights. This is a guideline only. You may find that midweek flights on a major business route are more expensive; the same goes for weekend flights to a leisure destination.

TICKET TIPS

- Fare-comparison websites don't always list all the airlines flying to a given destination; they may only list those that give them the best commission.
- Don't be fooled by the hype; booking directly with an airline is sometimes cheaper than with the well-publicised 'discount ticket' companies.
- Check the cheapest time to fly on an airline website by entering your destination and running several searches for different days and different times.
- Flights with a stopover are often cheaper than direct flights, but they do leave a larger carbon footprint.
- If you know a small independent travel agent it is worth talking to them, as they will be knowledgeable and up to date with any current deals. Telling them about your volunteer project may encourage them to go that extra mile for you. Don't bother with the well-known high-street tour operators; they are mainly geared up to sell their own packages.

- If you have a degree of uncertainty about your onward travel plans an 'open- jaw' ticket is the most flexible option, although it will be dearer
- Read and understand the airline small print about missed or changed flights. Some tickets will not permit changes, some will allow changes with advance notice and most will make a charge. The cheapest tickets have the least flexibility and larger airlines are usually more accommodating than smaller ones.
- If you plan to travel on to other destinations after volunteering a 'round-the-world' (RTW) ticket may be the best deal. These are special tickets that a group of airlines 'code share' (ie: One World Alliance, Star Alliance) to offer a wider range of destinations. Prices depend on how many continents you visit and the distance you fly above a basic 25,000 miles.

WHAT ABOUT MY CARBON FOOTPRINT?

The carbon footprint attributed to flying is sometimes misrepresented. The airline industry is responsible for just 2% of the world's total carbon emissions, in comparison to the 4% generated by the shipping sector and the 40% produced by the building industry.

Therefore, conservation volunteers shouldn't panic unduly about the carbon footprint they generate flying to and from an overseas project. Bradt believes you shouldn't avoid undertaking long-distance flights. By visiting a country you contribute to the local economy and by travelling positively, ie: engaging in the local lifestyle and taking part in projects such as tree planting, etc, you are effectively offsetting your carbon footprint.

If you do decide to offset your emissions when purchasing your plane ticket, it's worth bearing in mind that an 8,000-mile return flight to central Africa generates around 1.4 tons of CO_2, but if the volunteer stayed for a month two-thirds of this is likely to be offset by living a more low-tech and economical lifestyle. If they stayed six weeks their flights would potentially be carbon neutral. If they then chose to offset their emissions through companies like ClimateCare (*www.climatecare.org*) volunteers could in fact generate a personal carbon credit. Calculations of the carbon footprint associated with travelling to a particular country can be found under the relevant country listing in *Appendix 1*.

RED TAPE

When it comes to key documents – such as your agreement with your sending organisation, flight tickets, visa and travel insurance – reading the small print is absolutely vital. Voluminous terms and conditions are there to clarify what you are entitled to, but also to minimise a company's liability and therefore any claims against them. Some terms and conditions are outrageous so don't be duped by snazzy, colourful websites or friendly, chatty telesales teams who may hide, or be ignorant of, some very harsh small print.

PASSPORTS

Almost all countries require a passport to have at least six months to run before its expiry, so be sure to check it in far in advance of your travels so you have plenty of time to renew it if need be.

VISAS

Visa requirements and regulations differ for each country and can vary in response to sudden changes in the international political climate, so always check entry requirements – even if you've been to a country before. There are many countries where UK and US citizens do not need to purchase a pre-departure visa (typically Europe, parts of Africa, South America and east Asia) or simple electronic visa options (eg: Australia). The USA has special tourist visa-waiver agreements with many countries but from January 2009 the rules change. For security reasons the USA now require all visitors from agreed visa-waiver countries to obtain travel authorisation prior to travelling (unless arriving by land from Canada or Mexico) by using an 'Electronic System for Travel Authorisation' (ESTA). This can be completed on the American Embassy website; tourists are not required to attend an interview and no payment is required.

Rules for the different types of British passport holder – British dependent territories citizen, British overseas citizen, British national overseas or a British protected person, etc – vary and you may need to apply for a visa even if British citizens do not. Consult the Foreign & Commonwealth Foreign Office (🖰 www.fco.gov.uk/travel) for advice.

Be aware that some volunteer-sending organisations leave all responsibility for obtaining appropriate entry visas to the volunteer. Read the small print for clauses on visas: some specify that if customs and immigration don't let you in because your paperwork is wrong then it's your fault and you aren't eligible for a refund.

When filling out forms, make sure you apply for the correct type of visa. There are several categories, including tourist visas, transit visas, working visas, residence visas, and single- or multiple-entry visas. Normally conservation volunteering is classified as tourism, so don't confuse immigration officials by indicating you will be 'working', unless you will actually be undertaking paid employment. If you confuse the issue you can expect trouble, delays, extra costs, or even be refused entry. It is generally best to obtain your visa as early as possible; most countries permit applications three months ahead of travel.

DIY visas versus visa procurement agency

Applying for a visa independently can be a time consuming and stressful process, but the basic procedure is as follows:

1. Identify the embassy or consulate you need via 🖰 www.fco.gov.uk/travel. Check their requirements, procedures and costs then download the application form. Some embassies permit postal applications, but most require personal attendance, usually in London but occasionally elsewhere in the UK.

2. Obtain appropriate passport-sized photographs; you will need to leave your passport at the embassy, so make a photocopy.
3. You will probably have to queue at the embassy/consulate for hours especially during peak times. Many embassy visa sections only open in the morning and if you don't get there early you could get sent away if they've issued their daily quota or are going to close the office.
4. If you've made a clerical error on your application form, expect to be sent to the back of the queue and start again. Most embassy staff are busy and consummate bureaucrats, so don't expect anyone to say, 'Oh, let me help you sort that out.'
5. Pay the required fee and check whether cash only is accepted.
6. Go home with a ticket receipt and a date to return and collect your visa.
7. Return to the embassy and queue again. Hopefully it will be ready.
8. You must check that all the details are correct before accepting the visa. If errors are discovered after you have left the embassy, most will require you to make and pay for a fresh application.
9. A next-day or same-day service may be available for an additional fee.

Be aware that an increasing number of countries have begun out-sourcing visa processing; China and India started in 2008. Costs have increased as a result, so it's worth checking the embassy/consulate website for the latest details.

Alternatively, if you're prepared to pay a bit more, you could employ the services of a visa procurement company. They ensure the correct application form and your passport are delivered (often in person) to the embassy and pay the consular fees on your behalf, and they collect your passport, check the visa details and return everything to you by post, usually within three full working days.

Fees for an expensive country like Russia can range from £120–300 all-in (consular fee, VAT, courier service and agency fees), depending how fast you want it. Companies worth trying are: www.uk.cibt.com, www.thevisacompany.com, www.passportandvisaservice.co.uk, www.visaworld.co.uk, www.thamesconsular.com. Their fees vary so it's worth shopping around; services are available online and by post.

TRAVEL INSURANCE

A good travel insurance policy is not only important for your personal welfare, it is also a standard requirement made by most volunteer outfits who require proof that you will be covered in the event of an illness or accident. Don't leave it until just before you travel; take it out as soon as you have committed yourself by paying a deposit or booking flights, otherwise you will not have the full benefit of the policy's cancellation cover.

It's important to know what level of protection is provided by your chosen insurer. Out-of-the-ordinary activities such as zorbing and extreme sports like water-rafting, quite often aren't covered. Even manual labour is referred to as a 'risk' and most travel policies exclude any injury claim if you are engaged in 'manual work', so make sure you are covered for what you expect to be doing. Travel advisors often don't take the time to explain all the provisos, so ensure you read the small print. Below is a list of standard insurance terms:

Additional hospital benefits If emergency medical expenses have been authorised additional hospital expenses may be covered.

Baggage Only personal baggage is covered. Delayed baggage requires a written report from the carrier and receipts for any purchases, proof of damage and a police report if stolen. You are not covered if baggage is left unattended, checked-in (including on a bus), left in a car overnight, taken from a car without signs of forcible entry. And anything expensive is likely to be excluded.

Cancellation Only covers pre-booked flights and accommodation and where cancellation is 'necessary and unavoidable' – redundancy, jury service, and pregnancy after the policy is issued are normally good reasons, changing your mind is not.

Cash and documents Covers accidental loss or theft only if from your person or a locked safety deposit box. Shared accommodation is usually classed as unattended status.

Curtailment (ie: early return home) Only covers unused accommodation after you return home and only if it was originally pre-booked from your country of residence.

Hijack Very variable if covered at all and never if you have engaged in activity that could increase the risk of hijack. It's unclear what this means, but probably includes travelling to places where previous incidents have occurred.

Legal expenses Covers costs to claim compensation for injury or death during your trip. Exclusions are typically criminal or malicious acts, alcohol or drug involvement, actions by a relative or travelling companion, and claims against your insurance company.

Loss If drugs or alcohol are implicated in a loss claim, insurance companies reserve the right not to pay out.

Lost passport/driver's licence expenses Only covers reasonable costs over and above what you would normally have incurred, but there's no cover if it's lost or destroyed by Customs or other authorities.

Missed departures A police or roadside assistance report is required if your car breaks down or a report which confirms a public transport failure. You are not covered if you didn't leave sufficient time to reach your check-in, were not en route to the airport, or if a public transport strike was announced before booking your trip. Sometimes travelling by private car is not covered.

Personal accident Cash paid to your next of kin if you sustain a permanent disability or die, providing it is due to 'outward violence and visible means' during your trip.

Personal liability Covers legal claims made against you for any accidental damage to a person or property caused by you during your trip, but excludes your own and other people's possessions, criminal acts, as well as claims made by family, employees, or a travelling companion.

Repatriation/emergency medical expenses They will not cover any existing or recent medical conditions.

Sports cover There are endless exclusions, extra premiums are usually required and standard policies never provide cover for professional sporting activities.

Travel delay and abandonment Cover for adverse weather, mechanical breakdown, industrial action or security alerts. But there's no cover if you didn't check in or didn't leave sufficient time. EU airlines have a legal obligation regardless of your insurance policy.

Other typical exclusions
- Claims for depression, stress, mental disorders, HIV/AIDS or other sexually transmitted diseases, suicide, alcohol or drug abuse, pregnancy or any wilful exposure to exceptional risk.
- If the Foreign & Commonwealth office have an advisory notice against travelling to the country you visit.
- Failure by you or your travelling companion to comply with the law in the country visited.
- Driving a motorcycle over 125cc.
- Anything really serious like radiation contamination, war, invasion, terrorism, civil war or revolution.

It is useful to shop around after assessing your potential risks. Most policy variation is in the maximum amount payable, but extra cover may be available for search and rescue, resumption of your trip after curtailment, mugging and disaster – but they're often of dubious value when you read the small print.

Don't double-buy insurance because you do not get double cover. If you have home insurance or medical policy check whether you are already covered for personal items lost or stolen whilst abroad. Travel policies usually require you to claim from any existing insurance policy, so they may not actually cover you at all.

Insurance sold with general holiday packages is notoriously overpriced, so don't automatically accept the insurance offered by the organisation you plan to travel with. It has its advantages because you should be confident that it covers all the risks inherent in the project they are sending you on, but you might find the same cover elsewhere for less. Try to get at least three quotes that include the activities you will be engaging in. Useful comparison websites like ⁂www.moneysupermarket.com are a good place to start. Most standard and annual travel insurance is limited to a single 30-day trip or less. If you plan being abroad for longer than this, it will be necessary to get a more specialised and expensive policy.

It is possible that the organisation you plan to travel with includes insurance cover within its fee. However, this is likely to be restricted to medical and liability cover and not include other features of a typical policy – so check the details.

TRAVEL INSURANCE COMPANIES IN THE UK

Campbell Irvine 48 Earls Court Rd, Kensington, London W8 6EJ; ☎ 020 7937 6981; ⁂www.campbellirvine.com

Club Direct 19 Bartlett St, Croydon CR2 6TB; ☎ 0870 8902842; ⁂www.clubdirect.com

Endsleigh Insurance Shurdington Rd, Cheltenham, Gloucs GL51 4UE; ☎ 0800 028 3571; ⁂www.endsleigh.co.uk

Saga Travel Insurance ☎ 0800 015 8055; ⁂www.saga.co.uk

STATravel ☎ 0871 230 8481; ⁂www.statravel.co.uk

There are a vast number of alternative companies and if you have had positive experiences with one, it might be best to stay with them.

MAKING A CLAIM

Keep a record of everything that went wrong before you return home, including receipts, the sequence of events, witness details and get approval before incurring significant expenditure.

Don't be tempted to lie or omit any relevant information on an insurance application – it might appear to save money, but it will invalidate the policy when you attempt to claim against it.

Be wary, but don't be put off by all the exclusions; remember they have to deal with countless fraudulent claims. If you are honest, keep full records and receipts, and genuinely understand what is covered and what is not, a good travel policy is an invaluable travel companion. Just don't expect to come out in front in the money stakes if something goes wrong.

EUROPEAN HEALTH INSURANCE CARD (EHIC)

If you are travelling through Europe make sure you apply for the EHIC – the cross-border card that entitles the bearer to reduced or free medical treatment.

Insurance companies expect you to use the EHIC card to access local health care and if you generate costs that could have been covered by the possession of an EHIC then they are unlikely to reimburse you on your return to the UK. You can apply via post (application forms can be picked up from the post office), by phone (☏ *0845 6062030*) or online (✆ *www.ehic.org.uk*).

HEALTH
with Dr Felicity Nicholson
BEFORE YOU GO
Immunisations

The level of protection against infectious diseases will vary greatly depending on your destination, how long you stay, and the nature of your activities. Consult the 'Know Before You Go' section on the FCO website (✆ *www.fco.gov.uk/travel*) for advice about the general risks at your destination and visit the NHS website (✆ *www.fitfortravel.nhs.uk*) for a good overview of travel health matters and a country-by-country analysis of the health risks. Don't get too paranoid with their comprehensive lists of diseases!

You should also make an appointment with your GP well before departure and explain where you are going and what you will be doing. Ask for a general physical examination including blood pressure and advice about vaccinations and prophylactics (eg: malarial tablets) relevant for your destination and activities.

A minimal level of protection should include being up-to-date with diphtheria, tetanus, polio and hepatitis A but there are plenty more depending on your destination, how long you are staying, and whether you will be visiting rural areas. You should seek medical advice at least six weeks before travelling to allow enough time in case longer courses of vaccines, eg: for hepatitis B, rabies and Japanese encephalitis, are needed.

Teeth

Dental problems can occur at anytime, so have a check-up and any treatment well before departure; toothache will ruin your trip and overseas treatment might be a lot worse.

TRAVEL CLINICS

A full list of current travel clinic websites worldwide is available on ✆www.istm.org. For other journey preparation information, consult ✆www.tripprep.com. Information about various medications may be found on ✆www.emedicine.com/wild/topiclist.htm.

PERSONAL FIRST AID

A well-organised group-led project will have first-aid equipment, but many placements may not have one readily to hand. This is something to check out with your chosen organisation and the specific project you will be working on. A basic personal medical kit should contain the following:

- A good drying antiseptic, eg: iodine or potassium permanganate (don't take antiseptic cream)
- A few small dressings and plasters
- High factor suncream
- Insect repellent; anti-malarial tablets; impregnated bed-net or permethrin spray for clothing
- Aspirin or paracetamol
- Antifungal cream (eg: Canesten)
- Oral rehydration sachets
- Anti-diarrhoea tablets
- Ciprofloxacin or norfloxacin, for severe diarrhoea
- Tinidazole for giardia or amoebic dysentery
- Motion sickness tablets
- Antibiotic eye drops, for sore, 'gritty', stuck-together eyes (conjunctivitis)
- A pair of fine pointed tweezers (to remove hairy caterpillar hairs, thorns, splinters, coral, etc)
- Alcohol-based hand rub or bar of soap in plastic box
- Condoms or femidoms
- A digital travel thermometer
- Needle and syringe kit – and carry a doctor's letter to explain why carrying
- Any regular medication that you take including generic names and doses
- Sore throat lozenges

COMMON MEDICAL PROBLEMS

Ailments vary greatly depending on the destination, but taking the following precautions should guard against most common medical problems.

Protection from the sun

Give some thought to packing suncream. The incidence of skin cancer is rocketing as Caucasians are travelling more and spending more time exposing themselves to the sun. Keep out of the sun during the middle of the day and, if you must expose yourself to the sun, build up gradually from 20 minutes per day. Be especially careful of exposure in the middle of the day and of sun reflected off water, and wear a T-shirt and lots of waterproof suncream (at least SPF15) when swimming. Sun exposure ages the skin, makes people prematurely wrinkly; and increases the risk of skin cancer. Cover up with long, loose clothes and wear a hat when you can. The glare

LONG-HAUL FLIGHTS, CLOTS AND DVT
Dr Jane Wilson-Howarth

Long-haul air travel increases the risk of deep vein thrombosis. Although recent research has suggested that many of us develop clots when immobilised, most resolve without us ever having been aware of them. In certain susceptible individuals, though, clots form on clots and when large ones break away and lodge in the lungs this is dangerous. Fortunately this happens in a tiny minority of passengers.

Studies have shown that flights of over five-and-a-half-hours are significant, and that people who take lots of shorter flights over a short space of time can also form clots.

People at highest risk are:
- Those who have had a clot before – unless they are now taking warfarin
- People over 80 years of age
- Anyone who has recently undergone a major operation or surgery for varicose veins
- Someone who has had a hip or knee replacement in the last three months
- Cancer sufferers
- Those who have ever had a stroke
- People with heart disease
- Those with a close blood relative who has had a clot

Those with a slightly increased risk:
- People over 40
- Women who are pregnant or have had a baby in the last couple of weeks
- People taking female hormones, the combined contraceptive pill or other oestrogen therapy
- Heavy smokers
- Those who have very severe varicose veins

and the dust can be hard on the eyes too, so bring UV-protecting sunglasses and perhaps a soothing eyebath.

Prickly heat
A fine pimply rash on the trunk is likely to be heat rash; cool showers, dabbing dry, and talc will help. Treat the problem by slowing down to a relaxed schedule, wearing only loose, baggy, 100%-cotton clothes and sleeping naked under a fan; if it's bad you may need to check into an air-conditioned hotel room for a while.

- The very obese
- People who are very tall (over 6ft/1.8m) or short (under 5ft/1.5m)

A deep vein thrombosis (DVT) is a blood clot that forms in the deep leg veins. This is very different from irritating but harmless superficial phlebitis. DVT causes swelling and redness of one leg, usually with heat and pain in one calf and sometimes the thigh. A DVT is only dangerous if a clot breaks away and travels to the lungs (pulmonary embolus). Symptoms of a pulmonary embolus (PE) include chest pain that is worse on breathing in deeply, shortness of breath, and sometimes coughing up small amounts of blood. The symptoms commonly start three to ten days after a long flight. Anyone who thinks that they might have a DVT needs to see a doctor immediately who will arrange a scan. Warfarin tablets (to thin the blood) are then taken for at least six months.

Prevention of DVT
Several conditions make the problem more likely. Immobility is the key, and factors like reduced oxygen in cabin air and dehydration may also contribute. To reduce the risk of thrombosis on a long journey:

Exercise before and after the flight
- Keep mobile before and during the flight; move around every couple of hours
- Drink plenty of water or juices during the flight
- Avoid taking sleeping pills and excessive tea, coffee and alcohol
- Perform exercises that mimic walking and tense the calf muscles
- Consider wearing flight socks or support stockings (see ⁀ www.legshealth.com)
- Ideally take a meal each week of oily fish (mackerel, trout, salmon, sardines, etc) ahead of your departure. This reduces the blood's ability to clot and thus DVT risk. It may even be worth just taking a meal of oily fish 24 hours before departure if this is more practical.

If you think you are at increased risk of a clot, ask your doctor if it is safe to travel.

Sterilisation
Contaminated food and water are the most common causes of illness. As well as the well-known E coli, salmonella, campylobacter and norovirus sources of food poisoning there are also the more serious typhoid, hepatitis A and cholera. General advice is:

- Use bottled or boiled water rather than local tap water ; avoid ice in drinks and steer clear of ice cream served by disreputable sources.
- Only eat freshly and thoroughly cooked food that is still piping hot,

and avoid food that has been kept warm, ie: buffets.
- Avoid salads and uncooked food, unless you can wash, peel or shell it yourself.
- Be cautious with fish and shellfish.

And remember that money doesn't always buy hygiene; mass buffet-style catering on cruise ships and fancy hotels often produces outbreaks of food poisoning, whereas a street seller who cooks something in front of you might have a lower risk.

Skin infections

Any mosquito bite or small nick in the skin gives an opportunity for bacteria to foil the body's usually excellent defences; it will surprise many travellers how quickly skin infections start in warm humid climates and it is essential to clean and cover even the slightest wound. Creams are not as effective as a good drying antiseptic such as dilute iodine, potassium permanganate (a few crystals in half a cup of water), or crystal (or gentian) violet. One of these should be available in most towns. If the wound starts to throb, or becomes red and the redness starts to spread, or the wound oozes, and especially if you develop a fever, antibiotics will probably be needed: flucloxacillin (250mg four times a day) or cloxacillin (500mg four times a day). For those allergic to penicillin, erythromycin (500mg twice a day) for five days should help. See a doctor if the symptoms do not start to improve within 48 hours.

Fungal infections also get a hold easily in hot, moist climates so wear 100%-cotton socks and underwear and shower frequently. An itchy rash in the groin or flaking between the toes is likely to be a fungal infection. This needs treatment with an antifungal cream such as Canesten (clotrimazole); if this is not available try Whitfield's ointment (compound benzoic acid ointment) or crystal violet (although this will turn you purple!).

Malaria

Anti-malarial prophylactics may be essential for your destination, but remember they do not guarantee prevention if bitten by an infected mosquito. They reduce the odds enormously, but it is absolutely essential to minimise your chance of being bitten. This can be done by covering arms and legs, using insecticides (permethrin) on clothes, and insect repellents containing 50–55% DEET on exposed body areas. Ideally, you should sleep under a mosquito net again impregnated with permethrin and remember that although the highest risk of malaria is from dusk till dawn, when the specific mosquitoes fly, there are other diseases, eg: dengue fever, that are transmitted by day-biting mosquitoes, so be prepared to use repellents during the daytime, too. Seek current advice on the best antimalarials to take: usually mefloquine, Malarone or doxycycline. If mefloquine (Lariam) is suggested, start this two-and-a-half weeks (three doses) before departure to check that it suits you; stop it immediately if it seems to cause depression or anxiety, visual or hearing disturbances, severe headaches, fits or changes in heart rhythm. Side effects such as nightmares or dizziness are not medical reasons for stopping unless they are sufficiently debilitating or annoying. Anyone who has been treated for depression or psychiatric problems, has diabetes controlled by oral therapy, or who is epileptic (or who has suffered fits in the past) or has a close blood relative who is epileptic, should probably avoid mefloquine. In the past doctors were nervous about prescribing mefloquine to pregnant women, but experience has shown that it is relatively safe and certainly safer than the risk of malaria. That said, there are other issues, so it is essential you seek expert advice before departure.

Malarone (proguanil and atovaquone) is as effective as mefloquine. It has the advantage of having few side effects and need only be continued for one week after returning. However, it is expensive and because of this tends to be reserved for shorter trips. Malarone may not be suitable for everybody, so advice should be taken from a doctor. The licence in the UK has been extended for up to three months' use and a paediatric form of tablet is also available, prescribed on a weight basis.

Another alternative is the antibiotic doxycycline (100mg daily). Like Malarone it can be started one day before arrival. Unlike mefloquine, it may also be used in travellers with epilepsy, although certain anti-epileptic medication may make it less effective. In perhaps 1–3% of people there is the possibility of allergic skin reactions developing in sunlight; the drug should be stopped if this happens. Women using the oral contraceptive should use an additional method of protection for the first four weeks when using doxycycline. It is also unsuitable in pregnancy or for children under 12 years.

Yellow fever
Yellow fever vaccination is especially important when visiting or passing through the yellow fever belt – equatorial African countries and northern South America. If you do not have a yellow fever certificate proving vaccination you may be refused entry to certain countries.

SAFETY
Use the same common sense as you would at home. Don't leave valuables unattended and don't wander around alone after dark. Check the FCO website (⊕ www.fco.gov.uk/travel) for country-specific advice.

THEFT
Be aware of pick-pockets when in crowded markets or towns. Ideally, money should be concealed in a moneybelt or neck pouch about your person. Be sure to make copies of important documents like your passport, plane tickets, travel insurance and travellers cheques, etc, in case your bag is stolen.

DRUGS

The consumption or trafficking of drugs carries extreme penalties in most countries. Don't accept drugs and decline to carry any items or luggage belonging to others.

SWIMMING

Be aware of rips, strong currents and shallow rocks when swimming off unfamiliar beaches. Ask locals for advice.

TERRORISM

Check the FCO website (*www.fco.gov.uk*) for up-to-date reports. Any countries that carry a UK government advisory warning may render your travel insurance policy invalid, so be sure to check you're still covered.

WHAT TO TAKE

Choosing the right backpack is essential. It needs to be comfortable, so try on different styles, put it on and take it off a few times, trot up and down stairs and (if you can) go for a half-mile walk. Many travellers tend to opt for the 65-litre rucksack with another 25-litre daysack, but bear in mind that you will be picking it up and putting it down hundreds of times, perhaps carrying it long distances, and stowing it on luggage racks. The size and weight of your backpack must be within your personal capability. As a result, it's often better to purchase a medium-sized 45–50-litre backpack. It'll be worth its weight in gold when you're running for buses, or forced to stow it on your lap when the luggage compartments are full.

When it comes to packing your backpack, most people inevitably take far too much with them. The trick – as experienced backpackers will know – is to layout everything you think you might take, and then halve it. In most circumstances, you will be able to buy anything you may have forgotten upon reaching your destination. Remember to leave room at the top so you have space to pack the souvenirs and trinkets bought during the trip.

PACKING CHECKLIST

Packing checklists vary hugely depending on the nature of your conservation project, and it goes without saying that operators running diving, desert trekking, or rainforest expeditions will advise you on any specialist gear you may need to bring. However, the following checklist should help you remember the essentials:
- a mosquito net
- sleeping bag or liner
- pillowcase
- waterproof waist pouch
- water purification tablets
- wet wipes
- collapsible water bottle
- torch, padlock and chain.

- A personalised first-aid kit (see page 187)
- Some form of telecommunication plan or direct link with home (see page 195)
- An MP3 player with favourite music, space to download photographs and ideally a voice-recording function – very useful for making notes and capturing memories.
- A camera is probably essential but not necessarily a bulky expensive one that you will be paranoid about losing. New non-SLR 10MP cameras for £100 or less can produce newspaper- and even magazine-quality images if the light is good.
- Reading material, perhaps books that you have already read, but give you a comforting reminder of home – sometimes you'll want this. Take light paperback books you can swap or leave behind.
- Foot powder, especially for hot, humid climates
- A small daypack
- An inflatable neck/headrest pillow
- Earplugs
- A universal sink plug
- A head torch; it may look silly but it can be invaluable
- Pack a solar battery charger instead of stocking up on batteries that will either pollute the local environment or have to be lugged home again.
- Take some bin liners; they're very useful for keeping clothes dry and separating dirty laundry.

TIPS FOR LIGHTENING YOUR LOAD

- Take multi-purpose clothing such as T-shirts that can double as nightshirts.
- Take zip-off multi-pocket, cotton trousers that can double as shorts
- Opportunities for dressing up will be rare so dump smart outfits or fancy shoes.
- Plan to wash out clothes regularly and only take sufficient changes for four or five days.
- Buy clothes in local markets when you arrive; they will always be cheaper and you'll be supporting the local economy.
- If you have walking boots wear these bulky items instead of packing them.
- A good lightweight, multi-pocketed waterproof jacket is a good investment. Plenty of zip pockets mean you can carry as much as in a small bag, but more importantly you will be far less likely to lose it or have the contents stolen.
- Valuables are not covered by your travel insurance whilst in transit, so keep them with you. Store your carry-on valuables eg: camera, MP3, etc, either in a small daypack, or in a multi-pocketed coat.

MONEY

It's safer to take a mixture of travellers' cheques, US dollars and use a debit card to withdraw local currency on arrival. Credit cards should only be used for significant purchases from reputable shops, for car hire or hotels, and as an emergency back-up.

CASH

Generally having lots of cash with you is a hassle; you will have to continually plan where to leave it, how to carry it, and travel insurance normally only covers a few hundred pounds of stolen cash. It is far better to leave cash in the bank and draw it out as you go; few places do not have access to an ATM, even if only on a weekly visit to the town for supplies. Some countries still have a preference for US dollars, but it's always handy to take denominations of the local currency for small items, taxis, etc.

TRAVELLERS' CHEQUES

These are still a good idea, but you need advice on whether it's best to purchase them in the form of US dollars, euros, sterling or even Australian dollars. You will pay commission when you buy them and again when you cash them, but commission will be lower if the travellers' cheques are in a preferred currency. Also, because there is usually a minimum commission fee, you pay more by changing lots of small amounts rather than a few larger ones. On returning home, unused travellers' cheques can be paid back into your bank as a cash deposit with no additional commission fee. It's also essential to keep a record of when and where you cash each travellers' cheque – this is crucial information if you ever need to make a claim for their loss. Also keep the carbon copy details completely separate from the actual travellers' cheques.

CREDIT CARDS

These can be useless in some countries, but absolutely essential in others. They are often useful for getting local currency from an airport or city ATM and sometimes essential for car hire or hotel reservations. But beware the hidden costs. There will probably be a charge to use the ATM machine and a commission charge by your credit card company, as well as an additional charge for borrowing cash on your card. One or two larger withdrawals are cheaper than several smaller ones, as there is always a minimum fee.

A better option is to use a commission-free debit card (eg: Nationwide) and because it's your own money there is no borrowing charge. A relatively new option is a prepaid travel card, which is pre-loaded with dollars or euros. It is a useful way of controlling spending and if it is lost or stolen thieves only have access to the card's pre-loaded limit. The clever option is to keep topping the card up from a secure account at home by phone or online.

Keep a copy of your credit card and debit card details along with the company emergency telephone number in case you need to cancel a card that has been lost or stolen. It's a good idea to leave a record of all these crucial numbers at home just in case you lose all your baggage.

CULTURAL ETIQUETTE

It can't be over-stressed how important it is to get to know as much as you can about your destination before arriving. Its history is not just a matter of academic interest; it will have set many attitudes about how business is done, how its people are treated and how foreigners are viewed. Civil or international wars, interference by the major powers and a colonial past may all shape a country's ethos or leave a lingering resentment. Religion too may embody radically different concepts and attitudes than you are used to, and it can be very easy to offend local religious or official sensibilities without realising, via inappropriate dress, speech or behaviour.

For example, many travellers are aware that in Arabic and Asian countries it is considered rude to use your left hand when eating, passing things, or when greeting someone. But did you know that whilst blowing your nose into a handkerchief is considered good manners in the UK, it is considered vulgar in China? That a thumbs-up sign shows approval of something in Europe, but is used as a swearing gesture in Argentina? A quick background check for cultural etiquette like this pays dividends on arrival and prevents unnecessary embarrassment or upset on both sides.

Be aware too of the socio-economic status of the country you are travelling too; wearing expensive clothing, jewellery, etc, will attract trouble if you're visiting poor areas.

Finally, try to guard against being patronising when working on volunteer projects. This is an easier trap to fall into than you might think – as a paying volunteer you have power, money, company influence, choices and, at the end of the day, you can go back home to your comfortable previous existence. Local people may have none of these. Always remember that you are not just visiting the rainforest – it is someone's home. Try to learn as much of the local language as possible. It shows respect and most people are delighted even when you demonstrate the basics. For further discussion see pages 3–4.

KEEPING IN TOUCH WITH HOME

Using mobile phones abroad is the most expensive option, as both you and the person you're calling incur charges. However, there are plenty of cheaper alternatives:

1. If you're going to make a significant number of local calls, buy a local country SIM card on arrival.
2. If you are hooked on using your mobile there are also international SIM cards with significantly discounted international call charges, ie: SIM4travel (⌂ *www.sim4travel.com*) that you can buy in the UK before leaving.
3. Open an internet calling account with Skype (⌂ *www.skype.com*) or

Callserve (🖰 *www.callserve.com*). If you don't have a wireless-enabled laptop the drawback is that internet cafés may not have the relevant software on their computers and they are unlikely to allow you to install new software. But that need not be a problem. Before you go, get anyone you want to keep in touch with at home to sign up with Skype or Callserve. Friends can then ring you from their computer to a landline for a small fee (dearer to a mobile). Opening an account is free and the charges are paid as you go so you can instantly check the cost of each call on your web account.

4. Consider buying a v-phone from Vonage (🖰 *www.vonage.co.uk*). It's a USB flash-drive stick pre-loaded with software that – when plugged into any computer – connects with the internet phone service. You take out a monthly contract for unlimited free calls (including some mobiles) to a range of countries; the monthly tariff varies depending on which countries are chosen.

5. International phone cards for use on standard landlines are the cheapest way to make traditional phone calls but they are not available in all countries. You buy a pre-paid phone card in various denominations, which has a code number. Then you ring the local free number and follow the directions.

IF THINGS GO WRONG

When things go wrong it's often hard to know who you should turn to first. Approaching the correct contact saves you time and hassle. Depending on the seriousness of the event, I would suggest first contacting the local project supervisor or operator, then the company headquarters, then your insurance company, and finally the Foreign and Commonwealth Office. Should you require FCO assistance whilst abroad call: 📞 +44 (0)20 70081500. The lists below highlight what the Foreign and Commonwealth Office are able to assist with should you encounter problems.

FCO CAN...

* Issue replacement passports
* Provide information about transferring funds
* Provide appropriate help if you have suffered rape or serious assault, are a victim of other crime, or are in hospital.
* Help people with mental illness
* Provide details of local lawyers, interpreters, doctors and funeral directors (but not guaranteeing their quality).
* Do all they properly can to contact you within 24 hours of being told that you have been detained by the authorities.
* Offer support and help in a range of other cases, such as child abductions, death of relatives overseas, missing people and kidnapping.
* Contact friends and family for you
* Make special arrangements in cases of terrorism, civil disturbances or natural disasters.

FCO CANNOT...

- Get you out of prison, prevent the local authorities from deporting you after your prison sentence, or interfere in criminal or civil court proceedings.
- Help you enter a country; for example, if you do not have a visa or your passport is not valid, as they cannot interfere in another country's immigration policy or procedures.
- Give you legal advice, investigate crimes or carry out searches for missing people, although they can give you details of people who may be able to help you in these cases, ie: English-speaking lawyers.
- Get you better treatment in hospital or prison than is given to local people.
- Pay any bills or give you money (in very exceptional circumstances they may loan you money, from public funds, which you will have to pay back).
- Make travel arrangements for you, find you work or accommodation, or make business arrangements on your behalf.

RATHLIN ISLAND BIRD RESERVE
Christopher Margetts

I arrived on Rathlin Island, off the north coast of Ireland, in April not knowing what to expect. I had done some research on the RSPB website, but nothing prepared me for what I found – a sheltered harbour filled with eider ducks and drakes, basking common seals with black guillemots and red-breasted mergansers swimming and feeding nearby. High cliffs framed the spectacular view.

RSPB staff whisked me off to my lodgings at the well-equipped Kinramer Camping Barn where I met my fellow volunteer. After a period of training, induction and orientation I was soon greeting visitors to the RSPB viewpoint at the West Light, directing their gaze through telescopes and binoculars toward guillemots, razorbills, fulmars, kittiwakes and, to everyone's delight, puffins.

Days became weeks, and weeks became months; I found island life very much to my liking. I was due to leave in May but I am still here in June and hoping to remain until July. Why? Well, I don't know about your commute to work, but I look forward to mine. Skylark song is the only sound to break the silence; the fields I walk alongside are blanketed with daisies, pink heath-spotted orchids and buttercups; the air is filled with the scent of gorse and honeysuckle; and I meet no traffic as I wander past the freshwater lough to the office. There I spend the day making certain that all the visitors to the RSPB reserve experience the incomparable sights, sounds and smell of a seabird-nesting colony.

Christopher Margetts volunteered with the Royal Society for the Protection of Birds in Ireland

CHEETAHS

Eve Carpenter

I am crouching, head first, approximately 2ft away from a cheetah. This particular cheetah is pounding the ground with both its front paws, hissing and growling at the same time and glaring at me with what can only be described as extremely intimidating, large but painfully beautiful amber eyes.

'Och, just stare him down and make sure you show him who's boss,' says Cheetah Conservation Fund (CCF) research assistant, Mandy, as she jauntily sails past. This is all very well for a practised hand like her, but at this particular point in time I am wielding a child's red plastic spade, crouched in a curiously uncomfortable position as I try to flick the cheetah poo onto the spade with a twig. My sunglasses slip precariously off my nose, while I try to dominate in a duel of machismo with a 40kg young male cheetah. I feel slightly ridiculous, highly alert and extremely vulnerable, all at the same time.

I remove my sunglasses, stare in what I hope is a ferocious manner, and proffer my spade. Amazingly it works. This is not another bizarre television survival soap opera, but a real-life encounter on an Earthwatch project, which is managed, and run by the international conservation organisation CCF. I have joined an international team of volunteers who have travelled to the Waterberg Plateau in Namibia to give their time and money to the plight of the cheetah.

Of course, I am not in any real danger; Mandy is watching nearby and I am at a safe distance near the separated enclosure should I need to retreat. The above encounter is part of the daily enclosure clean-and-feed of the 27 cheetahs that have been brought to CCF – orphaned, injured, or rescued too late in their lives to be able to survive in the wild. CCF has huge enclosures that hold these animals and their daily care is one of the rewarding tasks that volunteers get involved with.

The CCF was founded in 1990 by Dr Laurie Marker, an exceptional woman whose vision and passion has been the backbone of the organisation, which focuses on ensuring the survival of this beautiful but endangered predator.

The cheetah can reach speeds up to 70 mph and must have been the inspiration behind the phrase 'poetry in motion'. There is little to compare to the sight of the sleek, golden, black-spotted body of a cheetah at full sprint, its beautifully painted face a blur as it gracefully races around a corner towards you.

Once found on four continents its numbers and distribution have now declined to the point where it is classified as endangered by the World Conservation Union. CCF is working to find out more about cheetah populations and their behavioural ecology so as to put in place practical conservation plans and mitigate the conflict between cheetahs, local livestock and game farmers.

Eve Carpenter travelled with the Earthwatch Institute on their cheetah project in Namibia

APPENDIX 1 COUNTRY GUIDE

This chapter lists all the countries covered by projects audited in the book, and includes basic practical information regarding climate, culture, language, visa requirements, health issues and carbon footprint, to help you plan your trip.

KEY TO COUNTRY GUIDE LISTINGS

Carbon footprint
Calculations vary considerably: those noted below are based on 0.25 tonnes of carbon dioxide per 1,000 air miles and on flying into the principle city. European flights are calculated from London and American flights from Chicago and will need to be adjusted up or down to take account of alternative destinations or stopover routes.

Wealth Indicators
It is not easy to briefly describe economic prosperity or the level of relative poverty. The indicators I have used are GNI – gross national income divided by mid-year population size (which presumes money is spread equally, which it never is) – mobile phone use and literacy levels. As a comparison, in 2006 the GNI for European countries averaged US$40,000 whereas India was US$820.

Risks, hazards and environmental issues
There is also a very rough indication of notable risks, hazards and environmental issues, but remember that road traffic accidents are always the greatest risk in any destination. Crime is endemic in every city, terrorism is also a threat in many countries and take it for granted that there are universal risks of credit card fraud, street crime, unlicensed taxi scams (especially at airports), and sexual assault.

Time zones and seasons
Time-zone differences are based on standard GMT, but do note that many countries introduce daylight-saving time in spring, which means clocks jump forward an hour and revert back in autumn. In the northern hemisphere summer runs from June to August, and winter from October to February. Countries in the southern hemisphere experience these seasons in reverse, whilst those in equatorial countries (where summer-winter seasons are non-existent) might be better described as wet or dry.

Visas
Where it's indicated that no visa is required, entry is always time limited, usually from 30 days to three months. Country guidelines for entry do change, so it's important to check the current status on each embassy's website.

AFRICA
Kenya
Essentials East Africa; capital: Nairobi; currency: Kenyan shilling (KES); GMT +3

Carbon footprint 8,465 return miles from London, generating 2.1 tonnes of CO_2 per person and 4.1 tonnes from Chicago

People Republic of 37 million people; principal religions: Christian 78%, Muslim 10%, indigenous beliefs 10%, other 2%; official languages: English and Kiswahili, plus many indigenous languages

Wealth indicators GNI = US$ 580; literacy 85%; 18% have mobile phones

Environment Equator; tropical along coast with an arid interior, low plains rising to central highlands bisected by the Great Rift Valley; fertile plateau in west; recurring drought and flooding

Risks and health hazards Political unrest, car jacking and terrorism risk; food or waterborne diseases: bacterial and protozoal diarrhoea, hepatitis A, cholera, typhoid fever, malaria is a high risk in some locations, bilharzia

Conservation opportunities Elephant behaviour monitoring, Sykes' monkey/human conflict, protecting Tsavo lions, cheetahs, hyenas, mangrove forest restoration, rhino protection, flamingo, Grevy's zebra, medicinal plant studies

Who to go with Earthwatch, BTCV, i-to-i, Frontier, GVI

Entry Most visitors require a visa to enter Kenya as a tourist (usually available on arrival)

Further information www.kenya.go.ke

Madagascar
Essentials Island off east Africa coast; capital: Antananarivo; currency: Malagasy Ariary (MGA) ; GMT +3.

Carbon footprint 11,300 return miles from London generating 2.8 tonnes of CO_2 per person and 4.6 tonnes from Chicago.

People Republic of 20 million; principal religions: indigenous beliefs 52%, Christian 41%, Muslim 7%; 3 official languages: English, French, Malagasy

Wealth indicators GNI = US$280; literacy 69%; 5% have mobile phones

Environment Southern hemisphere; tropical along coast, temperate inland, arid in south narrow coastal plain, high plateau and mountains in centre, drought, and locust infestation

Risks and health hazards Cyclones Jan–Mar; food or waterborne diseases, bacterial and protozoal diarrhoea, bilharzia, hepatitis A and typhoid fever, malaria and plague are high risks in some locations

Conservation opportunities Lemur behaviour, radio-tracking fossa (tree-dwelling cat like civet), rainforest, reef diving, sustainable development

Who to go with Blue Ventures, Azafady, i-to-i, Real Gap, Quest, Frontier, GVI, Earthwatch

Entry Most visitors require a visa to enter Madagascar as a tourist (usually available on arrival)

Further information www.wildmadagascar.org

Namibia

Essentials Southwest Africa; capital: Windhoek; currency: Namibian dollar (NAD); GMT +1.

Carbon footprint 10,437 return miles from London generating 2.6 tonnes of CO_2 per person and 3.9 tonnes from Chicago

People A republic of 2 million people; principal religions: Christianity and indigenous beliefs; main languages: Afrikaans, then German, then English

Wealth indicators GNI US$3,230; literacy 85%; 25% have mobile phone

Environment Southern hemisphere; mostly high plateau, hot, dry with erratic rainfall and drought risk; bounded by South Atlantic plus Namibian and Kalahari deserts

Risks and health hazards Not much risk in the predominant desert region, but the wet northwest includes bacterial diarrhoea, hepatitis A, typhoid fever, malaria, bilharzia

Conservation opportunities Leopard and cheetah tracking, animal sanctuaries, desert elephant monitoring and human/animal conflict issues

Who to go with Elephant Human Relations Aid, Earthwatch, Biosphere, GVI, Real Gap, Frontier, GlobalXperience,

Entry Visitors do not require a visa to enter Namibia as a tourist, visas are available on arrival

Further information www.namibiatourism.com.na

Seychelles

Essentials Indian Ocean, over 100 islands northeast of Madagascar; capital: Victoria; currency: Seychelles rupee (SCR); GMT +4.

Carbon footprint 10,100 return miles from London generating 2.5 tonnes of CO_2 per person and 4.5 tonnes from Chicago

People A republic of 82,000 people; principal religions: 93.2% Christian, 2.1% Hindu, 1.1% Muslim; languages: mostly Creole followed by English and French

Wealth indicators GNI = US$8,650; literacy 92%; 85% have mobile phones

Environment Northern hemisphere; the islands lie outside of the hurricane belt, so storms are rare; tropical marine, humid; cooler season during southeast monsoon (late May–Sep); warmer season during northwest monsoon (Mar–May). Mahe Island group is granitic with narrow coastal strip, rocky, hilly; others islands are coral reefs

Risks and health hazards Not many; car theft and potentially dengue fever

Conservation opportunities Coral reef monitoring, fish and turtle protection, whale shark, coastal ecology

Who to go with Earthwatch, GVI

Entry Most visitors do not require a visa to enter Seychelles as a tourist

Further information www.virtualseychelles.sc

South Africa

Essentials Southern tip of Africa; capital: Pretoria; currency: Rand (ZAR); GMT +2.

Carbon footprint 11,200 return miles from London generating 2.8 tonnes of CO_2 per person and 4.3 tonnes from Chicago

People A republic of 44 million people; principal religions: 79.7% Christian, 18.8% indigenous and 1.5% Muslim; main languages: tribal, Afrikaans and English

Wealth indicators GNI per capita US$5,390; literacy 86%; 66% have mobile phones

Environment Southern hemisphere; a vast interior plateau rimmed by rugged hills and narrow coastal plain, mostly semi-arid but subtropical along east coast with sunny days and cool nights

Risks and health hazards High crime rate; bacterial diarrhoea, hepatitis A, typhoid fever, haemorrhagic fever, malaria and bilharzia

Conservation volunteering Game ranger courses, animal sanctuaries, national park projects, meerkats, brown hyena, African penguins, sharks, dolphins, wildlife surveys, reforestation, reptiles, leopards, reforestation

Who to go with GVI, Africa Conservation Experience, Real Gap, Edge of Africa , Africa Guide, Earthwatch, Projects Abroad, Greenforce, BTCV, i-to-i, Frontier, GVI, Operation Wallacea, Travellers Worldwide, GlobalXperience

Entry Most visitors do not require a visa to enter South Africa as a tourist

Further information www.safrica.info

Zambia

Essentials South central Africa; capital: Lusaka; currency: Kwacha (ZMK); GMT +2.

Carbon footprint 9,850 return miles from London generating 2.4 tonnes of CO_2 per person and 4.1 tonnes from Chicago

People A republic of 11.5 million people; principal religions: Christian 50–75%, Muslim and Hindu 24–49%, indigenous beliefs 1%; main language: English with 75 indigenous languages

Wealth indicators GNI = US$630; literacy 87%; 10% have mobile phones

Environment Southern hemisphere; tropical; modified by altitude; rainy season Oct–Apr; mostly high plateau with some hills and mountains, periodic drought

Risks and health hazards Caution needed near the Congo border region; food or waterborne diseases; bacterial diarrhoea, hepatitis A, and typhoid fever, malaria and plague are high risks in some locations, bilharzia

Conservation opportunities Nile crocodile population studies, national park work, elephants

Who to go with Earthwatch, Frontier, GlobalXperience

Entry Most visitors require a visa to enter Zambia as a tourist (apply before departure)

Further information www.zambiatourism.com

NORTH AMERICA
Canada
Essentials Capital: Ottawa; currency: Canadian dollar (CAD); GMT varies from Eastern Time -5 to Pacific Time -8
Carbon footprint 6,660 return miles from London generating 1.66 tonnes of CO_2 per person and 0.32 tonnes from Chicago
People Constitutional monarchy, parliamentary democracy and a federation of 33.5 million people; principal religions: Christian 86.6%, Muslim 1.9%, other 11.8%, none 16%; official languages: English 59.3%, French 23.2%, other 17.5%
Wealth indicators GNI = US$36,170; literacy 99%; 50% have mobile phones
Environment Northern hemisphere; varies from temperate in south to sub-arctic and arctic in north; mostly plains with mountains in west and lowlands in southeast continuous
permafrost in north
Risks and health hazards Cyclones May–Sept; rabies
Conservation opportunities Minke and grey whale in the St Lawrence Gulf, bears, wolves, bobcat, small mammals, mammals of Nova Scotia, climate change studies
Who to go with Earthwatch, Ecovolunteer,
Entry British and American visitors do not require a visa to enter Canada as a tourist
Further information www.canada.travel

United States of America
Essentials Capital: Washington, DC; currency: American dollar (USD); GMT varies from Eastern Time -5, to Pacific Time -8
Carbon footprint 7,895 return miles from London generating 1.9 tonnes of CO_2 per person and 0.13 tonnes from Chicago
People Constitution-based federal republic of 304 million; principal religions: Christian 78%, Jewish 1%, Muslim 1%, other 20%; languages: English 82%, Spanish 11%, others 7%
Wealth indicators GNI = US$44,970; literacy 99%; 70% have mobile phones
Environment Northern hemisphere mostly temperate, but tropical in Hawaii and Florida, arctic in Alaska, semi-arid in the great plains west of the Mississippi River, and arid in the Great Basin of the southwest; low winter temperatures in the northwest, vast central plain, mountains in west, hills and low mountains in east; rugged mountains and broad river valleys in Alaska, volcanic topography in Hawaii
Risks and health hazards Street crime risk in urban areas; hurricane in south Jun–Nov, earthquakes and forest fires on the west coast, road deaths almost triple that of UK, West Nile virus,
Conservation opportunities Otter, bottlenose dolphin, grey whales, sharks, turtles, diamondback terrapin, prairie plants, coastal reserves, Alaskan sea birds, songbirds, moose, wolf, bear, bobcat, wild horses, Alaskan fur seals, sharks and rays, black sea turtle, Florida big cat sanctuary, New York

wildlife, Hawaii rainforest and sugar plantations

Who to go with Earthwatch, Ecovolunteer, BTCV, Real Gap

Entry Most visitors require a visa to enter America as a tourist, but most British visitors can use the visa waiver scheme but must first register via the American embassy website
from January 2009.

Further information www.usatourist.com

CENTRAL AMERICA
Bahamas

Essentials Central America in the Caribbean Sea; capital: Nassau; currency: Bahamian dollar (BSD); GMT -5.

Carbon footprint 8,680 return miles from London generating 2.17 tonnes of CO_2 per person and 0.65 tonnes from Chicago

People Constitutional parliamentary democracy of 306,000 people; principal religion: Christian 96.3%, other 3.7%; official language: English (near 100%)

Wealth indicators GNI = US$14,920; literacy 95%; 65% have mobile phones

Environment Northern hemisphere; tropical marine; moderated by warm waters of Gulf Stream; long, flat coral formations with some low rounded hills subtropical, hurricanes Jun–Nov

Risks and health hazards Watersports injuries are the biggest risk; possible malaria risk

Conservation opportunities Coastal ecology and mapping, coral reef surveys, whale and dolphin monitoring

Who to go with Earthwatch, Greenforce,

Entry Most visitors do not require a visa to enter the Bahamas as a tourist

Further information www.bahamas.com

Belize

Essentials Central America, bordering the Caribbean Sea; capital: Belmopan; currency: Belize dollar (BZD); GMT -6

Carbon footprint 10,460 return miles from London generating 2.6 tonnes of CO_2 per person and 0.85 tonnes from Chicago

People Parliamentary democracy of 300,000 people; principal religion: Christian 89%, 11% other; official language: English, but most speak Spanish 46%, Creole 32.9%, Mayan languages 8.9%, other 8.2%

Wealth indicators GNI = US$3,650; literacy 77%; 35% have mobile phones

Environment Northern hemisphere; tropical; very hot and humid; rainy season (May–Nov), dry season (Feb–May); flat, swampy coastal plain; low mountains in south, hurricanes (Jun–Nov) and coastal flooding

Risks and health hazards Dengue fever is endemic to Latin America

Conservation opportunities Coral reef monitoring, queen conch, coastal reserves, rainforest, marine mammals

Who to go with Earthwatch, GVI, Quest, i-to-i, Real Gap, Trekforce

Entry Most visitors do not require a visa to enter Belize as a tourist

Further information www.travelbelize.org.

Costa Rica

Essentials Central America; capital: San José; currency: Colón (CRC); GMT -6

Carbon footprint 10,480 return miles from London generating 2.7 tonnes of CO_2 per person and 1.1 tonnes from Chicago.

People Stable democratic republic of 4 million people; principal religion: Christianity 92%, 8% other; main languages: Spanish then English

Wealth indicators GNI = US$4,980; literacy 96%; 25% have mobile phones

Environment Northern hemisphere; coastal plains separated by mountain range; tropical and subtropical with active volcanoes, earthquakes, hurricanes, lowland flooding and landslides

Risks and health hazards Dengue fever is endemic to Latin America

Conservation opportunities Leatherback turtle, capuchin and howler monkeys, coral reefs, coastal reserves, sustainable rainforest use, caterpillars as forest indicators, sustainable coffee growing, volcanoes and wildlife

Who to go with Earthwatch, GVI, Quest, Frontier, i-to-i, Real Gap, Projects Abroad, GlobalXperience

Entry Most visitors do not require a visa to enter Costa Rica as a tourist

Further information www.tourism.co.cr

Mexico

Essentials Central America, bordering the Gulf of Mexico and Pacific Ocean; capital: Mexico City; currency: Mexican peso (MXN); GMT -7

Carbon footprint 10,970 return miles from London generating 2.74 tonnes of CO_2 per person and 0.9 tonnes from Chicago

People Federal republic of 110 million people; principal religion: Christian 76.6%, 23.4% other; official language: Spanish, but a number of Mayan languages are in use outside big cities

Wealth indicators GNI = US$7,870; 91% literacy %; 51% have mobile phones

Environment High, rugged mountains, low coastal plains, high plateaux, climate ranges from tropical to desert

Risks and health hazards Volcanoes and earthquakes in the centre and south, with hurricanes on the Pacific, Gulf of Mexico and Caribbean coasts; bacterial diarrhoea, hepatitis A, typhoid, dengue fever

Conservation opportunities Coral reef monitoring, rainforest, marine mammals

Who to go with GVI, Projects Abroad

Entry Most visitors do not require a visa to enter Mexico as a tourist. You do need an FMT tourist card – forms available at border crossings or on board flights to Mexico

Further information www.visitmexico.com

SOUTH AMERICA

Argentina

Essentials South, South America; capital: Buenos Aires; currency: Peso (ARS); GMT -3

Carbon footprint 13,835 return miles from London generating 3.45 tonnes of CO_2 per person and 2.7 tonnes from Chicago

People A republic of over 40 million people; principal religion: 94% Christian and 6% other; official language: Spanish
Wealth indicators GNI = US$5,150; literacy 97%; 65% have mobile phones
Environment Southern hemisphere; varied from subtropical rainforest in northeast, central pampas and sub-artic in the far south; Andes Mountains, natural hazards include earthquakes and fierce windstorms
Risks and Health hazards Yellow fever on its northern borders; dengue fever is endemic to Latin America
Conservation opportunities Big and small cats, condors, small mammals and reptiles
Who to go with i-to-i, GVI
Entry Most visitors do not require a visa to enter Argentina as a tourist
Further information www.turismo.gov.ar

Bolivia

Essentials Central South America; capital: La Paz; currency: Boliviano (BOB); GMT -4
Carbon footprint 12,420 return miles from London generating 3.1 tonnes of CO_2 per person and 2.3 tonnes from Chicago.
People Republic of 10 million people; principal religion: Christian 100%; official language: Spanish
Wealth indicators GNI = US$1,100; literacy rate 87%; 25% have mobile phones
Environment Southern hemisphere, varies with altitude; humid and tropical to cold and semi-arid, rugged Andes Mountains with a highland plateau, lowland Amazon Basin, flood risk
Risks and health hazards 'Express kidnapping' – short-term abductions to extort cash; dengue fever is endemic to Latin America
Conservation opportunities Caring for injured wildlife, giant otter survey
Who to go with GlobalXperience, Operation Wallacea, Inti Wara Yassi
Entry Most visitors do not require a visa to enter Bolivia as a tourist, but US Americans do
Further information www.boliviaweb.com

Brazil

Essentials East South America; capital: Brasilia; currency: Real (BRL); GMT -3 plus four other time zones
Carbon footprint 11,525 return miles from London generating 2.8 tonnes of CO_2 per person and 2.6 tonnes from Chicago
People A federal republic of 190 million people; principal religion: Christian 89%, 11% other; official language: Portuguese
Wealth indicators GNI = US$4,730; literacy 87%; 55% have mobile phones
Environment Southern hemisphere; mostly tropical, but temperate in south, mostly flat to rolling lowlands in north; some plains, hills, mountains and narrow coastal belt
Risks and health hazards Crime risk in big cities, especially in favelas (shanty towns); dengue fever in Rio and yellow fever generally

Conservation opportunities Puma and jaguar behaviour studies, ocelot, wolf, primate, humpback whale conservation, recording behaviour of the boto-cinza dolphins, field research on river otters, amphibians of Pantanal, toucan conservation, anaconda, caiman, birds, bats, rainforest reforestation, coastal reserves, deforestation, wildlife sanctuary

Who to go with Earthwatch, GVI, Quest, Frontier, i-to-i, Real Gap, Biosphere, Ecovolunteer, GlobalXperience

Entry Most visitors do not require a visa to enter Brazil as a tourist, but US Americans do

Further information www.braziltourism.org

Peru

Essentials Western South America; capital: Lima; currency: Nuevo sol (PEN); GMT -5

Carbon footprint 12,630 return miles from London generating 3.1 tonnes of CO_2 per person and 1.89 tonnes from Chicago

People A constitutional republic of 29 million; principal religion: Christian 83.1%, 16.9% other; official language: Spanish, but there are many indigenous languages

Wealth indicators GNI = US$2,920; literacy 88%; 35% have mobile phones

Environment Equatorial and southern hemisphere, varies from tropical in east to dry desert in west; temperate to frigid in the Andes, coastal plain, high Andes and central and eastern lowland jungle of the Amazon Basin; earthquakes, flooding and landslides in the wet season (Nov–Apr)

Risks and health hazards Traffic accidents, 'express kidnapping' – short-term abductions to extort cash; dengue fever, malaria (in wet lowlands) and yellow fever are endemic to Peru, while rabies is common in some areas

Conservation opportunities Primates, rainforest, marine mammals, macaw, manatee, river dolphin, giant river otter, peccaries, tapir, turtle

Who to go with Earthwatch, Ecovolunteers, GVI, Quest, Frontier, i-to-i, Real Gap, Biosphere Expeditions, Projects Abroad, Operation Wallacea, Travellers Worldwide, GlobalXperience

Entry Most visitors do not normally require a visa to enter Peru as a tourist

Further information www.peru.info/perueng.asp

EUROPE

Greece

Essentials Southern Europe, bordering the Mediterranean Sea; capital: Athens; currency: Euro (EUR); GMT +2

Carbon footprint 2,970 return miles from London generating 0.74 tonnes of CO_2 per person and 2.71 tonnes from Chicago.

People A stable parliamentary republic of 10.7 million people; principal religions: Christian (Greek Orthodox) 98%, Muslim 1.2 %; official language: Greek

Wealth indicators GNI = US$21,690; literacy 96%; close to 100% have mobile phones

Environment Northern hemisphere; mountainous peninsula with around 2,000 islands in the Aegean and Ionian seas. Mild, temperate climate with hot dry summers and wet winters. Natural hazards include earthquakes and summer fires

Risks and health hazards Road traffic injuries triple that of UK

Conservation opportunities Bottlenose dolphins, loggerhead turtles, marine protection

Who to go with Earthwatch, Archelon, Ecovolunteer, GVI, GlobalXperience,

Entry British and American visitors do not require a visa to enter Greece as a tourists; a Schengen country

Further information www.gnto.co.uk

Russia

Essentials West of the Urals is Europe to the east is Asia; capital: Moscow; currency: Rouble (RUB); 11 times zones from GMT +2 to GMT +12;

Carbon footprint 3,100 return miles from London generating 0.77 tonnes of CO_2 per person and 2.48 tonnes from Chicago

People A federation of 141 million people; principal religions: Christian (Russian Orthodox) 20%, Muslim 10–15%, other unknown; official language: Russian with many minority languages

Wealth indicators GNI = US$5,780; literacy 99.4%; close to 100% have mobile phones

Environment Steppe in the south through humid continental in much of European Russia; sub-arctic in Siberia to tundra climate in the polar north; broad plain with low hills west of Urals; vast coniferous forest and tundra in Siberia; uplands and mountains along southern border regions

Risks and health hazards Terrorist risk in Chechnya and the north Caucasus; volcanoes and earthquakes on the Kamchatka Peninsula; food poisoning, unsafe water, tuberculosis, rabies, bacterial diarrhoea and hepatitis A, haemorrhagic fever and tick-borne encephalitis, H5N1 avian influenza.

Conservation opportunities Brown bear rescue and release, tracking and monitoring released wolves

Who to go with Ecovolunteer, Projects Abroad

Entry Most visitors require a visa and a letter of introduction to enter Russia as a tourist

Further information www.russia.com

Slovakia

Essentials Central Europe; capital: Bratislava; currency: Slovak crown (SKK); GMT +1

Carbon footprint 1,630 return miles from London generating 0.4 tonnes of CO_2 per person and 2.35 tonnes from Chicago

People Parliamentary democracy of 5.5 million; principal religion: Christian 83.8%, other 16.2%; main languages: Slovak 83.9%, Hungarian 10.7%, Roma 1.8%, Ukrainian 1%, other 2.6%

Wealth indicators GNI = US$9,870 literacy 99%; 95% have mobile phones

Environment Northern hemisphere; temperate; cool summers; cold, cloudy, humid winters; rugged mountains in the central and northern part and lowlands in the south

Risks and health hazards Road traffic injuries double that of UK; pickpocketing in Bratislava; tick-borne encephalitis in forested areas

Conservation opportunities Big cats, bears, wolves, chamois

Who to go with Ecovolunteer

Entry British and American visitors do not require a visa to enter Slovakia as a tourist; a Schengen country

Further information www.slovakia.com

Spain

Essentials Southwestern Europe, bordering Mediterranean Sea; capital: Madrid; currency: Euro (EUR); GMT +1

Carbon footprint 1,570 return miles from London generating 0.39 tonnes of CO_2 per person and 2.09 tonnes from Chicago

People Parliamentary monarchy of 41 million; principal religion: Christian 94%, other 6%; official language: Castilian Spanish 74%, others spoken include Catalan 17%, Galician 7%, Basque 2%

Wealth indicators GNI = US$27,570; literacy 99%; close to 100% have mobile phones

Environment Northern hemisphere; temperate; clear, hot summers in interior, more moderate and cloudy along coast; cloudy, cold winters in interior, partly cloudy and cool along coast; large central plateau surrounded by rugged hills; Pyrenees in north

Risks and health hazards Road traffic injuries double that of UK

Conservation opportunities Iberian lynx, common dolphin, desert habitats, lammergeyer, capercaillie, vultures, Cordoba Zoo

Who to go with Biosphere Expeditions, Earthwatch, Ecovolunteer, GlobalXperience GVI, Quest

Entry British and American visitors do not require a visa to enter Spain as a tourist; a Schengen country

Further information www.spain.info

United Kingdom

Essentials Islands off western Europe; capital: London; currency: Pound sterling (GBP); GMT = 0

Carbon footprint 0 return miles from London generating 0 tonnes of CO_2 per person and 1.97 tonnes from Chicago

People Constitutional monarchy of 61 million; principal religions: Christian 71.6%, Muslim 2.7%, Hindu 1%, other 24.7%; official language: English, with some Welsh and Gaelic

Wealth indicators GNI = US$40,180; literacy 99%; close to 100% have mobile phones

Environment Northern hemisphere; temperate; moderated by prevailing southwest winds; more than half of the days are overcast; some rugged hills and low mountains; level to rolling plains in east and southeast

Risks and health hazards Road injuries and petty crime

Conservation opportunities Scottish and other reforestation, bottlenose dolphin, harbour porpoise, minke whale, beaked whale, grey whale, basking sharks, otter

Who to go with BTCV, Earthwatch

Entry EU, US, Canadian and Australian visitors do not normally require a visa to enter the UK as a tourist

Further information www.visitbritain.com

MIDDLE EAST
Oman

Essentials Middle East, bordering the Arabian Sea; capital: Muscat; currency: Rial (OMR); GMT +4

Carbon footprint 7,375 return miles from London generating 1.84 tonnes of CO_2 per person and 3.76 tonnes from Chicago.

People A monarchy of 3.25 million people; principal religion: Muslim 75% other 25%; official languages: Arabic, English

Wealth indicators GNI = US$9,070; literacy 86.8%; 43% have mobile phones

Environment Northern hemisphere; dry desert; hot, humid along coast; hot, dry interior; strong southwest summer monsoon (May–Sep) in far south central desert plain, rugged mountains in north and south, sandstorms in interior; periodic droughts

Risks and health hazards 48-hour prison sentences for traffic offences and 12 months for drink driving; some common prescription medicines are banned; and homosexual behaviour is illegal

Conservation opportunities Arabian leopard

Who to go with Biosphere Expeditions

Entry Most visitors require a visa to enter Oman as a tourist (available on arrival)

Further information www.omantourism.gov.om

CENTRAL AND SOUTH ASIA
China

Essentials East Asia; capital: Beijing; currency: Yuan (CNY); GMT +8

Carbon footprint 10,550 return miles from London generating 2.6 tonnes of CO_2 per person and 3.21 tonnes from Chicago

People Communist state of 1,322 million; officially atheist, predominant religions Taoist and Buddhist with Christian 3–4%, Muslim 1–2%; main language: Mandarin with many subsets and dialects

Wealth indicators GNI = US$2,010; literacy 91%; 30% have mobile phones

Environment Northern hemisphere; extremely diverse; tropical in south to sub-arctic in north, mountains, high plateaux, deserts in west; plains, deltas and hills in east; typhoons floods, tsunamis, earthquakes, droughts

Risks and health hazards Outbreaks of avian influenza, 1,000 cases per year of rabies, dengue fever in the south. The extreme altitude in Tibet can be a

hazard; drug trafficking carries a long prison sentence or the death penalty
Conservation opportunities Panda breeding centre, water and the Gobi Desert,
Who to go with Quest, Frontier, Greenforce, i-to-i, Real Gap
Entry Most foreign visitors require a visa to enter China (not Hong Kong) as
a tourist; application process outsourced to a commercial agent in 2008
Further information www.china.org.cn/english

India

Essentials South Asia; capital: New Delhi; currency: Indian rupee (INR); GMT
+5.5
Carbon footprint 8,330 return miles from London generating 2.08 tonnes of
CO_2 per person and 3.74 tonnes from Chicago
People Federal republic of 1,130 million people; principal religions: Hindu
80.5%, Muslim 13.4%, Christian 2.3%, Sikh 1.9%, other 1.9%; official
language: Hindi, but English is a key business language with many other
dialects
Wealth indicators GNI = US$820; literacy 61%; 15% have mobile phones
Environment Northern hemisphere; varies from tropical monsoon in south to
temperate in the north and the central upland plain (Deccan Plateau). Flat
to rolling plain along the Ganges, deserts in west, Himalayas in the north;
droughts, flash floods, as well as widespread and destructive flooding from
monsoon rains, severe thunderstorms and earthquakes
Risks and health hazards Road deaths alarmingly high, civil unrest and terrorist
threat especially in northwest provinces; bacterial diarrhoea, hepatitis A
and E, and typhoid fever, dengue fever, malaria, and Japanese encephalitis
are high risks in some locations; rabies; highly pathogenic H5N1 avian
influenza has been identified in birds
Conservation opportunities Pygmy hog is critically endangered, tiger, elephant,
sustainable development
Who to go with Projects Abroad
Entry Most visitors require a visa to enter India as a tourist (not available on
arrival)
Further information www.incredibleindia.org

Mongolia

Essentials Northern Asia, between China and Russia; capital: Ulaanbaatar;
currency: Tughrik (MNT); GMT +8
Carbon footprint 8,660 return miles from London generating 2.16 tonnes of
CO_2 per person and 3.01 tonnes from Chicago.
People A mixed parliamentary/presidential democracy of 3 million people;
principal religions: Buddhist Lamaist 50%, shamanist and Christian 6%,
Muslim 4%, other/none 40%; official language: Mongol 90%, Russian and
other 10%
Wealth indicators GNI = US$880; literacy figure unknown; 16% have mobile
phones
Environment Northern hemisphere; large daily and seasonal temperature

ranges, vast semi-desert and desert plains, grassy steppe, mountains in west and southwest; Gobi Desert south central, dust storms, grassland and forest fires, drought, and harsh winter conditions

Risks and health hazards Poor infrastructure outside Ulaanbaatar; safety concerns about domestic airlines

Conservation opportunities Przewalski's horses, pallas cats, Siberian ibex, mountain goats, leaping jerboa, cinereous vultures, small mammal research

Who to go with Earthwatch, Ecovolunteer, Projects Abroad

Entry British visitors require a visa to enter Mongolia as a tourist but Americans do not

Further information www.mongoliatourism.gov.mn

Sri Lanka

Essentials Southern Asia off the tip of India; capital Colombo; currency: Sri Lankan rupee (LKR); GMT +5.5

Carbon footprint 10,820 return miles from London generating 2.7 tonnes of CO_2 per person and 4.48 tonnes from Chicago

People Presidential parliamentary democracy of 21 million; principal religions: Buddhist 69.1%, Muslim 7.6%, Hindu 7.1%, Christian 6.2%, unspecified 10%; main languages: Sinhala 74%, Tamil 18%, other 8%, English is widely used

Wealth indicators GNI = US$1,300; 91% literacy; 35% have mobile phones

Environment Southern hemisphere; tropical monsoon; northeast monsoon (Dec–Mar); southwest monsoon (Jun–Oct); mostly low, flat to rolling plain; mountains in south-central interior, occasional cyclones and tornadoes

Risks and health hazards Civil unrest and terrorist risk in the north and east (Tamil Tigers); dengue fever, chikungunya and malaria; monsoon; Volcanoes and earthquakes on the Kamchatka Peninsula

Conservation opportunities Elephants, tigers, leopards, monkeys, hawksbill, leatherback, olive ridley, loggerhead and green turtles, sustainable development

Who to go with Travellers Worldwide, Real Gap, Earthwatch, Frontier, GVI

Entry Most visitors require a visa to enter Sri Lanka as a tourist (available on arrival)

Further information www.srilankatourism.org

SOUTHEAST ASIA

Indonesia

Essentials Equator, southeast Asia, archipelago between Indian and Pacific oceans;
capital: Jakarta; currency: Rupiah (IDR); GMT +7

Carbon footprint 14,550 return miles from London generating 3.64 tonnes of CO_2 per person and 4.9 tonnes from Chicago.

People Republic of 235 million people; principal religions: Muslim 86.1%, Christian 8.7%, Hindu 1.8%, other 3.4%; main language: Indonesia (a form of Malay), English and Dutch

Wealth indicators GNI = US$1,420; literacy 90%; 23% have mobile phones
Environment Southern hemisphere, tropical; hot, humid; more moderate in highlands, mostly coastal lowlands; larger islands have interior mountains; occasional floods, severe droughts, tsunamis, earthquakes, volcanoes, forest fires
Risks and health hazards Civil unrest and terrorism risk, safety concerns about domestic airlines; bacterial and protozoal diarrhoea, hepatitis A and E, typhoid fever, dengue fever, malaria and chikungunya; highly pathogenic H5N1 avian influenza, leprosy, anthrax are high risks in some locations. Gambling is illegal and convicted traffickers or users of hard drugs face the death penalty
Conservation opportunities Orang-utan field research and sanctuaries, caring for injured wildlife, rainforest and reef monitoring
Who to go with Way Out Experiences, GVI, Ecovolunteer, Quest, Frontier, i-to-i, Travellers Worldwide, Real Gap, Trekforce, Operation Wallacea, GlobalXperience
Entry Most visitors require a visa to enter Indonesia as a tourist (available at major airports and some sea port arrival points)
Further information www.indonesia-tourism.com

Malaysia

Essentials Equator, southeast Asia, peninsula bordering Thailand and northern third of the island of Borneo; capital: Kuala Lumpur; currency: Ringgit (MYR); GMT +8
Carbon footprint 13,100 return miles from London generating 3.27 tonnes of CO_2 per person and 4.63 tonnes from Chicago
People Constitutional monarchy of 25 million people; principal religions: Muslim 60.4%, Buddhist 19.2%, Christian 9.1%, Hindu 6.3%, Confucianism and Taoism 2.6%, other 2.3%; main languages: Malay, English, Chinese and several indigenous languages
Wealth indicators GNI = US$5,490; 89% literacy; mobile phones uncommon
Environment Southern hemisphere; tropical; annual southwest (Apr–Oct) and northeast (Oct–Feb) monsoons; coastal plains rising to hills and mountains
Risks and health hazards Food or waterborne diseases: bacterial diarrhoea, hepatitis A, typhoid fever, dengue fever and malaria are high risks in some locations; as are forest fires flooding, landslides. Homosexual acts are illegal. Drug trafficking incurs a mandatory death penalty; possession incurs a custodial sentence or whipping
Conservation opportunities Bats, rainforest, orang-utan, pygmy elephant,
Who to go with Way Out Experiences, GVI, Ecovolunteer, Quest, Frontier, i-to-i, Travellers Worldwide, Real Gap
Entry Most tourists do not need a visa to enter Malaysia as a visitor
Further information www.tourism.gov.my

Thailand
Essentials Southeast Asia, bordering the Andaman Sea and the Gulf of Thailand; capital: Bangkok; currency: Thai baht (THB); GMT +7
Carbon footprint 11,840 return miles from London generating 2.96 tonnes of CO_2 per person and 4.89 tonnes from Chicago
People Constitutional monarchy of 65 million people; principal religions: Buddhist 94.6%, Muslim 4.6%, Christian 0.7%, other 0.1%; official language: Thai, English widely spoken, plus ethnic and regional dialects
Wealth indicators GNI = US$2,990; literacy 93%; 65% have mobile phones
Environment Northern hemisphere; tropical; rainy, warm, cloudy southwest monsoon (mid-May–Sep); dry, cool northeast monsoon (Nov–mid-Mar); southern isthmus always hot and humid; central plain; Khorat Plateau in the east; mountains elsewhere
Risks and health hazards Civil unrest and terrorism in the southern provinces; 38 people die everyday on motorcycles and drug-related road accidents, exceptionally high for visiting Europeans; dive operators are not always qualified; bacterial diarrhoea and hepatitis A, dengue fever, malaria, Japanese encephalitis, and plague are high risks in some locations; rabies, leptospirosis, highly pathogenic H5N1 avian influenza. Insulting the royal family is an imprisonable offence. Drug trafficking carries a long prison sentence or the death penalty
Conservation opportunities Coral reef monitoring, mangrove restoration, elephant sanctuary, rainforest, gibbon rescue, macaque, gibbon and loris sanctuary, turtle nesting protection, sustainable development
Who to go with Earthwatch, GVI, Starfish Ventures, Quest, Africa Conservation Experience, Travellers Worldwide, Frontier, Ecovolunteer, Projects Abroad, GlobalXperience
Entry Most visitors can acquire a tourist visa on entering Thailand
Further information www.tourismthailand.org

OCEANIA
Australia
Essentials Oceania, continent between the Indian and South Pacific oceans; capital: Canberra; currency: Australian dollar (AUD); Western Standard Time (Western Australia) GMT+8, Central Standard Time (South Australia and Northern Territory) GMT +9.30, Eastern Standard Time (New South Wales, Victoria and Queensland) GMT +10
Carbon footprint 21,100 return miles from London generating 5.27 tonnes of CO_2 per person and 4.69 tonnes from Chicago
People Federal parliamentary democracy of 20.5 million people; principal religions: Christian 67.4%, Buddhist 1.9%, Muslim 1.5%, other 1.2%, unspecified 12.7%, none 15.3%; main languages: English 79.1%, Chinese 2.1%, Italian 1.9%, other 11.1%, unspecified 5.8%
Wealth indicators GNI = US$35,990; literacy 99%; 98% have mobile phones
Environment Southern hemisphere; sub-tropical in the north, central desert region, temperate southern coastal region mostly low plateau with deserts;

fertile plain in southeast; limited freshwater resources, cyclones along the coast (Nov–Apr); severe droughts; forest fires

Risks and health hazards Wildlife, road trains on rural roads, tidal rip currents cause 100 deaths and 10,000 rescues per year Mosquito-borne diseases such as dengue fever, Ross River fever and Murray Valley encephalitis (MVE) are a risk in northern tropical areas also tropical cyclones

Conservation opportunities Barrier reef coral and fish, whale shark, northern rainforests, hawksbill turtle, fish, koala, arboreal marsupials, kangaroo, bettong, cockatoo, echidna, goanna, national park maintenance

Who to go with CVA, Earthwatch, GVI, Real Gap, Frontier, i-to-i, GlobalXperience

Entry British and American visitors require a visa to enter Australia (electronic visa (ETA) is available for most tourists)

Further information www.australia.com

New Zealand

Essentials South Pacific Ocean, southeast of Australia; capital: Wellington; currency: New Zealand dollar (NZD); GMT +12

Carbon footprint 23,400 return miles from London generating 5.85 tonnes of CO_2 per person and 4.17 tonnes from Chicago

People Parliamentary democracy of 4 million people; principal religions: Christian 53.5%, other 3.3%, unspecified 17.2%, none 26%; official languages: English and Maori

Wealth indicators GNI = US$27,250; literacy 99%; 90% have mobile phones

Environment Southern hemisphere; climate with sharp regional contrasts, mountainous with some large coastal plains; earthquakes but usually not severe; some volcanic activity

Risks and health hazards Road deaths nearly twice that of UK; extreme adventure sports are a risk

Conservation opportunities Marine mammals, forests, birds, national park maintenance

Who to go with CVNZ, GVI, Real Gap, Frontier, BTCV, GlobalXperience

Entry British and American visitors do not require a visa to enter New Zealand as a tourist (visa wavier scheme)

Further information www.newzealand.govt.nz/aboutnz

Papua New Guinea

Essentials Eastern half of island of New Guinea in Coral Sea; capital: Port Moresby; currency: Papua New Guinea Kina (PGK); GMT +10

Carbon footprint 18,000 return miles from London generating around 4.5 tonnes of CO_2 per person and 4.22 tonnes from Chicago

People Constitutional parliamentary democracy of 6 million people; principal religions: Christian 66% and indigenous beliefs 34%; main language; English is the business language, but pidgin dialects are more widespread, along with 820 indigenous languages

Wealth indicators GNI = US$770; literacy 57%; 1–2% have mobile phones

Environment Warm to hot and humid throughout the year, driest (May–Dec); mountainous rainforest, fertile coastal plains and flooded delta regions
Risks and health hazards Volcanoes and earthquakes; dengue fever, malaria, bacterial diarrhoea, hepatitis A and typhoid fever
Conservation opportunities Rainforest conservation, coral reef surveying, sustainable eco-developments
Who to go with Trekforce, GVI, Coral Cay Greenforce, Real Gap
Entry A 60-day visa is available to most visitors on arrival and costs 100 PNG kina
Further information www.pngtourism.org.pg

CONSERVATION VOLUNTEERING IN THE UK

Don't automatically think you have to travel abroad to do meaningful conservation volunteering. Here in the UK we have been devastating our wildlife and environment for centuries. We have destroyed most of our native forest and driven many endemic species to extinction. Britain is probably more in need of conservation volunteers than many faraway countries and there are wildlife surveys of endangered species, reforestation projects, environment restoration and plenty more that needs doing.

WEEKEND CONSERVATION

The British Trust for Conservation Volunteers (*www.btcv.org.uk*) runs hundreds of conservation volunteer projects throughout the UK during weekdays and at weekends (see page 108).

ENDANGERED WILDLIFE

Every part of the UK has its local Wildlife Trust (*www.wildlifetrusts.org*) working on a host of endangered wildlife and environmental restoration projects (see page 156).

REFORESTATION

Trees for Life (*www.treesforlife.org.uk*) is a conservation charity dedicated to the regeneration and restoration of the Caledonian Forest in the Scottish Highlands. Ninety-nine per cent of this native forest has been destroyed, but they have planted 600,000 trees in recent years and aim to continue planting 100,000 each year (see page 152).

RENEWABLE RESOURCES

The Centre for Alternative Technology (*www.cat.org.uk*) in Powys, Wales, has been pioneering low-impact and renewable energy solutions for over 25 years. There are long- and short-term volunteer opportunities, hands-on courses and getting-in-touch-with-nature holidays (see page 146). Not only are these organisations doing vitally important work to preserve and restore Britain's natural environment, they offer great opportunities for volunteers to experience conservation work without having to travel across the globe or spend a lot of money.

APPENDIX 2
FURTHER INFORMATION

BOOKS

Ausenda, Fabio *Green Volunteers: The World Guide to Voluntary Work in Nature Conservation* Green Volunteers, 2005

Benjamin, Alison & Brian McCullam *A World Without Bees* Guardian Newspapers, 2008

Boyle, Godfrey *Renewable Energy* Oxford University Press,1996

Bradt, Hilary, Derek Schuurman & Nick Garbutt *Madagascar Wildlife* Bradt Travel Guides, 2007

Cheshire, Gerard, Huw Lloyd & Barry Walker *Peruvian Wildlife* Bradt Travel Guides, 2007

De Silva Wijeyeratne, Gehan *Sri Lankan Wildlife* Bradt Travel Guides, 2005

Finn, Adharanand *Make a Difference at Work* Think Publishing, 2008

Ford, Liz *The Guardian Guide to Volunteering* Guardian Newspapers, 2007

Fossey, Dian Fossey *Gorillas in the Mist: A Remarkable Story of Thirteen Years Spent Living with the Greatest of the Great Apes* Hodder and Stoughton, 2001

Garbutt, Nick, *100 Animals to See Before They Die* Bradt Travel Guides, 2007

Goodall, Jane *My Life with the Chimpanzees* Simon & Schuster, (revised ed) 2008

Lovelock, James *The Revenge of Gaia: Why the Earth is Fighting Back and How We Can Still Save Humanity* Penguin, 2006

Monbiot, George *Amazon Watershed* Abacus,1992

Pullin, Andrew *Conservation Biology* Cambridge University Press, 2002

Sinclair, Tony, John Fryxell, and Graeme Caughley *Wildlife Ecology, Conservation and Management* Blackwell, 2005

Walters, Martin *Chinese Wildlife* Bradt Travel Guides, 2008

Woodroffe, Rosie, Simon Thirgood and Alan Rabinowitz *People and Wildlife Conflict or Co-existence* Cambridge University Press, 2005

*Griffin, Tom *A Discourse Analysis of UK-sourced Gap Year Overseas Projects* MA study, University of the West of England

MAGAZINES

BBC Wildlife (🖱 *www.bbcwildlifemagazine.com*) spotlights specific animal species and wildlife-rich destinations.

Biological Conservation (🖱 *www.elsevier.com/wps/find/journaldescription. cws_home/405853/description#description*) is a scientific research journal of the Society of Conservation Biology

National Geographic (🖱 *www.nationalgeographic.com*) carries news stories, articles and features about animals, the environment and cultures.

The Ecologist (🖱 *www.theecologist.org*). is a good source of information about current environmental issues.

WEBSITES

Official government websites
Those listed below are government websites containing travel warnings, passport and visa information, health and safety advice, emergency assistance abroad and much more. Although aimed at their nationals, much of the information is generally useful to all travellers.

🖱 **www.fco.gov.uk** British Foreign and Commonwealth Office

🖱 **www.fco.gov.uk/knowbeforeyougo** British Foreign and Commonwealth Office travel information

🖱 **www.fitfortravel.scot.nhs.uk** NHS website

🖱 **www.foreignaffairs.gov.ie** Irish Department for Foreign Affairs

🖱 **www.smarttraveller.gov.au** Australian Department of Foreign Affairs and Trade

🖱 **www.travel.state.gov** US Department of State

🖱 **www.cdc.gov/travel** Centers for Disease Control and Prevention (US)

🖱 **www.voyage.gc.ca** Canadian Foreign Affairs and International Trade C

General
🖱 **www.who.org** World Health Organisation. Global health and welfare overview applicable to everyone.

🖱 **www.cia.gov/cia/publications/factbook** CIA World Factbook. Has good global coverage with lots of useful information, but plenty of dull facts as well.

🖱 **www.embassyworld.com Embassy World.** A useful listing of official government contacts around the world.

Ethical Travel

🖰 **www.tourismconcern.org.uk** Tourism Concern. An organisation focusing on fighting exploitation in tourism.

🖰 **www.ethicalvolunteering.org** Ethical Volunteering.

Focusies on advice and information for people who are interested in international volunteering and want to make sure that what they do is of value.

🖰 **www.ecotourism.org International Ecotourism Society.** Founded in 1990, TIES is the largest and oldest ecotourism organisation in the world dedicated to promoting ecotourism. As a non-profit, non-governmental and multi-stakeholder association, it aims to provide guidelines, standards, training, technical assistance, research and publications to foster sound ecotourism development.

🖰 **www.thetravelfoundation.org.uk** Travel Foundation. Focuses on improving the eco-credentials of the travel trade.

🖰 **www.responsibletravel.co.uk** Responsible Travel. An ethical search engine where all listed organisations have to meet some ethical standards.

🖰 **www.comhlamh.org Comhlamh.** An Irish activists group focusing on social justice, human rights and global development issues.

Environment

🖰 **www.panda.org/ World Wildlife Fund.** Focuses on global conservation issues and what everyone can practically do to help.

🖰 **www.panda.org/news_facts/publications/living_planet_report/ index.cfm** Living Planet Report. Outlines the global consequences of the way we currently live and what the future holds. .

🖰 **www.iucnredlist.org** IUCN Red List (International Union for Conservation of Nature and Natural Resources). Identifies endangered species around the world.

🖰 **www.climatecare.com** and **www.carbonfootprint.com** Carbon offsetting. Focuses on offsetting your carbon footprint.

🖰 **www.cheatneutral.com/** Anti carbon offsetting. Raising awareness that offsetting your carbon footprint could be an excuse for not doing what really matters; really funny, but makes you think.

🖰 **www.wwf.org.uk/livingplanet** Living Planet Report. Focusing on global environmental issues eg: major threats, species extinction rates, and what needs to happen to prevent future disasters for humankind as well as wildlife.

Miscellaneous

⌐ **www.tradingstandards.gov.uk** Trading Standards. Useful resources for regulations related to fundraising events.

⌐ **www.food.gov.uk** Food Standards Agency. Useful resources for fundraising events if selling food is involved.

⌐ **www.fundraisingdirectory.com** The Fundraising Directory. Useful resources to aid fundraising events.

ECO-SCHOOL PROJECT
Yolanda Barnas

On returning from a UK-based Earthwatch conservation volunteer trip, I thought, 'This is not the end, it is just the beginning.'

I applied for an Earthwatch community action grant, sometimes available to returning volunteers, and set about transforming a run-down, muddy patch in the school grounds into a wildlife garden.

Working at lunchtimes and in our spare time, the students and I built a herb garden, started growing our own vegetables and bought plants to create a mural of sunflowers, tulips and daffodils.

The wildlife area is now used for a raft of learning and teaching purposes, there have been assemblies on the environment and we came third in a recent 'Ealing in Bloom' competition.

The original idea was to involve students and make them more aware of their environment and the difference they can make. But not content to stop there, the school has gone one step further by registering as a European eco-school. The Eco-Schools programme provides a framework for schools to analyse their operations and become more sustainable. Pupils are engaged in the whole process, from monitoring and action planning to decision making.

The Ellen Wilkinson School now has an eco-team and an eco-action plan concentrating on litter and recycling and is also part of an international group of schools working towards a programme of bronze, silver and green flag awards.

The students are really committed to making a difference and their enthusiasm and dedication to the project have allowed the school to accomplish a great deal. I work at an inner London girls' school, and for some this is the only opportunity they have to connect with nature.

Yolanda Barnas is a London schoolteacher

APPENDIX 3 WHAT IS BS8848:2007+A1:2009?

The British Standard Specification for the provision of visits, fieldwork, expeditions and adventurous activities, outside the United Kingdom

Produced by the British Standards Institute and first published in April 2007 with an updated amendment in Spring 2009, this comprehensive document is the national standard for the safe operational management of visits, fieldwork, expeditions, and adventurous activities outside the UK.

It was developed because of consumer concerns about the risks associated with overseas adventurous pursuits and the variable levels of competence, training and fitness of participants. Peter Eisenegger, whose daughter Claire died of heat stroke on a gap year expedition in 1999, originally proposed the idea to BSI. Discussions with the Royal Geographical Society brought together an extensive network of stakeholders and experts to develop this new British standard.

The new British Standard will help companies assess the risks involved in trips abroad and take appropriate steps to manage them. It also provides organisations with a set of rules that can demonstrate their organisation is following good practice in managing trips safely.

It is intended for organisers of adventure, gap year, university and school fieldwork, research expeditions, charity challenges and general conservation activities taking place outside the UK. Many conservation volunteer organisations sub-contract part or all of their projects to third parties, which can blur responsibilities so the BS8848:2007 is an important way of ensuring that UK standards are applied by any third party contractors.

It aims to establish best practice for organisers, by helping users recognise whether a venture is as safe as possible (it doesn't have to be entirely risk free), how they should prepare participants for the risks involved and how users can reduce the risk of injury. A key way in which it does this is by ensuring clear accountability and defining the roles for everyone involved.

It tells organisations what they must do to comply but does not specify *how* they should to do it, so there is scope for variation in how organisations put the standard into practice. The Royal Geographical Society is the main organisation involved in rolling out training. Furthermore, it's only a standard, not a mandatory regulation, so an organisation can either ignore it, self-declare that they meet the standards, or at the highest level have an external audit to demonstrate their compliance.

It is a substantial document of 40 pages and costs £100
(*www.bsi-global.com/en/Shop/Publication-Detail/?pid=000000000030185211*)

INDEX

Entries in **bold** indicate main entries.